Lecture Notes in Computer Science 2580

Edited by G. Goos, J. Hartmanis, and J. van Leeuwen

T0233036

Springer
Berlin
Heidelberg
New York
Barcelona
Hong Kong
London
Milan
Paris
Tokyo

Hakan Erdogmus   Tao Weng (Eds.)

COTS-Based
Software Systems

Second International Conference, ICCBSS 2003
Ottawa, Canada, February 10-12, 2003
Proceedings

 Springer

Series Editors

Gerhard Goos, Karlsruhe University, Germany
Juris Hartmanis, Cornell University, NY, USA
Jan van Leeuwen, Utrecht University, The Netherlands

Volume Editors

Hakan Erdogmus
Tao Weng
National Research Council Canada
Institute for Information Technology
M50, 1200 Montreal Road
Ottawa (Ontario) K1A 0R6, Canada
E-mail:{Hakan.Erdogmus/Tao.Weng}@nrc-cnrc.gc.ca

Cataloging-in-Publication Data applied for

Bibliographic information published by Die Deutsche Bibliothek
Die Deutsche Bibliothek lists this publication in the Deutsche Nationalbibliografie;
detailed bibliographic data is available in the Internet at <http://dnb.ddb.de>.

CR Subject Classification (1998): K.6.3, D.2, J.1

ISSN 0302-9743
ISBN 3-540-00562-5 Springer-Verlag Berlin Heidelberg New York

Springer-Verlag Berlin Heidelberg New York
a member of BertelsmannSpringer Science+Business Media GmbH

http://www.springer.de

© Springer-Verlag Berlin Heidelberg 2003
Printed in Germany

Typesetting: Camera-ready by author, data conversion by DA-TeX Gerd Blumenstein
Printed on acid-free paper   SPIN 10872378   06/3142   5 4 3 2 1 0

Preface

It is with great pleasure that I introduce the Proceedings from the 2nd International Conference on COTS-Based Software Systems (ICCBSS). The theme for ICCBSS 2003 is "Multiple Paths – Multiple Solutions," representing the fact that developers of commercial off-the-shelf (COTS)-based systems choose from a set of potentially competing products the best interacting suite for a particular context. It is a task that is becoming more familiar, but no less challenging, with each new system under development. The possible solutions often differ from each other in ways that are difficult to assess, but, in the end, one of those solutions will be implemented.

By combining good research with the practical application by knowledgeable developers and systems integrators of those research results, we are beginning to develop roadmaps that will help ensure success. We believe that ICCBSS 2003 was a major step forward, providing attendees and all those who read this volume with the means to interact and network. As with the previous conference, the attendees represented a worldwide network of like-minded people, who are committed to the principles of COTS-based systems. We had submissions from all major continents, with attendees representing academia, business, government, and industry. This bodes well for the future of the field and for this conference series.

These proceedings are proof that there is a dynamic community of software researchers and practitioners who are expanding the scope of their interest in developing systems using COTS software products, whether standalone applications or commercial components. The papers presented here were written by both old friends and new acquaintances and represent the best of a significant number of submissions. We regret that we could not choose more papers for presentation in the conference program but we know that the Program Committee reviewed critically and chose wisely.

Last year's conference was a success in many ways, not the least of which was the interaction of the attendees. A number of new collaborations were started and new friendships begun. ICCBSS 2003 in Ottawa, Canada offered a unique opportunity to celebrate our accomplishments and to cement these relationships. The conference organizers, the European Software Institute, the National Research Council Canada, the Software Engineering Institute, and the University of Southern California Center for Software Engineering, welcomed the chance to showcase this work from many outstanding researchers, developers, and integrators in this ongoing forum. We look forward to many years of successful conferences.

February 2003   John C. Dean

International
Conference
on COTS-Based
Software Systems

Planning Committee

General Chair: John Dean
                                     National Research Council Canada

Conference Coordinator: Pierre Lamoureux
                                     National Research Council Canada

Panels/Tutorials Chair: Chris Abts
                                     Texas A&M University

Poster Chair: Fred Long
                                     University of Wales, Aberystwyth

Proceedings Chair: Hakan Erdogmus
                                     National Research Council Canada

Program Co-chairs: Patricia Oberndorf
                                     Software Engineering Institute
                                     Sandy Tay
                                     European Software Institute

Publicity Chairs: John Robert
                                     Software Engineering Institute
                                     David Morera
                                     European Software Institute
                                     Pierre Lamoureux
                                     National Research Council Canada

Program Committee

Program Committee Co-chairs:
Patricia Oberndorf, Software Engineering Institute, USA
Sandy Tay, European Software Institute, Spain

Chris Abts	Texas A&M University, USA
Sergio Bandinelli	European Software Institute, Spain
David M. Bennett	POWERflex Corporation, Australia
David P. Bentley	South Carolina Research Authority, USA
Ljerka Beus-Dukic	University of Westminster, UK
Jørgen Bøegh	DELTA, Danish Electronics, Light & Acoustics, Denmark
Alan Brown	Rational Software Corporation, USA
Daniel Duma	IBM Belgium Software Group, Belgium
Anthony N. Earl	Sun Microsystems, Inc., USA
Rose F. Gamble	University of Tulsa, USA
Göran V. Grahn	Volvo Information Technology, Sweden
Mark Jennings	Department of National Defence, Canada
Anatol Kark	National Research Council Canada
Ron Kohl	R.J. Kohl & Associates, USA
Lech Krzanik	University of Oulu, Finland
Anna Liu	Microsoft, Australia
Fred Long	University of Wales, Aberystwyth, UK
Michael Looney	University of Portsmouth, UK
Jean-Christophe Mielnik	Thales Research and Technology, France
Maurizio Morisio	Politecnico di Torino, Italy
Cornelius Ncube	City University London, UK
Thuy Nguyen	Electricité de France, France
Michael Ochs	Fraunhofer Institute for Experimental Software Engineering (IESE), Germany
James R. Odrowski	ComponentWave, Inc., USA
Dan Port	University of Southern California, USA
Marco Torchiano	Norwegian University of Science and Technology, Norway
Mark Vigder	National Research Council Canada

Keynote Speakers

Dr. Robert Balzer
Chief Technical Officer
Teknowledge Corporation

Dr. Victor R. Basili
Professor of Computer Science
Computer Science Department, University of Maryland

Sponsoring Institutions

European Software Institute

The European Software Institute (ESI) has now established itself as one of the world's major centers for software process improvement. Our strength lies in our close partnership with industry. ESI's business-driven approach focuses on issues that result in a genuine commercial impact, such as reduction of costs and improving productivity.

ESI's work is divided into four key technology areas: Software Process Improvement, Measurement, System Engineering, and Product-Line-Based Reuse, where COTS Research is allocated.

Learn more about the ESI at `http://www.esi.es`.

NRC · CNRC

National Research Council Canada

The National Research Council (NRC) Canada's premier science and technology research organization, is a leader in scientific and technical research, the diffusion of technology, and the dissemination of scientific and technical information.

Working in partnership with innovative companies, universities, and research organizations, NRC enhances Canada's social and economic well being and creates new opportunities for Canadians. Through knowledge, research, and innovation, NRC and its partners are expanding the frontiers of science and technology.

Learn more about the NRC at `http://www.nrc.ca`.

Software Engineering Institute

The Software Engineering Institute (SEI) provides leadership in advancing the state of software engineering practice. We collaborate with industry, academia, and the government to learn about the best technical and management practices and then use what we learn to benefit the software engineering community.

The institute is based at Carnegie Mellon University and is sponsored by the US Office of the Under Secretary of Defense for Acquisition, Technology, and Logistics [OUSD (AT&L)].

Learn more about the SEI at `http://www.sei.cmu.edu`.

USC Center for Software Engineering and CeBASEC-CSE

The USC Center for Software Engineering (USC-CSE) focuses its research and teaching efforts toward helping industry and government address multiple new challenges of concern to software system procurers, developers, and users. We work in partnership with the members of our Affiliates Program, which includes some two dozen organizations representing a mix of commercial industry, aerospace, government, nonprofit FFRDCs, and consortia. The Center for Software Engineering is based at the University of Southern California.

Learn more about USC-CSE at `http://sunset.usc.edu`.

Tutorials

Evaluating COTS Using Function Fit Analysis
Presenter: Steven Woodward (Q/P Management Group of Canada)

Today many organizations are attempting to reduce software development effort and schedules by purchasing off-the-shelf solutions rather than developing them from scratch. This strategy can be very cost effective if the COTS solution meets the customer requirements. Unfortunately, in numerous situations, the extent to which COTS solutions satisfy requirements is not quantified. This can result in overall higher-priced COTS solutions or the selection of COTS when "make" is actually a more cost-effective alternative.

Conducting complete and accurate quantified assessments of the "COTS fit" and not relying on vendor claims of high compatibility can improve the probability of successful COTS selection and project completion. This tutorial will provide attendees with practical examples on Function Point Analysis, plus "Functional Fit Analysis" techniques that have proven to be successful for the US DoD and in large projects in identifying the compatibility of COTS products with customer requirements. The technique called "Function Fit Analysis" is based on function point analysis (FPA). Function point analysis is the decomposition of an existing or planned system based on the customer perspective of functional requirements. Function points therefore can be used to evaluate various COTS solutions, select the best solution, and determine the degree of enhancement work required to meet customer requirements.

This session provided attendees with specific details of the process, including a Function Point Analysis overview, plus practical examples and cases utilizing the Function Fit Analysis process. The following topics were addressed in this session.

– The Function Fit Analysis Process
  – Function point analysis of requirements
  – Rules of FPA
  – Examples/cases of applying FPA rules
– Evaluation and Quantification of COTS
  – Function gap analysis
  – Calculating COTS fit
  – COTS project estimation
  – The make/buy/punt decision
– Leveraging the Information in Various Scenarios

Function Fit Analysis has been successfully used by the US Navy and a number of government agencies in the US and Canada to evaluate and select specific COTS solutions. The attendees gained practical knowledge of how to make the process operational for use on their own projects in order to ensure successful implementation of COTS projects.

MSG/ESS ITSEP
Presenters: Gail Brown (MSG/ESS); Billie Common (MSG/ESS, BTAS);
Todd Trickler (MSG/ESS, BTAS); David Bentley (MSG/ES, SCRA)

The Integrating Technology by a Structured Evolutionary Process (ITSEP) is
a powerful and straightforward approach to selecting, fielding, and supporting
Commercial-Off-The-Shelf (COTS) and other reuse solutions in complex environments. ITSEP provides a framework to develop, field, and support a solution composed of an integrated assembly of hardware and software products,
the required custom code, linkage to enterprise architecture, and end-user business process changes. ITSEP uses concurrent discovery and negotiation of four
spheres of activity that influence the solution. These spheres comprise: user needs
and business processes, industry and the marketplace (including commercial and
government), engineering and design, and programmatic constraints (including
risk management). The Materiel Systems Group (MSG) has used ITSEP to develop solutions for several projects such as the Air Force Technical Order (TO)
Concept of Operations, TO Transformation, Aircraft Battle Damage Assessment
and Repair (ABDAR), Depot-X planning, Manufacturing Resource Planning II
(MRP II)/Maintenance, Repair & Overhaul (MRO), and MSG Business Development.

The tutorial incorporated MSG's experience to date using ITSEP and provided attendees with practical knowledge useful in developing and supporting
COTS-based solutions. The tutorial consisted of a four-part presentation that
taught the basics of ITSEP and related MSG's experience with the process. Part
one of the tutorial covered an overview of ITSEP. Part two covered the practical
application of ITSEP through a review of MSG projects. Part three covered:
more on practical application, this time focusing on marketplace evaluations;
what the MSG has learned, both good and bad; and the mistakes made and the
changes incorporated to avoid mistakes in the future. Part four continued with
practical application of the process. This final part of the tutorial addressed the
infrastructure support that needs to be developed and functioning before gaining
the full strength and benefit of the ITSEP process.

Trouble spots, worthwhile efforts, and practical lessons learned were presented throughout the tutorial. We hope that customers or users, program and
project managers, developers, commercial vendors, and anyone considering and/
or involved with putting together a COTS-based solution benefited from this tutorial. Since this conference was a forum to exchange ideas and results, discussion
was strongly encouraged as a component of the tutorial.

Marketing Principles for COTS Developers and Acquirers
Presenters: Eileen Forrester and Suzanne Garcia (Software Engineering Institute)

One of the challenges inherent in the development of COTS-based systems is
that marketing communications surrounding components is not effective at help-

ing practitioners to make appropriate matches between available components and system needs. Basic marketing principles and practices could improve the rate of effective matches. In this tutorial, attendees learned marketing ideas and techniques that will make them better at communicating the attributes of components that make for better fits. Deployers of COTS-based systems can also use these principles and techniques to further the appropriate adoption of systems.

Poster Sessions

Title: **"Competitive Development of Solutions Based on COTS Technology"**
Presenters' Names: Vladimir Lilov (Rila Solutions, Bulgaria) and
Sylvia Ilieva (Sofia University, Bulgaria)

Title: **"Fast Multi-team Development Using COTS Components –
A Case Study"**
Presenter's Name: Pedro Falcão Gonçalves (iBest S/A, Brazil)

Title: **"Meta-Model Based Component-Level Interaction Analysis"**
Presenters' Names: Fan Ye and Tim Kelly (University of York, UK)

Title: **"Composable Process Elements for Developing COTS Based Applications"**
Presenters' Names: Jesal Bhuta, Barry Boehm, and Daniel Port (Center for Software Engineering, University of Southern California)

Title: **"Evolutionary Process for Integrating COTS-Based Systems (EPIC)"**
Presenter's Name: Cecilia Albert and Lisa Brownsword (Software Engineering Institute)

Title: **"COTS Evaluation & Selection Process Based on DESMET and AHP Methodologies"**
Presenter's Name: David Morera (European Software Institute, Spain)

Title: **"Software Acquisition Model for New Component-Based Software Systems"**
Presenter's Name: David Morera (European Software Institute, Spain)

Experience Report

Title: **"Tools for Successful COTS Software Implementation and Integration"**
Author: Gail M. Talbott (Program Director, Lockheed Martin Asset Solution Integration)

Government and commercial industries are relying more and more on the successful integration of Commercial-Off-The-Shelf (COTS) software to reduce systems development and maintenance costs and keep pace with technological advances. The use of COTS software in systems development introduces the need for a unique software engineering approach and expertise. COTS products integration combined with expertise in the research, analysis, and selection of technologies for a particular market is essential to the successful implementation of COTS-based systems. The presentation outlined the Lockheed Martin (LM) Asset Solution Integration (ASI) Service's practical experience as a solution integrator in the Enterprise Asset Management (EAM) domain, and explored valuable lessons learned when faced with the challenge of successfully architecting, implementing, and delivering COTS-based systems. It combined a Business Model, which defines the methodology used for COTS solution integration, and the Defined Software Engineering Process that identifies the approach to the successful delivery of integrated COTS solutions.

Table of Contents

Protective Wrapper Development: A Case Study

Tom Anderson, Mei Feng, Steve Riddle, and Alexander Romanovsky

School of Computing Science
University of Newcastle upon Tyne,
Newcastle upon Tyne, NE1 7RU, UK

Abstract. We have recently proposed a general approach to engineering protective wrappers as a means of detecting errors or unwanted behaviour in systems employing an OTS (Off-The-Shelf) item, and launching appropriate recovery actions. This paper presents results of a case study in protective wrapper development, using a Simulink model of a steam boiler system together with an OTS PID (Proportional, Integral and Derivative) controller. The protective wrappers are developed for the model of the system in such a way that they allow detection and tolerance of typical errors caused by unavailability of signals, violations of constraints, and oscillations.

1 Introduction

There are many economical reasons why integration of Off-The-Shelf (OTS) components into systems with high dependability requirements (including the safety-critical ones) is becoming a viable option for system developers (see, for example, [1]). The main obstacle is that employing such components can undermine overall system dependability unless special care is taken. Considerable evidence supports the judgement that complex systems built using OTS components could have a higher risk of failure. This is due to a number of reasons:

- OTS components are typically aimed at a mass-market and are often of a lower quality than bespoke components.
- OTS components are seldom intended for the specific setting and environment in which they are employed—consequently a system in which an OTS component is integrated may misuse or misinterpret it.
- information about the COTS item which the system integrator has at his/her disposal is often incomplete, ambiguous or, even, erroneous.

We take a pragmatic view in developing our approach by accepting that, in spite of all efforts to improve the quality of OTS components and of the system in which they are to be integrated, their use will be a source of failure. The solution we are advocating is a defensive strategy of employing specialised fault tolerance techniques during system integration.

H. Erdogmus and T. Weng (Eds.): ICCBSS 2003, LNCS 2580, pp. 1–14, 2003.

1.1   Protective Wrappers

Fault tolerance [2] as a general means for improving overall system dependability has been an area of very active research and development over the last 30 years. Many fault tolerance techniques proceed by employing redundant software in some form; for example, recovery blocks, N-version programming, exception handling [3,4]. The main phases of providing fault tolerance are error detection, error diagnosis and error recovery [5]. At the first phase an erroneous state is identified as such; after that error diagnosis is used to examine the damaged area to allow it to be replaced by an error-free state during error recovery. Employing proper system structuring techniques (e.g. classes, processes, layers, modules) is vital for achieving fault tolerance because it allows erroneous information to be contained within structural units. Our work aims to apply these general fault tolerance techniques in the context of integrating OTS items into complex systems.

Component wrapping is an established technique used to intercept data and control flow between a component and its environment [6]. Typical applications include adding data caching and buffering, simplifying the component interface, and providing transparent component replication.

In a component-based system development the OTS items are natural units of system structuring. Unfortunately, as we have explained above, they usually do not provide enough assurance of correct behaviour. In previous work [7] we proposed the development of *protective wrappers* as part of system integration activities. A protective wrapper is a piece of redundant, bespoke software intercepting all information going to and from the OTS item. Such a wrapper may detect errors or suspicious activities, and initiate appropriate recovery when possible.

A wrapper is a piece of software and, clearly, may contain software defects itself. Deploying a wrapper to perform protection functions obliges us to take considerable care over issues such as relative complexity and common-mode failures between the wrapper and the wrapped component. For this reason, wrappers must be rigorously specified, developed and executed as a means of protecting OTS items against faults in the Rest Of the System (ROS), and the ROS against faults in OTS items. Information required for wrapper development is obtained by analysing several sources of information [7], including:

- Specification of the OTS item behaviour, as provided by both the item designers and the integrated system designers. The latter characterises the behaviour the system designers require of the OTS item in order to integrate it with the system.
- "Erroneous" behaviour of the OTS item, for example a known failure to react to stimuli as specified by the item designers (these may be known, for example, from testing or from previous experience in using the OTS item), or behaviour which the system designer especially wants to protect against.
- Specification of the correct behaviour of the ROS with respect to the OTS item.

1.2   Case Study

In this paper we report the results of applying the proposed approach to developing a protective wrapper for an Off-The-Shelf PID (Proportional, Integral and Derivative) controller. It is our intention to demonstrate how the approach could be applied in practice. The results of this study will be used to aid the development of a generic approach for wrapping OTS items.

Rather than conduct an experiment with protective wrapping in the real world environment, with all the associated cost and potential damage to equipment and life, we have employed software models of the PID controller and of the steam boiler system in which it is to be integrated. Employing software models of the controller and the boiler system is an active area of R&D carried out by many leading control product companies (including Honeywell [8]). We believe that the decision to use a third-party model adds credibility to our results.

A related case study in steam boiler control specification was examined at the Dagstuhl seminar on Methods for Semantics and Specification [9]; the seminar was run as a competition to show the strengths and weaknesses of particular formal methods. Rather than adapt this specification to our needs, we chose to use a model developed within a research project conducted by Honeywell for their control products [8]. This model simulates a real controller and the controlled steam boiler system, enabling us to investigate the effect of wrapping with a more representative model than the idealised specification employed at Dagstuhl. In the course of our work we extended the Honeywell model by incorporating protective wrappers.

1.3   Roadmap

The remainder of this paper is organised as follows. In the following section we describe the simulation environment, the controller and the boiler models we are using, and our approach to monitoring the model variables. Section 3 discusses the requirements for a protective wrapper and outlines the categories of errors to be detected and tolerated at the level of the wrapper. The next section outlines design and implementation of the wrapper to detect these categories of error. Section 5 concludes the paper by summarising the results, discussing the limitations of our approach, and indicating avenues for future work.

2   Simulation

2.1   Simulink

Simulink (Mathworks) [10] is one of the built-in tools in MATLAB, providing a platform for modelling, simulating and analysing dynamical systems. It supports linear and nonlinear systems modelled in continuous time or sampled time, as well as a hybrid of the two. Systems can also be multi-rate, i.e., have different parts that are sampled or updated at different rates. Simulink contains a comprehensive block library of sinks, sources, linear and nonlinear components, and connectors to allow modelling of very sophisticated systems. Models can also be developed through self-defined blocks by means of the *S-functions* feature of Simulink or by invoking MATLAB functions. After a model has been defined, it can be simulated and, using scopes and other display blocks, simulation results can be displayed while the simulation is running.

Simulink provides a practical and safe platform for simulating the boiler system and its PID control system, for detecting operational errors when boiler and control system interact, and for developing and implementing a protective wrapper dealing with such errors.

2.2   The Structure of the Model

The abstract structure of the system we are modelling is shown in Fig. 1. The overall system has two principal components: the boiler system and the control system. In turn, the control system comprises a PID controller (the OTS item), and the ROS which is simply the remainder of the control system.

The ROS consists of :

- the boiler sensors. These are "smart" sensors which monitor variables providing input to the PID controller: Drum Level, Steam Flow, Steam Pressure, Gas Concentrations and Coal Feeder Rate.
- actuators. These devices control a heating burner which can be ON/OFF, and adjust inlet/outlet valves in response to outputs from the PID controller: Feed Water Flow, Coal Feeder Rate and Air Flow.
- configuration settings. These are the "set-points" for the system: Oxygen and Bus Pressure, which must be set up in advance by the operators.

Smart sensors and actuators interact with the PID controller through a standard protocol.

Simulink output blocks can be introduced into the model in such a way that the variables of the MATLAB working space can be controlled as necessary. Working with the Simulink model we were able to perform repeatable experiments by manipulating any of the changeable variables and the connections between system components so as to produce and analyse a range of possible errors that would be reasonably typical for the system we are simulating.

2.3   The Simulink Model

The Simulink model (shown in Fig. 2) actually represents the OTS item as three separate PID controllers that handle the feed water flow, the coal feeder rate and the air flow. These controllers output three eponymous variables: Feed Water Flow (F_wf), Coal Feeder Rate (C_fr) and Air Flow (Air_f); these three variables, together with two external variables (Coal Quality and Steam Load) constitute the parameters which determine the behaviour of the boiler system. There are also several internal variables generated by the smart sensors; some of these, together with the configuration set-points, provide the inputs to the PID controllers. Table 1 lists all of the variables used in the model.

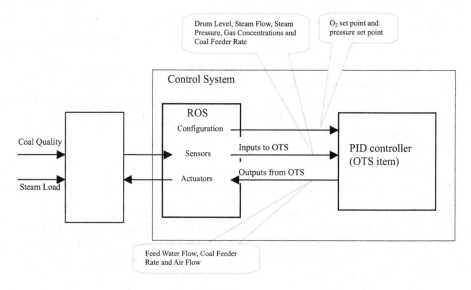

Fig. 1. Boiler System and Control System (including the PID Controller)

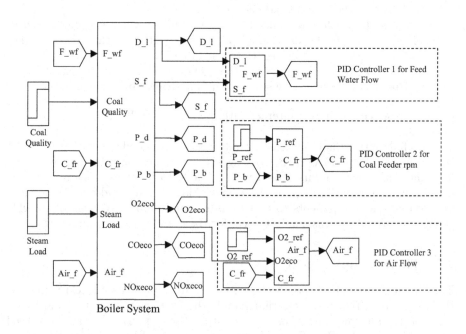

Fig. 2. Simulink Model of the Boiler System with PID Controllers

2.4   Variable Monitoring

Simulink scopes and other display blocks enable us to develop modelling components that monitor the intermediate results while the simulation is running. In our experiments we can monitor and display a total of 15 variables, comprising all the variables listed in Table 1 (except for the two set-points), plus three internal variables which represent two internal air flows and one internal steam flow. The simulation time for all of our experiments is set to 12000 steps. Some monitoring results are presented in Fig. 3. This particular chart demonstrates the behaviour of the three PID outputs and two external inputs of the boiler system when at step 2000 the steam load is increased, and at step 5000 the coal quality changes: in both these scenarios the boiler system returns to steady operation reasonably soon.

Table 1. Variables used in the model

Variable	Representation	Variable	Representation
Coal Quality	Coal quality, ton per hour	D_l	Drum level
Steam Load	Steam Load, fraction of pure combustibles	S_f	Steam flow
F_wf	Feed water flow	P_d	Steam pressure /drum
C_fr	Coal feeder rate	P_b	Steam pressure / bus
Air_f	Air flow (controlled air)	O2eco	O2 concentration at economizer
P_ref	Bus pressure set-point	COeco	CO concentration at economizer
O2_ref	O2 set-point	NOxeco	NOx concentration at economizer

2.5   Properties of the Boiler System and the PID Controllers

In this section we summarise the information which we collected to guide us in developing the protective wrappers. The basic boiler specification provides information on steam flow, bus pressure, output temperature and coal calorific value. As the OTS item (the PID controller(s)) is treated as a black box, any information about its properties must be deduced from the interface or from relevant sources where available. In an ideal world the system designer will have a complete and correct specification of the boiler system, the PID controller and the ROS. Unfortunately, we only had access to limited information about the boiler system and the ROS (which is typical for many practical situations). From an investigation of the boiler model and information acquired from all available sources, we have formulated the following description.

Information from the documentation available to us is:

– Output temperature: 540 deg C.
– Coal calorific value: 16-18 MJ/kg.

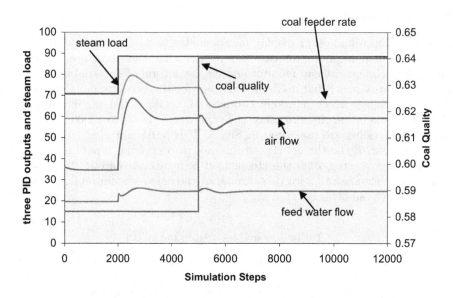

Fig. 3. Normal Performance of the Boiler System with PID Controllers

- Steam load: 50-125 ton/hour.
- Coal quality is measured as a fraction of pure combustibles (where pure = 1; actual value about 0.55-0.7).
- Three controlled outputs (F_wf, C_fr, Air_f) are each given as a percentage.

Information obtained by analysing the interface and by investigating the simulated model:

- Set-point of bus pressure ranges from 0 to 20 (actual value about 9.4).
- Set-point of O2 concentration at economiser ranges from 0 to 0.1 (actual value about 0.03).
- Internal variables input to PID controllers:
  - Drum level: output value between -1 and +1 (actual value close to 0).
  - Steam Flow: 0 to 125.
  - Bus pressure: 0 to 20 .
  - O2 concentration at economiser: 0 to 0.5.

3 Requirements for a Protective Wrapper

In the previous section we presented an outline specification of the modelled boiler system, as deduced from the model and other sources. In this section we consider the errors which could arise from integrating an OTS PID controller in the system, in order to derive the requirements for a protective wrapper. We make the following assumptions:

- The value of each variable can be detected instantaneously through micro-processors. In particular, we assume that the values of input and output variables of the PID controller are detected instantaneously. This (highly) simplifying assumption enables us to illustrate the method for protective wrapper development without regard to issues relating to response times.
- The wrapper program can be inserted into the control system, either by a partial hardware implementation which intercepts the physical connections, or purely in software. We are not concerned at this stage with the details of this implementation.

In order to clarify the requirements for a protective wrapper, it is necessary to form a view of what the PID controller and the ROS can, and cannot, do at their shared interface. This view can be formulated as a collection of *Acceptable Behaviour Constraints (ABCs)* [7] defined from the perspective of the systems integrator. Once defined, these ABCs can be thought of as contracts [11] which a system designer could use as the basis for defining a protective wrapper, which would employ conventional mechanisms for error detection, containment and recovery [2].

3.1   Types of Cues, and Examples

For our case study, Table 2 provides a list of error symptoms (cues) and asso-ciated actions, following a structural analysis of the possible errors detectable at the interface between the ROS and the PID controller. Since the OTS PID controller is a black box item we can only reason about errors concerning the inputs and outputs to the PID from the ROS. This gives four groups for the cues, as shown in first column of the table.

The second column classifies the type of error we are concerned with, and the third column gives an example of each type of error. The recovery action given in the fourth column is a suggested action which a protective wrapper could be designed to launch; we do not claim that these illustrative actions are the most appropriate in each case. The cue highlighted in bold is selected as an example for further discussion.

The example, "Input to PID which is known to be untrustworthy", is illus-trated in Fig. 4. Steam load is kept constant at 70.8 ton per hour during the operation. After 5000 simulation steps, the coal quality is increased from 0.5 to an artificial value just under 3, and as a consequence some inputs to the OTS would approach untrustworthy values which are close to the boundary of the PID controller's practical specifications. The curves shown on Fig. 4 converge to a steady state, but if the overshoots of the initial oscillations were of greater magnitude than the specification of the boiler system permits, or the oscillations kept going longer than the boiler system can support, the situation would be regarded as critical.

A more extreme version of this example is shown in Fig. 5. Here, the coal quality (not shown on the figure) is increased unrealistically to almost 4.5 at step 1000, with steam load constant as before. The curves are no longer convergent, leading to a dangerously unstable situation.

Table 2. Cues for protective wrapper

	Types of cues	Examples	Actions
Errors in PID inputs w.r.t. ROS output constraints	Illegal output from ROS (according to ROS specification)	An output from ROS is disconnected from PID	Shutdown
	Output from ROS is detectably erroneous	ROS sampling rate suddenly exceeds the normal rate	Alarm
	Output from ROS is illegal w.r.t. the system designer's specification of system operation	A ROS output is outside the envelope of values anticipated by the system designer	Alarm
Errors in PID inputs w.r.t. PID constraints	Input to PID is illegal (according to PID specification)	Set-point values are mis-configured and violate the PID specification	Alarm
	Input to PID that is suspect	The measured derivative of a PID input exceeds the maximum level for which it has been tested	Alarm
	Input to PID which is known to be untrustworthy	**A PID input (or its derivative) is close to the boundary specified for the PID, at a level which is known to create problems**	**Alarm**
Errors in PID outputs w.r.t. PID constraints	Illegal output from PID (according to PID specification)	An output from PID is disconnected from ROS	Shutdown
Errors in PID outputs w.r.t. ROS input constraints	Illegal input to ROS (according to ROS specification)	The PID controller changes its rate of processing and sends messages to ROS too frequently	Alarm

3.2   Summary Analysis

Errors may occur anywhere in the boiler system or the PID. However, a protective wrapper for the OTS PID controller can only check for error conditions as cues at the PID/ROS interface. In the previous subsection we have characterized these cues in terms of their sources, but the wrapper can only detect them by their behavioural attributes. We have therefore placed the cues into three distinguishable categories:

1. Unavailability of inputs/outputs to/from the PID controller.
   Either the PID controller crashes, resulting in no output from the PID controller to the ROS (and beyond), or the boiler system or ROS (or some connections between these and the PID) is disrupted, so that inputs to the PID controller are unavailable.
2. Violation of specifications of monitored variables.
   Set-points to the PID controller, or any monitored variable, violate their specification.
3. Oscillations in monitored variables.

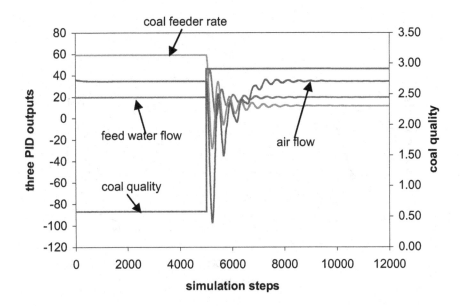

Fig. 4. Input to the PID for which it is known to be untrustworthy: A PID input exceeds the boundary specified for the PID controller

Monitored variables, and their derivatives, take on excessive and rapidly changing values.

This categorization of error types informs the design of a protective wrapper, which is addressed in the next section.

4   Design and Implementation of a Wrapper

4.1   Design of Wrapper

In this section we address the design of a wrapper to be implemented using MATLAB functions.

The main function of the wrapper is to cyclically check for each type of error identified in the previous section (3.2). It uses two sub-functions:

- *no_signal_alarm*, to check for absence of a signal after a given period of time.
- *check_oscillate*, to check whether oscillating variables revert to a stable state before a maximum number of oscillations.

The "given period of time" and "maximum number of oscillations" referred to here should in general be determined after consulting the specification of the system. Since this information was not available, we have set the number of

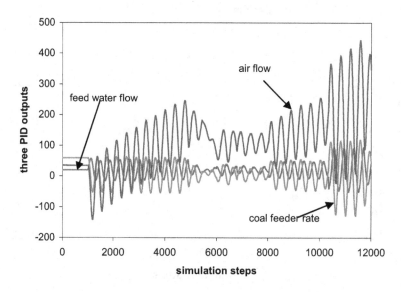

Fig. 5. Input to the PID for which it is known to be untrustworthy: A more extreme example leading to dangerous oscillations

steps for detecting absence of signal to 1000 (the simulation itself runs for 12000 steps), as this serves to illustrate the protective wrapper design.

The wrapper implements a number of ABCs based on the properties (discussed in Sect. 2.5) of input and output variables F_wf, C_fr, Air_f, D_l, S_f, P_b, P_ref, O2eko and O2_ref, with an addition of two more ABCs stating that the signals cannot be lost and that the variables cannot oscillate beyond the maximum number of oscillations. (we view these as dangerous conditions which have to be prevented). If the signals do not violate any of the ABCs they go through the wrapper unchanged otherwise an alarm is raised, or the system is shut down.

Thus, in this case we are adopting an elementary monitoring and alerting strategy, as an obvious starting point on the way to the development of a more general engineering methodology for wrapper design. Our approach, as outlined in Sect. 3 above, is to derive wrapper requirements from a consideration of possible interface errors classified by their symptoms (cues); this leads to the formulation of a set of ABCs. We touch on more general issues in [7] but clearly there is considerable scope for further research.

4.2 Wrapper Implementation

Although there are many pragmatic considerations to be addressed in order to achieve an effective implementation of wrapper technology, the choice of the appropriate mechanism will be largely determined by the environment. A more detailed discussion is presented in [7].

4.3 Example

We now illustrate the operation of the wrapper for the error discussed in Sect.
3.1 (Fig. 4), due to oscillation of signals. Fig. 6 demonstrates the case where the
boiler system can only withstand three oscillations in signals. This is the same
situation as was presented in Fig. 4.

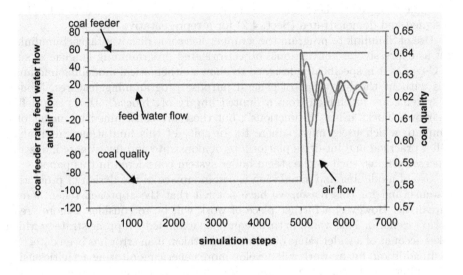

Fig. 6. Demonstration for wrapper working on signal oscillations

A maximum peak plus one minimum peak is counted as one oscillation. After
the forth oscillation was generated, the wrapper shut down the boiler system.

5   Conclusions

This paper has investigated the types of error which can occur in the modelled
boiler system (Sect. 3.2) and then addressed the design of a wrapper to detect
these errors.

We would like to emphasise that this work focuses on error detection and
error recovery preventing systems from failure rather than on fault diagnosis and
fault treatment [2]. The protective wrappers detect erroneous information going
to and coming from the PID controller and perform recovery actions (raising
alarms or shutting the system down). In real systems employing PID controllers
such errors can be clearly caused by various reasons (faults), such as design faults
in the PID or in the system employing it, mismatches between these two entities
(in which case it may be impossible to identify the fault location), failures of the
underlying hardware, etc.

The errors were categorised as:

1. Unavailability of signals to/from PID controllers, either through the controllers themselves not working or a fault in the boiler system.
2. Violation of limitations specified for variable(s), due to a fault in the boiler system or mis-configured set-points.
3. Oscillations in the values of some variable(s).

A simple wrapper to check for these errors and take appropriate action has been designed and demonstrated (Sect. 4.2) for a representative example.

Use of Simulink to program the wrapper has some disadvantages. Simulink is not as expressive as conventional object-oriented programming languages, such as C++, as it is specifically designed to allow mathematical modelling and analysis without the full range of general purpose programming features. Models of systems are assembled from a limited library of "blocks". Users can define their own blocks using "S-functions", but these are constrained by means of a template which users must adhere to. In spite of this limitation, Simulink is still a practical and intuitive platform to demonstrate and investigate industrial process systems, such as the steam boiler system considered in this paper.

Use of modelling and simulation is commonplace in the design of protection systems, and for this reason we have not felt that the approach taken here is unrealistic. However, a further piece of work will be to consider a more "real-world" scenario. This would in turn require an extended wrapping strategy which takes account of a wider range of actions to be taken if an error has been detected.

In addition, future work will develop more generic monitoring activities using a combination of error detection and fault injection techniques, to measure the effect a wrapper has on the overall system dependability. Other avenues could include investigating the potential use of wrappers to capture behaviour that has not been explicitly specified.

Acknowledgements. This work is supported by the UK EPSRC project DOTS: Diversity with Off-The-Shelf Components (www.csr.ncl.ac.uk/dots). A. Romanovsky is supported by the European IST project DSoS: *Dependable Systems of Systems*.

We are grateful to Vladimir Havlena for sharing with us some of the results of his research, and to Prof. Lorenzo Strigini for comments on an early draft of this paper.

References

1. Special Issue on COTS. In: IEEE Computer 31(6) (1998)
2. Lee, P. A., and Anderson, T.: Fault Tolerance: Principles and Practice. Wien-New York (1991)
3. Lyu, M. R.: Software Fault Tolerance. John Wiley and Sons (1995)
4. Romanovsky, A.: Exception Handling in Component-based System Development. In: 25th International Computer Software and Application Conference, Chicago, IL, October (2001) 580–586

5. Laprie, J. C.: Dependable Computing: Concepts, Limits, Challenges. In: 25th International Symposium On Fault-Tolerant Computing, IEEE Computer Society Press, Pasadena, CA, June (1995) 42–54
6. Voas, J.: Certifying Off-The-Shelf Software Components. In: IEEE Computer 31(6) (1998) 53–59
7. Popov, P., Riddle, S., Romanovsky, A., and Strigini, L.: On Systematic Design of Protectors for Employing OTS Items. In: Procedings of the 27th Euromicro Conference, Warsaw, Poland, September (2001) 22–29
8. Havlena, V.: Development of ACC Controller with MATLAB/SIMULINK. In: MATLAB 99, Praha: VSCHT-Ustav Fyziky a Merici Techniky (1999) 52–59
9. Abrial, J. R., Börger, E., and Langmaack, H.: Formal Methods for Industrial Applications: Specifying and Programming the Steam Boiler Control. LNCS 1165, Springer Verlag, October (1996)
10. Mathworks, Using Simulink: Reference Guide. Available at: http://www.mathworks.com
11. Mandrioli, D., and Meyer, B.: Advances in Object-Oriented Software Engineering. Prentice Hall (1992)

Establishing Trust in COTS Components

Adnan Bader[1], Christine Mingins[1], David Bennett[2], and Sita Ramakrishan[1]

[1] School of Computer Science and Software Engineering
Faculty of Information Technology
Monash University, Australia
{abader, cmingins, sitar}@csse.monash.edu.au
[2] PowerFlex Corp., Australia
dmb@pfxcorp.com

Abstract. Increased use of COTS software components means increased demand for trust in these artifacts. The problem lies in the fact that trust is mainly a philosophical concept. We all deal with trust issues in our daily life yet it is hard for us to identify the attributes of trust. In the context of software components certain aspects and features can be classified as trust attributes. In this paper we attempt to identify these attributes and describe a mechanism to effectively use these in the selection and integration of COTS components. We also emphasize the important connection between the production and procurement processes and discuss how it can help us establish better trust in software components.

1 Introduction

The growing use of COTS (commercial-off-the-shelf) components in building software systems during recent years has caused an increased demand for trust in such components. Trust is a well-understood philosophical concept but it is still unclear what constitutes trust and how human mind measures and uses it. Despite the difficulty in managing and measuring trust, it is still the most important element of communication, collaboration and cooperation. We need to trust human and non-human entities to a reasonable degree before we can relate to them. In this paper we try to extend the *abstract* idea of trust from trusting humans to trusting software components.

Like other off-the-shelf products, trust in COTS Software components also depends on factors like the market reputation of the vendor/producer, customer loyalty, length of our experience with a partciular component or vendor, information gathered about the component by general evaluation and initial testing, and the apparent and hidden risks associated with using the component.

Trust in software components is also directly related to the testability of these components. Extensive research has been conducted on increasing the testability of components (e.g. [5] and [6]) and testing the interaction of components with their host environment (e.g. [2]). But little attention has been given to how testing relates to establishing trust in components and what are the other factors that affect trust.

H. Erdogmus and T. Weng (Eds.): ICCBSS 2003, LNCS 2580, pp. 15–24, 2003.

The most common problem in building trust between two parties is lack of common understanding of the fundamental ideas. For instance, the term *security* may have completely different meanings for both the parties. For software components it is the specifications of these components and the requirements of the users that need to speak the same language. The problem of accurately specifying consumer/integrator requirements has been emphasized by a number of different researchers. In [12] the authors even suggested the addition of a new job role—*vendor manager* for the integrators' organization (where an organization deals with number of different COTS vendors) with the sole purpose of negotiating and maintaining the relationship with the vendors.

In order to analyze and increase the amount of trust in COTS software components we look at them first from the perspective of their consumers to determine what consumers expect from a trustable component and then from the perspective of the vendors to establish how these expectations can be met in the *off-the-shelf* form of COTS components.

2 Usage of COTS Components

Off-The-Shelf software has been developed and used in many different ways over the past decades. Different definitions and even different terminologies exist for these software components, e.g. COTS (Commercial-Off-The-Shelf), MOTS (Modifiable Off-The-Shelf), GOTS (Off-The-Shelf software owned by the government) and NDI (Non-Developmental Item). Attempts have been made to define and characterize COTS software by many researchers (e.g. [1] and [3]).

From the consumers' perspective, once the requirements for required COTS component have been established, the typical procurement process involves the following steps (as shown in Fig. 1):

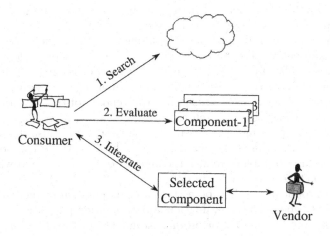

Fig. 1. Process of COTS Component Procurement

1. searching for any components satisfying (or closely satisfying) these requirements in a components marketplace or through search engines (represented
   by a cloud in Fig. 1).
2. evaluating the candidate components.
3. integrating the most suitable component in the system. This may involve
   interaction with the vendor of the selected component in certain circumstances.

For the purpose of this study we consider a software system that needs to integrate a COTS component for compressing/decompressing data. The functional
requirements were very simple; ability to compress data and decompress data
compressed with the same COTS component. Since there is a large number
of vendors who provide COTS components with this functionality, we had the
chance to look very closely at the non-functional specifications of these components. This process led us to our strong view on the importance of non-functional
attributes of COTS components in the context of building trust.

Following the process of requirements specifications for the COTS component
we start searching for a suitable component. The immediate problem encountered as soon as a candidate component is found is the comparison between the
components specifications and our requirements. Since the two specifications are
written by two different parties without any common protocol, even when both
parties belong to the same domain of software development there can be drastic
differences between the terminologies used and features specified. We, therefore,
recognize the need for such a protocol but do not address this problem here.

3   Need for Trust

Trust is inversely proportional to risk. Increase in trust results from a decrease
in risk, which in turn can be achieved by increasing the amount of useful information available. In general, a highly trusted component needs to be highly
testable and have a low degree of risk associated with its usage.

Once the fundamental functional requirements are satisfied, the process of
evaluating different COTS components for a given set of requirements mainly
aims at assessing the amount of trust offered by each component. COTS component consumers always take a risk, small or large, in using a component developed
by someone else. They have to trust what the vendors of those components say
and most of the times also research the worthiness of those vendors in the market. The amount of testing performed on such components also directly affects
the amount of trust the consumer is going to have in those components. All
this is done in an attempt to reduce the amount of risk associated with using a
particular COTS component.

COTS components need to be as trustable as possible in their *off-the-shelf*
form in order to speed up the evaluation and integration process. Unfortunately,
this is not so due to the lack of product standards in the IT industry. In our
industry, we have a healthy collection of process standards but the fact remains
that an excellent process does not guarantee an excellent product. With the

availability of highly trustable COTS components the speed of building software systems increases and the cost goes down since there is no need for the integrators to repeatedly perform acceptance testing or cover the untested risk associated with a COTS component.

Consumers are more likely to select a component that offers more information about itself. In our example scenario, we evaluated a number of COTS components that compress/decompress data and the selection was based on the criteria that whether a given component is compatible with the standard PKZIP format [14] or not and whether it offers an API on Microsoft .Net platform. Any components that specified these two features clearly were selected and further evaluated against each other. Components that do satisfy these requirements but did not state it got discarded simply due to the fact that although they offered the features they failed to offer the required trust to the consumers.

4   Attributes of Trust for COTS Components

Trust is often related to the transfer of risk from one party to the other while COTS components prohibit the transfer of ownership. This results in a greater risk to be taken by the consumers and hence the demand for more trust. The degree of risk associated with the usage of COTS components can be lowered by communicating useful information to the potential consumers. The key concern then is to identify what constitutes useful information and how can it be made available to the consumers. We address the first part in this section and discuss the second part in the later sections.

4.1   Functional Specifications

Consumers have to test and evaluate functional correctness of components as much as possible before they can make a decision about integrating a component in their system. Furthermore, consumers may be interested in only a subset of functionalities offered by a given COTS component. Testing the entire component using the information provided by the vendor is not desirable in such circumstances. In addition, certain features of components are extremely hard to test due to their nature and leave the consumers with the only option to use the components with an accepted degree of risk. For instance, the major functionality of a data compression component deals directly with the file system. The compressed data is written directly to the disk and the component only responds with a notification of successful completion. But successful completion, in this case, does not guarantee a valid compression unless we explicitly validate the resulting compressed data and it may not be feasible to test every possible output in this manner.

The time consuming process of acceptance testing COTS components can be expedited and facilitated if information from the analysis and design phase (and maybe even from the implementation) of the component's development is communicated to the consumers in a useful manner. Such information can be beneficial for both the evaluation and integration of COTS components.

Design By Contract (DBC) is a very useful means for this communication but at a much lower level than may be required for establishing trust at component or sub-component level. We believe that this concept needs to be extended and contracts should be added to every layer of a component to ensure correct functionality at each level. These contracts should then be included in the specifications of the COTS form of the component for the benefit of the consumer.

4.2   Non-functional Specifications

While testability of a component is critically important for establishing trust it does not eliminate the requirement of having useful non-functional information available about the component. Testing may cover some non-functional aspects like performance and resource usage but its main focus remains on functional aspects of a component. Non-functional aspects of software components play an equally important role in building trust.

Traditionally, non-functional requirements (NFRs) of software systems are synonymous with quality of service (QoS) issues—a view based on the context of dealing with NFRs during the early phases of the development process rather than delaying it till the implementation and testing stages ([7] and [8]). We believe that NFRs also play the major role in building trust in software components. However, QoS issues are not the only ingredients of trust-building NFRs. We extend the concept of NFRs to include issues like dependency requirements of the component, reputation of the vendor and the support extended by vendor to the consumers/integrators.

We propose a useful specification of all the non-functional attributes (QoS, dependency, reputation) for a COTS component. Some of these non-functional attributes are listed in Table 1. This information is *useful* in the sense that it is used by vendors (for publishing/advertising), brokers (for matchmaking, as discussed later in Sect. 5) and consumers (for evaluating and integrating).

Table 1. Initial Categorization of Non-Functional Attributes

Category	Sample Non-Functional Attributes
Quality of Service	Accuracy, security, performance
Implementation	Dependency, Standards, OS, platforms, Languages
Stability	Backward/forward compatibility, 24x7 support, technical documentation
Reputation	Company ranking/standing, user-base

4.3   Degree of Associated Risk

Trust is not an absolute or binary concept. Although we may trust some components to a certain degree and for a certain kind of functionality, complete (100%)

trust is unthinkable at least in the current era of software components. For instance, we may trust that the selected data compression component in our case will successfully compress and decompress all the data in different standard file formats but we cannot be completely certain that the compression performed will always be efficient. An even bigger risk is that there may exist a specific file (or set of data) that will cause the component to fail and that we shall encounter such a file only in the future. It is not feasible for the vendor to test the component with all possible files (or combination of data). Therefore, the consumer is always taking that unknown risk when they integrate this component in their system.

Another important feature of trust is that it cannot be measured accurately. We can rate trust as total, very high, high, adequate, moderate, low, very low or no trust at all, but we can not assign numbers to it. Most of the non-functional attributes that we have identified earlier can only be specified as ranges of values and some times even as averages.

4.4   Time & Usage History

Trust builds over time. Vendors of COTS components need to deal with this fact as they produce and update components and consumers have to be wary of trust as they integrate and use these components. Another important observation is that it is easier for us to trust a vendor whose components have already been successfully integrated and used by us in the past or vendors with a wide and known user-base.

Once a consumer has established an acceptable degree of trust in a COTS component, the problem for them is to keep that level or achieve an even higher level of trust in the face of different usage patterns and, especially, new and updated releases of the same component. In most cases, the consumers test and trust only a subset of features offered by a component at the time of integration. As the needs change and the system matures the consumers may need an increased level of trust in the component. Therefore, monitoring and maintaining the usage history of COTS components in host/target systems is critical for establishing trust in these components.

Consumers of COTS components also share trust and benefit from the lessons learned by early consumers. Early consumers of a component always take a bigger risk integrating it into their system than the later ones. Trust has to be maintained and improved as consumers integrate and use the components over time so the degree of trust established by early consumers can be transmitted to the later ones. Conventionally, this is achieved by having special interest groups or mailing lists for a component (or a group of similar components) that the consumers can subscribe to and share knowledge through. This is generally facilitated by vendors. This mechanism needs to progress towards automation so components can trust other components with a minimal intervention from their developers.

Vendors need to keep the functional and non-functional specifications of the COTS component up-to-date as they release new updates to their components.

In order to achieve higher trust, these updates should highlight any changes to the functional and non-functional specifications of the previous version.

Proper feedback has to be facilitated from the consumers to the vendors. For instance, the vendor of our selected data compression component may not have tested the component for compressing data in our in-house file format, or maybe one of the possibly hundreds of consumers of the component may discover the file that causes the component to fail. If a feedback mechanism exists such information can be easily communicated back to the vendor and in turn to other consumers of the same component.

5   Publishing Trustable Components

We use the wrapper mechanism to include all the trust attributes of a component in its COTS form (Fig. 2a). A wrapper generator tool is used to compile these attributes and produce a wrapper around the functional component. This tool interrogates the component for the features offered and allows the vendor to interactively include non-functional specifications in the wrapper. The wrapped component can then be published, registered with any brokers or made available to consumers via any other means. The responsibilities of the wrapper are to:

- facilitate the communication of the trust attributes to the consumers.
- monitor the usage of the component in the context of any dynamically changing attributes (e.g. QoS).
- provide useful feedback to the vendor.

At this stage, we introduce the role of a *broker* (Fig. 2b). A broker is a lot like real-estate agents in that vendors register their COTS components with the broker and consumers use a broker to find and perform the initial filtering of these components. A broker, therefore, needs to maintain a database of all the registered COTS components. Since the components already have all the functional and non-functional specifications included in the wrapped form, the registration process is straightforward and does not require much intelligence on the broker's part.

The broker facilitates usage of COTS components by helping the consumers locate suitable components for their requirements. It knows about both the consumer requirements and component specifications and implements the match-making logic based on these specifications. The final decision of component selection rests with the consumer.

6   COTS Procurement and *Usage Contracts*

Different methods have been suggested for the selection and procurement of COTS components by the consumers (e.g. PORE [4], CARE [9] and PECA [10]). While these approaches focus at evaluating different candidate COTS components for a given set of requirements, they do not look at the big picture of how the processes of COTS components *production* and *usage* affect each other and how these can be improved to achieve better trust.

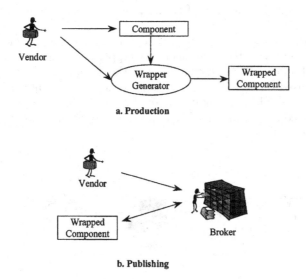

a. Production

b. Publishing

Fig. 2. Publishing a Trustable COTS Component with a Broker

A *broker*, as described in Sect. 5, fills up the gap between the production and usage of COTS components. It can play a vital role in the selection process (Fig. 3a), especially, when the selection is based on non-functional specifications of COTS components. The importance of brokers in the usage of COTS components has been recognized by other researchers as well [13].

We have concentrated on the post-evaluation process of integrating the selected COTS component in the target/host system. Based on the specifications of trust attributes of a COTS component, as discussed earlier, we create a *usage contract* between the consumer and the component. A usage contract contains all the trust attributes for the component that the consumer is interested in. This includes functional level constraints as well as non-functional attributes of the component.

Usage contract is a technical agreement between the consumer and the COTS component and includes all the specifications as promised by the vendor and as accepted by the consumers. For instance, the data compression component specifies that it can encrypt the compressed data with any password string up to a length of 65 characters, but our host system allows its users to key in a maximum of only 32 characters. The usage contract between our host system and the selected data compression component will, therefore, be established on and the component tested only against the maximum password length of 32 characters. If at a later stage we change our system to increase the length of password string to 64 characters, we will need to re-establish the usage contract by testing the component for this new length of password string. We will not be concerned with any issues/bugs of the component caused by a password string of 65 characters or more.

We use the contract generator tool to generate usage contracts (Fig. 3b). This tool interacts with the component's wrapper to get all the available trust attributes and allows the consumer to select the attributes of interest from this list. This is based on the fact that consumers are mostly interested in only a subset of features and functionalities offered by a component and in the context of a particular consumer of a given component it would be wasteful to monitor everything offered by it.

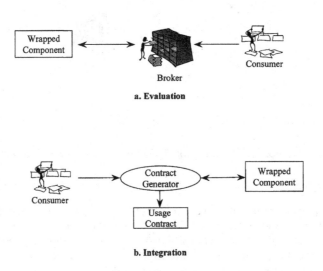

Fig. 3. Procuring a Trustable COTS component through a Broker

Usage contracts play the key role in the integration and monitoring of COTS components. They serve as a service-level agreement between the vendor and the consumer without necessarily requiring any direct communication between the two parties since they originate from the functional and non-functional specifications of the component as included in the wrapper. Once negotiated, a usage contract is then used for monitoring the behavior of the component from the consumers' perspective as it is used in different scenarios.

7   Conclusion

Trust in COTS components can be achieved either by thoroughly and exhaustively testing the components or by actually using the components over a period of time with an accepted degree of risk. Since complete testing is neither feasible nor possible the consumers are left with the only option to take the risk. The critical issue then is to lower the amount of this risk in order to increase the usage of COTS components. We have identified the reasons behind this risk and proposed a mechanism to achieve better trust by improving both the production and integration processes. Consumers can benefit from this mechanism and evaluate components more effectively for trust-worthiness rather than merely depending on factors like market reputation and user-base of the vendor.

Transfer of risk is inevitable in COTS components usage but transfer of useful information can significantly reduce the amount of risk transferred from vendors to consumers and in turn result in better trust between the two parties.

References

1. Carney, D., and Long, F.: What Do You Mean By COTS—Finally, a Useful Answer. In: IEEE Software (2000) 83–86
2. Bader, A., Sajeev, A.S.M., and Ramakrishnan, S.: Testing Concurrency and Communication in Distributed Objects. In: International Conference on High Performance Computing, IEEE Computer Society Press (1998) 422–428
3. Morisio, M., and Torchiano, M.: Definition and Classification of COTS: A Proposal. In: ICCBSS 2002, LNCS Vol. 2555, Springer-Verlag (2002) 165–175
4. Ncube, C., Maiden, N.: COTS Software Selection: The Need to Make Tradeoffs Between System Requirements, Architectures and COTS Components. In: International Conference on Software Engineering, Limerick, Ireland (2000)
5. Freedman, R. S.: Testability of Software Components. In: IEEE Transactions on Software Engineering 17(6), IEEE Computer Society Press (1991) 553–564
6. Gao, J., Gupta, K., Gupta, S., and Shim, S.: On Building Testable Software Components. In: ICCBSS 2002, LNCS Vol. 2555, Springer-Verlag (2002) 108–121
7. Boehm, B. et al.: Characteristics of Software Quality. North-Holland (1978)
8. Chung, L., Nixon, B. A.: Dealing with Non-Functional Requirements: Three Experimental Studies of a Process-oriented Approach. In: Procedings of 17th International Conference on Software Engineering, Seattle, WA, USA (1995) 25–37
9. Chung, L., Cooper, K., Huynh, D.: COTS-Aware Requirements Engineering Technique. In: Procedings of the 2001 Workshop on Embedded Software Technology (2001)
10. Comella-Dorda, S., Dean, J. C., Morris, E., and Oberndof, P.: A Process of COTS Software Product Evaluation. In: ICCBSS 2002, LNCS Vol. 2555, Springer-Verlag, (2000) 86–96
11. Beus-Dukic, L.: Non-Functional Requirements of COTS Software Components. In: International Conference on Software Engineering, Limerick, Ireland (2000)
12. Helokunnas, T., and Nyby, M.: Collaboration Between a COTS Integrator and Vendors. In: ECSQ 2002, LNCS Vol. 2349, Springer-Verlag (2002) 267–273
13. Periorellis, P., and Thomas, N.: Mutuality and the CLARiFi Component Broker. Technical Report 03/00, Department of Computer Science, University of Durham, August (2000)
14. PKZIP Application Note (2001)
   Available at: http://www.pkware.com/support/appnote.html

Incorporation of Test Functionality into Software Components

Franck Barbier, Nicolas Belloir, and Jean-Michel Bruel

LIUPPA, Université de Pau et des Pays de l'Adour
BP1155, F-064013 Pau cedex, France
{barbier, belloir, bruel}@univ-pau.fr

Abstract. COTS components trustworthiness is a key issue to be addressed within the field of component-based software engineering. This problem relies on the duality between development and deployment. COTS components vendors may prove varied properties for their components but purchasers may want to validate these properties in different execution environments. Built-In Test is thus the ability to endow components with extra functionality in order to develop in-situ tests. This paper stresses a Java library that supports Built-In Contract Testing. Complex component behaviors are ruled and observed based on states and reactivity to client requests. A large component consisting in a Programmable Thermostat illustrates the Built-In Contract Testing technology and the offered Java library.

1 Introduction

Component-based software engineering (CBSE) is currently the most recommended technique in terms of reuse and of reduction of development costs. The development of applications in this context is based on the principle of composition of components interacting together. In particular, this composition is carried out by connecting component interfaces that provide services, with clients requiring these services. However, composition of components remains syntactical and thus raises many problems. Among possible investigations, let us mention semantic interoperability [1], composability [2], prediction of assembly behaviors [3].

Experience shows that, whatever the level of certification/quality of service announced by a component, it is fundamental to give to its customers the possibility of testing it in situation in its new environment (which is called "run-time testing" in the remainder of this paper). In this context, it is necessary for a component to be able to show that it behaves according to its specification in the final phase of development (contract testing), or in the phase of deployment (quality of service testing). In this purpose, we have developed a Java library that implements these principles. In order to attenuate component integration, we advocate a special design technique for COTS components based on complex state machines (vendors side) and/or some customisation (users side) that adapts and allows to plug a given COTS component into our library. One recurrent feature

H. Erdogmus and T. Weng (Eds.): ICCBSS 2003, LNCS 2580, pp. 25–35, 2003.

of COTS components is the obstacle to access source code. In the Java context, we thus use the reflection capabilities of this language to permit dynamic access at run-time to internal properties. Test protocols are especially written once for all and greatly help the way COTS components may be acquired, assessed and finally (re)used.

We present in this article the main orientations of our approach, and we illustrate the use of our library. Thus, in Sect. 2 we present the general context of components testing. Our approach is illustrated by means of a concrete example in Sect. 3. Finally we conclude in Sect. 4 and present some perspectives.

2   Component Testing

As for electronic components, software components "are integrated" in software architectures without modification. In some extreme cases, components can even be incorporated into applications at run-time (such as in CORBA platforms). This kind of development results in increasing the importance of the assembling and the validation phases compared to the implementation phase. The developer thus builds the tests that are suitable for unit testing. The customer, on the other hand, generally does not test the component itself (it is supposed to be validated, even certified, by the supplier) [4]. It is nevertheless essential to test its integration in real execution contexts (e.g., communication with other components, appropriateness of interfaces, fault tolerance, conformance to specified behavior). Thus we are not actually and directly interested in testing a component. We want to provide the component with a certain degree of functionality allowing to assess its behavior in its deployment environment.

Previous works in the field of Built-In Test (BIT) rather deal with self-test [5] (i.e., automatic triggering of tests), or with the improvement of tests set definition [6]. Approaches close to ours is that in [7]. They define the notion of testable component that supports remote testing based on a generic testing interface and an architectural model. We enhance such an approach in dealing with the deep and detailed internal behavior of components within tests, allowing contract and quality of service testing.

2.1   Built-in Contract Testing

We consider a COTS component as an aggregate of sub-components that are implementations of several operations that it provides. In Java, such a component is realized through a class that possesses fields whose type is that of these sub-components, recursively. Figure 1 describes the micro-architecture in which an anonymous COTS component is connected with the predefined classes of our library. A BIT component is built such that it "acquires" all of the properties of "Component". In Fig. 1, a UML dependency is used in order to defer the choice of an adequate programming mechanism (inheritance is often useful). The BIT testability contract interface, detailed in Sect. 3, is a set of operations that are systematically used within BIT test case, itself systematically used by

BIT tester. BIT test case is a Java class that has frozen test protocols, namely "initialize the test", establish "execution conditions", "get results and/or failures" and "finalize the test". Any BIT component may customize (i.e. override) these basic actions in taking care, opportunistically, of the property values of "Component". BIT tester allows to develop test scenarios: sequences, expected results, aborting/completion policies, etc. A great benefit of this approach is that most of the test stuff is not dependent upon the specificity of the evaluated COTS component. For instance, competing components that may be bought in order to satisfy very special requirements, can be compared based on the same test framework. Moreover, the test stuff is actually built in "BIT component". BIT component (instead of Component) may be deployed in order to measure the quality of service at run-time. Notice however that in this case, one has to pay attention to performance and resource burden: BIT component creates some overload compared to Component. A drawback of our approach is that sub-components are fully encapsulated entities, and as such, analysis and diagnoses are difficult to determine at a deep level of aggregation. We have thus extend the library to cope with nested and concurrent states of components, in order to supply a better access to the internal of a component.

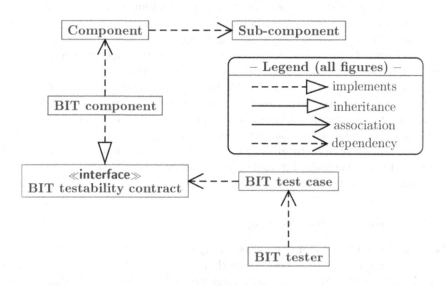

Fig. 1. Dependencies in Built-In Contract Testing

2.2   State-Based Contract Testing

Figure 2 shows an extended interface called State-based BIT testability contract from which a BIT component can be linked to. The white arrows with dotted line is the Java "implementation" relation between classes and interfaces. This second way of running Built-In Contract Testing is more coercive in the sense that a state machine is need for the tested COTS component. While such a specification is common in real-time systems for instance, one cannot always expect that. Some reengineering work is thus sometimes required to extract a behavioral specification from an existing component.

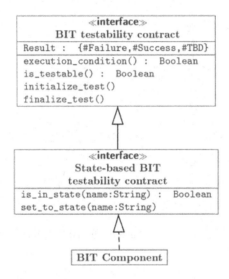

Fig. 2. Extension of the BIT/J library for state-based contract testing

3   A Concrete Example of the BIT/J Library Usage

In order to show the applicability of the concepts presented above, we first present a Programmable Thermostat component. Next, we discuss the construction of the corresponding BIT component, while insisting on a precise step-by-step process.

3.1   The BIT/J Library

Figure 3 is a complete overview of the BIT/J library. Built-In Test can first be simply carried out by means of the three main elements named BIT testability contract, BIT test case and BIT tester. In this case, BIT just copes with assessment of computation results, execution environment and faults. In the more complicated case, three equivalent state-oriented facilities are required: State-based BIT testability contract, State-based BIT test case and State-based BIT tester. Since these three last one use Harel's formalism called Statecharts [8], a underlying sub-library ("Statecharts" package: top, left of Fig. 3) is reused (i.e. Statechart and Statechart monitor). BIT state and BIT state monitor are contextual specializations of the sub-library in order to create a connection with State-based BIT testability contract, State-based BIT test case and State-based BIT tester.

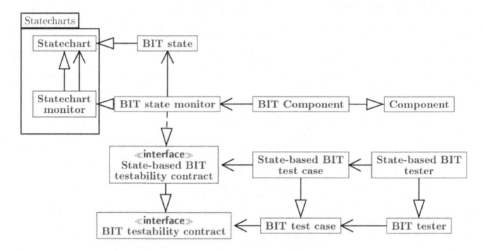

Fig. 3. Architecture of the BIT/J library

3.2 The Programmable Thermostat Component

We give here the specification of the interface provided by a Programmable Thermostat component (see Fig. 4). The operations in the interface are requested by clients. They mask the inside of the Programmable Thermostat component. Traditional testing is thus confined to activating operations while intermediate hidden results, states and possible faults have to be known to assess deployement compliance.

3.3 The BIT Implementation of the Programmable Thermostat Component

The realization of a BIT component and its evaluation occur within four phases. The first one can have different shapes according to the component nature: whether it was derived "from scratch", i.e. conceived since the beginning as a BIT component, or whether it was built from an existing component. Our method first consists in linking the BIT part to the original component. The

Programmable_thermostat
+ambient_temperature_changed()
+fan_switch_turned_on()
+f_c()
+hold_temp()
+run_program()
+season_switch_turned_off()
+set_clock()
+set_day()
+temp_down()
+temp_up()
+time_backward()
+time_forward()
+time_out()
+view_program()
+auto()
+on()
+cool()
+heat()
+off()
+propertyChange(event:PropertyChangeEvent)

Fig. 4. Programmable Thermostat interface

second step consists in implementing the behavioral specification in the BIT part. The third step consists in providing an implementation for the interface relating to the standard testability contracts. Lastly, at the time of the fourth step, a given customer of the BIT component defines specific test cases handled by testers.

Step 1: Linking the BIT part to the original component. There are several ways for bounding a component to its BIT incarnation. Firstly, the BIT part can inherit from the component. This method is interesting because it allows to directly manipulate the component itself. Indeed, it is then possible, for example, to have access to protected attributes and operations, in order to setup the component in a particular state before execution of a specific test. That also allows to directly describe its behavior in terms of its attribute values if the component was initially designed to support the BIT technology. Secondly, the component can be included as a particular field value in its BIT version. The major advantage is encapsulation respect since the protected attributes and operations are then not activable. In the remainder, we use the first approach.

Step 2: Description of the behavior with a state machine. To describe the component behavior, it must be specified via a state machine that conforms to Harel's formalism (Fig. 5). Each state is an attribute of the BIT component whose type is BIT_state (or Statechart). A unique special attribute is also implemented within the BIT component whose type is BIT_state_monitor (or Statechart_monitor). Below, we have the declaration of two states: Run and Hold :

```
1  protected Statechart _Run;
2  protected Statechart _Hold;
3    //...
4  protected Statechart_monitor _Programmable_thermostat;
```

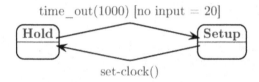

Fig. 5. An extract of the Programmable Thermostat state machine

Below, instantiation of simple states occurs. It is also possible to build complex (i.e. nested) states, recursively. In order to connect them together, the *and* (concurrency between states) and *xor* (common exclusiveness between states) operators are used. As for nesting, it is managed through assignment (e.g. _Operate is assigned with an expression mixing its sub-states).

```
1  // declaration of the state machine in the BIT component
2  _Run = new BIT_state("Run");
3  _Hold = new BIT_state("Hold");
4  //...
```

```
1  // complex BIT_state
2  _Operate=((_Run).xor(_Hold)).and(...)).name("Operate");
3
```

It is possible to associate an operation with an incoming (or an outgoing or an internal) transition. This operation is then automatically triggered. *These operations can be those of sub-components.* This permits the correlation between the BIT component states and the activation of sub-components. This also permits the trace of execution paths in case of faults at a deep level of nesting.

```
1  // Automatic dynamic access to the "set_time" internal
2  // action through the "time_out" operation belonging
3  // to the BIT component's interface
4    _Operate = (((_Run)).name("Operate")).internalAction(
5      "time_out", this,"set_time",null);
6  //...
```

Once all of the states defined, the state machine of the BIT component must be declared and instantiated:

```
1  // State machine
2    _Programmable_thermostat =
3    new BIT_state_monitor((_Operate).xor(_Setup)...);
```

Finally, the initial states of the state machine must be established. In our example, the initial states are Hold and Current_date_and_time_displaying.

```
1    _Hold.inputState();
2    _Current_date_and_time_displaying.inputState();
```

Step 3: Definition of the testing interface. The BIT/J library provides general-purpose operations which may be overloaded to pay attention to contextual phenomena (see "execution_condition()" for instance in Fig. 2). These operations are supported by two entities of the library. The first is the BIT_testability_contract interface. It allows to develop *traditional* contracts. In contrast, the is_in_state() and set_to_state() operations are members of the State_based_BIT_testability_contract interface and rule the setup of states before a test (see below), and the evaluation of target, expected or unexpected, states after a test.

```
1  // In the BIT Component
2  public boolean Configuration_1() throws ... {
3      set_to_state("Hold");
4
5      // execution of the "set_clock()" operation
6      set_clock( );
7  }
```

Step 4: Instantiation and execution of the test case objects. The tester instantiates a BIT component. Then, it can run the test sets that embody a given policy. For that, it instantiates test cases (i.e. instances of BIT_test_case and/or State_based_BIT_test_case) by specifying operations that have to be run. The global test process relies on the test() operation and result/fault interpretation depends upon the interpretation() operation. The code below shows the realization of a test concerning the set_clock() Programmable Thermostat's operation. The expected result is the arrival at the *Setup* state.

```
1  // bc is a BIT component
2  bc = new BIT_programmable_thermostat (temperature);
3
4  // Put the BIT component in a specific state before the test
5  bc.set_to_state("Hold");
6
7  // Definition of the test case. The third argument
8  // is the expected result
9      sbbtc1 = new State_based_BIT_test_case (bc,
10 "set_clock", null, null, "Setup");
11
12 // Execution of the test case
13 sbbtc1.test();
14
15 // Get the test case result
16 System.err.println("Interp: "+ sbbtc1.result());
```

Quality of service analysis. Below is an example of malfunctioning that the BIT technology may help to detect. The Programmable Thermostat is designed for automatically be forced in the Hold state if previously in Setup and no action performed for 20 seconds. We simulate a defect by means of a undesired delay. Different computer operating systems may lead to different results for specific test.

```
1  /* Instantiation of the BIT component */
2  public boolean Configuration_2 () throws ... {
3
4      set_to_state("Setup");
5
6      /* Starting of a timer for 20 s */
7      try {
8          Thread.sleep(20000);
9      } catch(Exception e){...}
10
11     /* Test if the BIT component is in the Hold State */
12     if (is_in_state("Hold"))...
13     else...
14 }
```

4   Conclusion

Individual comprehensive behaviors of COTS components often remain buried within their hidden part. Formal behavioral specifications is a first step to make trustworthiness effective but is insufficient. Built-In Test is another step to create confidence. Vendors may equip their COTS components with test stuff in order to run it online, especially within unknown (at development time) execution environments. We enhance in this paper Meyer's "design by contract" idea in allowing first the description of assertions (pre-conditions, post-conditions and invariants) based on complex nested, and sometimes concurrent, states of components that largely hinge on sub-components. Next, we ground our approach on Java reflection capabilities that ensure that test protocols are written once and for all. In such a context, properties of components are dynamically accessed at run-time. Test stuff is launched within test case objects subject to interfaces embodying testability contracts, are implemented by BIT components. They are in fact two ways for working: either vendors adhere to our component design technique or purchasers need to build BIT components from ordinary components. In the first case, providers add value to their COTS components by delivering customizable testing functionality. In the second case, components have to be adapted in order to be plugged into the BIT/J library. Limited to the Java world, our approach is however a concrete support for the notion of Built-In Test that has been defined more theoretically in some other papers. The Programmable Thermostat component is in this respect, a representative example. We measure for instance the timer event quality of service that may greatly vary from an environment to another one. Finally, we also supply a step-by-step component design process that is based on rationality. The most significant perspective is nowadays the submersion of the BIT/J library in the JMX (Java Management eXtensions) framework. BIT components may thus be evaluated through Web browsers. We intend in a near future to develop remote testing as part of a project that intends to offer component acquirement facilities on the Web.

References

1. Heiler, S.: Semantic Interoperability. In: ACM Computing Surveys 27 (1995) 271–273
2. Meijler, T.D., and Nierstrasz, O.: Beyond Objects: Components. In: Cooperative Information Systems—Trends and Directions, Academic Press, San Diego, CA (1998) 49–78
3. Crnkovic, I., Schmidt, H., Stafford, J., and Wallnau, K.: Anatomy of a Research Project in Predictable Assembly. In: Fifth ICSE Workshop on Component-based Software Engineering (2002)
4. Harrold, M.J.: Testing: A Roadmap. In: ICSE—Future of SE Track (2000) 61–72
5. Wang, Y., King, G., Patel, D., Court, I., Staples, G., Ross, M., and Patel, S.: On Built-in Test and Reuse in Object-Oriented Programming. In: ACM Software Engineering Notes 23 (1998) 60–64
6. Jézéquel, J.M., Deveaux, D., and Le Traon, Y.: Reliable Objects : Lightweight Testing for OO Languages. In: IEEE Software 18 (2001) 76–83

7. Gao, J., Gupta, K., Gupta, S., and Shim, S.: On Building Testable Software Components. In: Proceedings of First International Conference on COTS-Based Software Systems, LNCS Vol. 2255, Orlando, FL, USA, February (2002) 108–121
8. Harel, D.: Statecharts : a Visual Formalism for Complex Systems. In: Science of Computer Programming 8 (1987) 231–274

Not All CBS Are Created Equally: COTS-Intensive Project Types

Barry W. Boehm, Dan Port, Ye Yang, and Jesal Bhuta

Center for Software Engineering
University of Southern California
{boehm, dport, yey, jesal}@cse.usc.edu

Abstract. COTS products affect development strategies and tactics, but not all CBS development efforts are equal. Based on our experiences with 20 large government and industry CBS projects assessed during our development of the COCOTS estimation model, and our hands-on experience with 52 small e-services CBS projects within USC's graduate level software engineering course, we have identified four distinct CBS activity areas: assessment intensive, tailoring intensive, glue-code intensive, and non-COTS intensive. The CBS activity type fundamentally affects the COTS related activity effort and project risks. In this work we define the three COTS activity intensive CBS types and discuss their strategic comparisons based on an empirical study of the spectrum of large and small CBS projects.

1   Introduction

Much has been written regarding the various ways in which commercial off-the-shelf (COTS) products affect the way we develop systems. In particular, how we define requirements, evaluate products, manage risks, and relate the activities of product evaluation and system design (for example see [1] and [14]). We have seen a number of patterns among these, ranging across large government and industry projects to smaller e-service projects. In our experiences since 1996 in both areas, we have observed three main strategies for developing COTS based systems (CBS): find and use COTS products without modification to cover all desired capabilities, find and adapt COTS as needed, find and integrate multiple COTS as components in a custom built application. The decision as to which approach to use is driven primarily by the systems shared vision, economic constraints, and desired capabilities & priorities (DC&P's). In projects where a significant amount of COTS related development effort is expended relative to the overall development effort (which we will later refer to as COTS Based Applications or CBA), we have observed within our USC e-services CBS projects that these approaches will differ considerably in regards to the development focus, critical activities, and project risks.

Although there are some significant differences between our large industry CBS projects and our smaller USC e-services CBS projects, we have found that

H. Erdogmus and T. Weng (Eds.): ICCBSS 2003, LNCS 2580, pp. 36–50, 2003.

they share many common factors such as client demand for sophisticated functionality, fixed time schedules, limited developer resources and skills, lack of client maintenance resources, and many others. As a result, we believe our USC e-services COTS experiences are particularly representative of CBS development in general [10]. In particular, we have observed that, the degree that our comprehensive software development guidelines (MBASE [24]) used by the developers of the e-services projects, have to be adapted is proportional to the intensity of effort within performing COTS related activities such as product assessment, tailoring, and glue-code development. We have also observed that there are considerable risks in these areas and strategic guidance on the management of these is critical to a successful project [13]. Analogous observations have been made for our larger, industry based CBS projects studied for calibration of the COCOTS [23] CBS cost estimation model.

While developing COCOTS, it was found that there is no "one size fits all" CBS effort estimation model. Instead, effort estimates are made by composing individual assessment, tailoring, and glue-code effort sub-models. Following this lead, we surmised that there are four major types of CBS projects: those that are assessment intensive, tailoring intensive, glue-code intensive, or non-COTS activity intensive. To elaborate this:

1. An *assessment intensive* project will have the DC&P's covered without much modification (or tailoring) by a single COTS package or through the simple integration of several. The primary effort is focused on identifying a collection of candidate COTS products and evaluating (i.e. assessing) a feasible set of products whose existing capabilities directly address a desired operational concept.

2. A *tailoring intensive* project is where the DC&P's are covered by a single (or very few) COTS package(s). The primary effort is on adapting a COTS framework whose existing general capabilities can be customized (i.e. tailored) in a feasible way to satisfy the majority of a systems capabilities or operational scenarios.

3. The *glue-code intensive* project will have non-trivial DC&P's covered by multiple COTS packages and components, The primary effort is to identify COTS packages that can feasibly used and integrated as components to address subsets of the required system capabilities and integrate them to develop the system. Typically there is a significant amount of glue code design and development in order to integrate such packages.

4. A *non-COTS intensive* project is any CBS in which all the non-trivial DC&P's are not covered with COTS package(s), and many DC&P's must be covered by custom development. The primary effort in such systems in the custom design and development. Typically there are significant "Buy versus Build" decisions. Critical factors are: available COTS products, schedule limitations, budget limitations, and desired current and future capabilities.

Although non-COTS intensive project development encompasses a large number of CBS projects, it is not the primary focus of this research. Instead, this paper will discuss the empirical motivation for distinguishing between CBS project types, their development characteristics and considerations, basic development guidelines, and use in strategic project planning and risk management.

1.1   Previous Work

A number of researchers [1,2,7,20] have identified the existence of different types of CBS, and have affirmed that the process and activities involved to be followed in developing each type of system largely differs. There are several proposed CBA development processes such as described in [1,2,3,4,6,7,20].

The authors of [20] have classified COTS based systems based on the manner in which the COTS product is used in the system. While this work includes similar terminology and indicates analogous CBA project types, the present work refines and justifies these types via empirical data gathered from COCOTS calibrations and our hands-on project experience with the various e-services projects.

1.2   COTS, COTS Based Systems, and COTS Based Applications

There are a multitude of definitions for COTS [14,25,26,27], but for the purposes of this work we adopt the SEI COTS-Based System Initiative's definition [7] of a *COTS product:* "A product that is sold, leased, or licensed to the general public, offered by a vendor trying to profit from it, supported and evolved by the vendor, who retains the intellectual property rights, available in multiple identical copies and used without source code modification."

We also will adopt the definition of a COTS based system (CBS) as any system that makes use of a COTS package. COTS based systems however, may range from simple 'turnkey' systems such as Microsoft Office, Common Desktop Environment or Netscape Communicator, where a single system meets most of the DC&P's to systems that rely on a specific COTS product such as Oracle, but involve a large amount of custom development specific to the application [1]. Making clear distinctions between such systems is difficult, particularly when mainly COTS assessment is involved and no COTS customization. We are primarily concerned with the COTS related development effort required to satisfy the DC&P's relative to the overall development effort, not percentage of COTS used in the system or other such measures. For our purposes, we define a *COTS-Based Application* (CBA) as a system for which at least 30% of the end-user functionality (in terms of functional elements: inputs, outputs, queries, external interfaces, internal files) is provided by COTS products, and at least 10 % of the development effort is devoted to COTS considerations. The numbers 30% and 10% are not sacred quantities, but approximate behavioral CBA boundaries observed in our CBS projects. Here we observed a significant gap observed in COTS-related effort reporting where projects either reported less than 2% or over 10% COTS-related effort, but never between 2-10%.

The above empirical definition is based on our observations of CBS projects that required a great deal of COTS "special handling" with respect to overall development effort in order to succeed. The percentages are only approximate and are likely to change (perhaps in relation to increasing COTS availability and maturity levels). However, we have noted that the majority of special handling for CBA projects lies in managing assessment, tailoring and glue-code efforts along with their associated project risks and value tradeoffs and other project lifecycle activities such as requirements modeling and system design. A critical element of this is to evaluate the COTS effort and risks within the feasibility analysis and project business case [18]. For example the "USC Collaborative Services" project from USC e-service projects was asked to identify a variety of COTS packages to support distributed project collaboration (e.g. message board, chat). The team quickly identified a number of potentially useful COTS packages and after a cursory assessment settled on an open source product called DotProject. At first DotProject seemed to satisfy nearly all of the desired operational capabilities and better still, it was free and easily customized. However, since the package was still in its beta version and had a lot of bugs that needed to be fixed, and most importantly, most of its collaborative features only supported one type of user, there would have to be a lot of customization for each feature to satisfy the projects needs. As a result, a round of business case analysis concluded that DotProject would be unfeasible due to the high demand of glue code effort needed to address its shortcomings. Though the team had already spent tremendous time on adapting this product into system requirements and architecture design, they chose to switch to another COTS package after a re-negotiation of the requirements with the client.

2   Motivation for CBA Project Typing

Many researchers have identified the necessity to use a special process to develop and implement CBSs [1,8] and some have proposed a generic process for CBS development [2]. However within the CBS domain there is a large variation in development approaches (e.g. turnkey, adaptation, integration) for which a single generic CBS process is unable to provide adequate development guidance. We have tried to incorporate such generic CBS processes with limited success. This was evidenced by observing numerous teams succumbing to effort allocation pitfalls. For example performing too much COTS assessment and neglecting to allocate enough time for training, tailoring and integration, resulting in project delays, inability to implement desired functional capabilities, and so forth. In some cases some developers did not perform enough assessment, which resulted in problems and delays during construction phases. For example in case of a project titled 'Quality Management through Bore' where the developers were mandated the use of the BORE product, the developers did not perform enough assessment which resulted in delays due to lack of product stability, promised features that were unavailable etc. resulting in serious losses due to schedule delays and unsatisfied capability requirements.

Such losses may be minor when it comes to implementing small e-service applications, however in case of large scale systems and systems required to meet a 'specific window of opportunity,' such losses may be extremely significant. Our experience in USC e-service projects has led us to conclude that a generic CBS process is insufficient for CBA projects. To this end we have introduced guidelines for the early identification and continuous monitoring of a CBA project along with development guidance *based on the CBA project type*. A CBA project can be classified as *assessment intensive, tailoring intensive, or glue-code intensive*.

These classifications provide an overview of the potential risks, characteristics, and development effort priorities and are useful for strategic and tactical development planning. Early identification of the CBA type can help a project team identify a clear development process and mitigate risks especially risks due to COTS effort allocation.

2.1   Increase in CBA Projects

Our keen interest in CBAs is due to an observed dramatic increase in the number of CBA projects from 28% in 1997 to 60% in 2001 over a 5-year period as evidenced in Fig. 1.

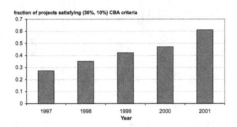

Fig. 1. CBA Growth in USC E-services Projects

Some of our USC-CSE affiliates have reported similar qualitative trends, but this is the first quantitative data they and we have seen on the rate of increase of CBA projects under any consistent definition and in any application sector (we note that e-services applications probably have higher rates of increase in recent times than many other sectors). We have experienced many notable effects of this increase: for example, programming skills are necessary but not sufficient for developing CBA's [8,9,10,11].

2.2   CBA Effort Distributions

Based on 2000-2002 USC-CSE e-services data and 1996-2001 COCOTS calibration data, we observed a large variation of COTS-related effort (assessment, tailoring, and glue code) distributions. This is clearly illustrated in the e-services and COCOTS COTS effort distributions of Fig 2. and Fig. 3 respectively.

Some CBA approaches, including our initial approach to COCOTS, just focus on one CBA activity such as glue code or assessment. As shown in Fig. 2, some

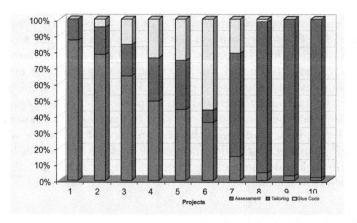

Fig. 2. CBA Effort Distribution of USC e-Service Projects

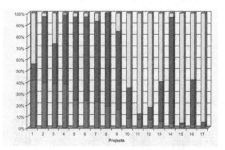

Fig. 3. CBAs Effort Distribution of COCOTS Calibration Data

projects (projects 7, 8, 9, 10) are almost purely tailoring efforts, while others (projects 1, 2, 3) spent most of the time on COTS assessment, and still others focused on glue code (project 6). The industry projects in Fig. 3 show similar variation. While some projects did not have glue code (projects 1, 9, 10), all projects had some degree of assessment and tailoring, but never tailoring or glue code only efforts, or a mix of just tailoring and glue code.

The industry projects in Fig. 3 were a mix of small-to-large business management, engineering analysis, and command control applications. Assessment effort ranged from 1.25 to 147.5 person-months (PM). Tailoring effort ranged from 3 to 648 PM; glue code effort ranged from 1 to 1411 PM.

This data indicates that the CBA types described in the introduction do indeed manifest themselves as usually one of the effort areas dominates and there is clearly are patterns in how COTS effort is distributed.

3   CBA Project Types

The three CBA types were defined briefly in Sect. 1. In this section we elaborate on the assumptions, some of the primary characteristics, critical activities, and risks for each type. To see the overall similarities and differences between the CBA types, the section closes with an overall summary comparison of the CBA types.

3.1   Assessment Cots Based Application

Implied by the definition of assessment CBA (ACBA) in Sect. 1, the intent is to avoid doing custom development by finding COTS to handle the DC&P's. In this, an ACBA is based on two assumptions. First, that COTS packages are available to cover most of desired system capabilities identified according to system shared vision among stakeholders. Second, a considerable number of COTS packages need to be assessed against established evaluation criteria, or a few must be assessed in great depth. In another words, an ACBA will have the DC&P's covered without much modification (or tailoring) by a single COTS framework or through the simple integration of several.

Characteristics. The primary effort is focused on identifying collection of candidate COTS products and evaluating a feasible set of products whose existing capabilities directly address a desired operational concept. About 60-80% of COTS related effort is assessment effort, and accounts for 24% of overall effort.

Custom development, glue-code, and tailoring effort are undesirable. There must be high degree of flexibility in the requirements and design due to COTS capability uncertainties. COTS impose requirements based on their existing capabilities that typically do not match precisely with a systems needs. As a result, even after final COTS selection the system requirements may change to be kept compatible with the chosen COTS package and its evolutionary path.

A business case analysis is critical for a detailed COTS assessment. Early assessment effort may greatly reduce overall system cost, risk, and schedule by helping to establish a sound business case for a particular feasible set of COTS packages.

Critical Activities. The following are some critical activities that an ACBA must perform.

1. Plan: set the evaluation procedures and provide a baseline and guide for evaluation process.
2. COTS Identification: search for COTS candidates based on the DC&P's and filter out the risky COTS packages based on observation or other initial filtering criteria.
3. Establish evaluation criteria: Produce the evaluation criteria necessary for detailed evaluation. Identification of evaluation criteria is based on functional, performance, architectural, and financial characteristics of DC&P's.

4. Detailed Evaluation: Perform multiple cycle of evaluation to collect evaluation data. One type of detailed evaluation is scenario-based evaluation testing, focusing on verifying vendor's claim and test the feasibility and performance of COTS package(s) in the proposed system context.
5. COTS Recommendation: Analyze the evaluation data captured from each candidate and make trade-offs among the results to choose the final COTS package.

3.2 Tailoring COTS Based Applications

Following the definition of a tailoring CBA (TCBA) from Sect. 1, there is an implied desire to avoid complex custom development by identifying COTS for the DC&P's, but there is expectation that some customization must be done to adapt the selected COTS to the particular needs of the organization. This makes the following two obvious assumptions. There are COTS package(s) that can satisfy most of the requirements or DC&P's of the system. Owing to this, a TCBA must always include some amount of assessment effort—even if the COTS packages are pre-selected or are mandated for use. In this latter circumstance, assessment must be performed in order to identify the extent the COTS packages satisfy the DC&P's and the degree of tailoring required. Another trivial, yet vital assumption is that the COTS packages have some sort of a customization interface or capability for which the product can be tailored to meet the requirements of the system.

Characteristics. The primary effort is on tailoring the COTS package to meet the system requirements. Approximately 60-80% COTS related effort is spent on tailoring the system, which accounts for approximately 10% of overall development effort.

Custom development is undesirable and as such there is a need for moderate flexibility in requirements and design due to COTS uncertainties for similar reasons for an ACBA. The primary difference is that some of the requirements will not be totally negotiable. In such cases, the COTS package and the requirements will have to be adapted until they are mutually compatible. Typically this involves GUI and hardware requirements. For example a function selection menu may always need to include the company logo, a selected COTS package may require a certain amount of free disk space to operate.

The focus of system architecture depends upon the type of tailoring features available in the COTS package and the amount of tailoring required in order to satisfy the DC&P's. The different types of tailoring interfaces available include GUI based tailoring interface (e.g. Spearmint [28]) where no design involved, parameter based tailoring interface (e.g. Windows Media Player [29]) where little design may be involved in terms of passing of parameters or programmable tailoring interface (e.g. Hyperwave [30]) where detailed procedural or object oriented design may be required. Some COTS packages may have a combination of one, two or all three types of tailoring interfaces (e.g. Microsoft Office [31]).

Critical Activities. The critical activities for tailoring intensive systems include:

1. Assessment: Some assessment may be required in identifying the right COTS product to be used for the system. The amount of assessment shall be dependent upon the number of available COTS products, the number of constraints, available budget, type of tailoring interface etc.
2. Tailoring Interface Identification: The tailoring interface utilized in order to tailor the COTS product to satisfy the desired capabilities and priorities shall determine the future activities to be implemented.
3. For a GUI Based Tailoring Interface: Plan and Tailor the COTS product and document the actions and activities performed during the GUI tailoring of the system.
4. For a parameter based tailoring system: Design the interactions between the components within the COTS and implement the design.
5. For a programmable tailoring system: Design the procedures and objects required to implement the desired capabilities and priorities and implement the system.

3.3   The Glue-Code COTS Based Application

As specified in the definition in Sect. 1, the intent of a glue-code CBA (GCBA) is to use COTS as basic system components. The GCBA assumes that COTS packages are available to satisfy significantly valuable subsets of system capabilities or project limitations dictate use (e.g. schedule, skill, or complexity factors). This implies there is a reasonable buy versus build cost-benefit return on investment. In particular, the integration overhead is minimal with respect to custom development cost and that there is low assessment and tailoring effort needed. As with the TCBA, some amount of assessment will always be required.

Characteristics. The primary effort is focused on identifying system components and requirements that may be risky to custom implement and mapping them to a collection of candidate COTS products. Further, the COTS packages are expected to implement core system requirements; there is little flexibility in these requirements.

It is expected that the packages will require a significant amount of custom integration effort (glue-code) as the COTS packages used are not specialized to a particular application domain and there generic capabilities will need to be adapted to the particular system needs. Custom code development is typically necessary to satisfy requirements not covered by the selected COTS or where the business case indicates that 'build' considerations outweigh investing in COTS. In general, the COTS components utilized are not designed to execute independently and must be built application to function. Typically many possible COTS packages may apply and some cursory assessments must be performed to identify which best match the requirements. There may be many evolutionary requirements with respect to the custom components and anticipated COTS features.

Critical Activities

1. Identify Implementation Risks: Consider risky development areas due to schedule limitations, skill limitations, high complexity, etc.
2. COTS Identification: search for COTS candidates based on the DC&P's and implementation risk areas.
3. Assessment: Evaluate the COTS candidates with respects to DC&P's, determine COTS risks due to requirements mismatch, faulty vendor claims, vendor support, familiarity with COTS packages, etc.
4. Buy Versus Build: Compare expected cost of utilizing individual COTS packages with building a component with similar capabilities, choose best mix of COTS, custom components.
5. Implement: Tailor COTS or develop glue code or integrate COTS or develop custom components as needed.
6. Integrate: Integrate COTS and custom components and tests.

Table 1. CBA Type Comparison

CBA type Project Type	ACBA	TCBA	GCBA	Non-CBA
Number of COTSs	Various single COTS or COTS mix solutions	Usually one leading COTS product much covers the system functions.	A mix of many COTS products.	Varies, but not any one or a combination of many intensively drives the system.
Requirements Covered by COTSs	Should be covered as much as possible based on assessment and business case analysis.	Mostly covered by adapting existing capabilities	Covers effort intensive or risky subsets	Few
Requirements Flexibility	High, requirements depend on COTS selection	Moderate (Change non-critical requirements if needed)	Low to moderate	Varies, but usually low
COTS Assessment	Significant (75%)	Little to moderate (1%)	Little to moderate (19%)	Varies
COTS Tailoring	None or little (22%)	Significant (89%)	Little to moderate (42%)	Varies
COTS Glue Code	None to little (3%)	None or little (10%)	Significant (39%)	Varies
Domain Specificity	Generic to domain or COTS is domain specific; organization will adapt to COTS	General to domain and can be refined to specific organization or mission	Independent of domain	Usually highly domain specific
Custom Development	None or very little	None or very little	Little	Significant development to implement custom capabilities
Evolution Requirements Degree	Generally Very Low, but included within assessed products	Limited to what is tailorable	High with respect to custom components and anticipated COTS features	Generally Very High
Top-10 Risks (see Table 2)	1, 2, 3, 4, 5, 6, 7, 8, 9, 10	7, 10, 14, 4, 8, 6, 13, 12, 15	4, 13, 11, 12, 16, 5, 13, 1, 7, 10	7, 13, 16, 2, 3, 4, 5, 14, 10, 12, 15

Table 2. Top CBA Project Risks from USC e-service projects 2000-2002

Risk	Common Mitigation Plan
1. Requirements changes and mismatches	Prototyping and business case analysis can help to estimate the effect of change and corresponding team effort and schedule needed. Win Win negotiation among all stakeholders must be maintained in each development phase.
2. Many new non technical activities are introduced in the Software Engineering Process	Stakeholders with Domain Expertise, Evaluation expertise must be included in the evaluation process
3. Miss possible COTS candidates within the COTS process	Stay as broad as possible when doing the initial searching for candidates
4. Too much time spent in assessment due to too many requirements and too many COTS candidates	Identify the core 'showstopper' requirements and filter all the COTS candidates that do not meet these during the initial assessment and then proceed for a more detailed assessment with the remaining COTS candidates
5. Might not include all key aspects for establishing evaluation criteria set. (Inadequate COTS assessment)	Involve experienced, knowledgeable stakeholders for reviewing evaluation criteria and weight distribution judgments
6. Introducing new COTS candidates is likely and requires replanning	Develop a contingency plan in cases of addition of a new COTS product. Identify the limits on schedule and budget while making the introduction
7. Faulty Vendor Claims may result in feature loss and/or significant delays	Detailed analysis provides greater assurance of COTS characteristics with respect to vendor documentation (although at significant effort). Detailed assessment beyond literature review or vendor provided documentation should be performed in the form of hands-on experiments and prototyping (especially of core capabilities to be utilized).
8. Ability or willingness of the organization to accept the impact of COTS requirements	The project operational concept must identify such risks and they must be conveyed to the higher management
9. Difficulty in coordinating meetings with key personnel may result in significant delays	The key decision making personnel must be well accounted for the project life cycles. The project manager must make them aware of the approximate time required to be spent be them during the process of assessment etc. The decision making personnel must be kept as minimal as possible
10. Inadequate vendor support may result in significant project delays	The licensing of COTS products must account for vendor support details. In case of contracting labor the developers with experience in using the COTS must be selected
11. COTS package incompatibilities may result in feature loss and significant project delays (Integration Clash)	COTS integration issues must be considered during assessment. The number of COTS products must be kept as minimal as possible.
12. Added complexity of unused COTS features	The number of unused features could be identified and the added complexity because of the presence of such features must be calculated during COTS assessment
13. Overly optimistic expectations of COTS quality attributes	Significant quality features must be tested before selecting COTS products. Special testing packages may be used. Evaluations could be carried out at sites where the COTS is actually being used
14. Overly optimistic COTS package learning curve	An most likely COTS package learning curve must be accounted for during planning the schedule
15. A version upgrade may result in re-tailoring of COTS package	Ensure that the features used to implement the capabilities still exist in the new version before the version upgrade.

Risk	Common Mitigation Plan
16. Imposed black box testing of COTS components	A risk based testing plan must be developed and accounted for in the project life cycle schedule. The test cases must be designed to satisfy at least the high priority capabilities that the COTS package is responsible for implementing. In case of mission critical systems 'all' the capabilities being satisfied by the COTS package must be tested to the appropriate level of service. Additionally, the developers should ensure that the capabilities that were not tested are NOT implemented or used in the system (one way to do this is to build wrappers around the COTS components to ensure that the system can access only the capabilities that have been tested).

In Table 1, *Number of COTS* indicates the number of COTS used to develop the application. COTS *Requirements Coverage* indicates the number of requirements covered by the COTS application (s). *Requirements Flexibility* indicates the willingness of the organization (or project team) to modify the requirements based on the available capability of the COTS application. *Glue Code* indicates the custom development needed to integrate COTS packages within an application external to the packages themselves. *Tailoring* indicates the activities relating to adapting COTS packages internally for use within an application. *Assessment* indicates the suitability evaluation and analysis of the desired attributes of the COTS packages for an application. *Domain specificity* indicates how specific the application is within a given domain (e.g. A library management system is highly specific to the library domains). *Custom Development* indicates the custom development required to satisfy requirements for the system. *Evolution Requirements Degree* indicates the degree to which the system can evolve once it has been developed.

Based on the developers weekly top risk reports, our architecture review board comments and observations (which are performed twice each semester), the risks in Table 2 have been identified for CBA's.

4   CBA Project Type Lifecycle Effort Comparisons

Up to this point, we have discussed three types of CBA's. Though the typing is based on the intensity of certain COTS related activities, most of other activities as well as the entire development process will also be significantly affected by the CBA type [10]. This section will examine such differences among CBA types.

The following chart illustrates the effort sources comparison among four CBA categories based on effort data reported by 9 CBA projects from year 2001 to 2002.

From Fig. 4, the following observations show the impact of different CBA types on development effort:

1. Both CBA projects and non-CBA projects have a lot (around 15%) of total effort spent on team interactions (activity 1).
2. ACBA has more than 15% of total effort on COTS assessment (activity 2), while TCBA and GCBA have less, but larger than 1% assessment effort.

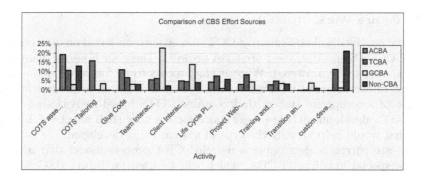

Fig. 4. Comparison of USC e-service CBA Projects Effort

3. CBA projects have spent about twice as much effort on client interaction as non-CBA projects as shown by activity 3. It is known that at least 5% of client interaction is unreported assessment or tailoring effort.
4. Life Cycle Planning (activity 4) also accounts for about 5% of both Assessment and TCBA's total effort, which corresponds to life cycle re-planning caused by COTS uncertainty and volatility.
5. CBA projects require equal or more effort on training and preparation (activity 6) to thoroughly research an application. This effort is included as assessment effort (note that non-CBA projects did not report COTS assessment directly).
6. The reported effort data shows there is about 8% COTS tailoring effort (activity 7) for TCBA, however, we believe the number should be certainly much higher since according to our investigation on those teams, at least one team has reported most of their tailoring effort as critical component development (activity 10).
7. GCBA has about 3% of glue code effort (activity 9) compared to that it only has 1% of critical component development effort (activity 10) as well.

5   Conclusions

5.1   Benefits of CBA Typing

Our empirical data and hands-on experience has confirmed that the three major CBA types have a significant impact on CBS project development. That is, not all CBA projects are created equally. Insight into the characteristics and risks of these types can help a project rapidly converge on a successful development focus. Further, more specific guidance ('special handling') can be provided within a CBA development process. In particular, enabling more effective use of COCOTS to estimate CBA development cost and effort via its three CBA activity submodels. With this, COCOTS also provides a detailed set of assessment and tailoring checklists, glue-code activities, cost drivers, and risk assessments.

5.2   Future Work

We have provided a classification of COTS based systems based on data obtained from COCOTS and USC e-service CBA projects. There are however many questions are yet to be answered. What is the process to be followed for the development of each type of COTS intensive systems? What is to process followed in case of a composite system that contains COTS based activities as well as non-COTS development? Are there more factors that shall affect the business case that would help identify the type of system being developed?

We are currently developing a detailed CBA process model that accounts for the special handling of CBA, which will be used for future USC e-service CBA projects and its effectiveness, tested in terms of risk management, schedule management and other project success factors.

References

1. David C.: Assembling Large Scale Systems from COTS Components: Opportunities, Cautions, and Complexities. In: SEI Monograph on the Use of Commercial Software in Government Systems
2. Morisio, M., Seaman, C. B., Parra, A. T., Basili, V. R., Kraft, S. E., and Condon S. E.: Investigating and Improving a COTS-based Software Development Process. In: Proceedings of the 22nd International Conference on Software Engineering, Limerick, Ireland, June (2000)
3. Jyrki, K.: A Case Study in Applying a Systematic Method for COTS Selection. In: Proceedings of the 18th International Conference on Software Engineering, Berlin, Germany, May (1996)
4. Braun, C. L.: A Life Cycle Process for Effective Reuse of Commercial Off-the-Shelf (COTS) Software. In: Proceedings of the Fifth Symposium on Software Reusability, Los Angeles, California (1999)
5. Boehm B., and Abts, C.: COTS Integration Plug and Pray. In: IEEE Computer, January (1999)
6. Vigder, M. R., and Dean, J. C.: Building Maintainable COTS Based Systems. National Research Council of Canada
7. Dean, J., Oberndorf, P., Vigder, M., Abts, C., Erdogmus, H., Maiden, N., Looney, M., Heineman, G., and Guntersdorfer, M.: COTS Workshop: Continuing Collaborations for Successful COTS Development
8. Carney, D.: Requirements and COTS-based Systems: A Thorny Question Indeed. Available at:
   http://interactive.sei.cmu.edu/news@sei/columns/the_cots_spot/2001/1q01/cots-spot-1q01.htm
9. Seacord, R. C.: Building Systems from Commercial Components: Classroom Experiences. Available at:
   http://interactive.sei.cmu.edu/news@sei/columns/the_cots_spot/cots-spot.htm
10. Hissam, W. S., and Seacord, R.: Building Systems from Commercial Components. Addison-Wesley (2002)
11. Boehm, B., Port, D., Abi-Antoun, M., and Egyed, A.: Guidelines for the Life Cycle Objectives (LCO) and the Life Cycle Architecture (LCA) Deliverables for Model-Based Architecting and Software Engineering (MBASE). USC Technical Report USC-CSE-98-519, University of Southern California, Los Angeles, CA, February (1999)

12. Boehm, B., and Port, D.: Educating Software Engineering Students to Manage Risk, Software Engineering. In: ICSE 2001 (2001)
13. COTS Risk Mitigation Guide.
    Available at: http://www.faa.gov/aua/resources/COTS/Guide/crmg122101.pdf
14. Victor R. B., and Barry W. B.: COTS-Based Systems Top 10 List. IEEE Computer 34(5) (2001)
15. Vidger, M. R., Gentleman, W. M., and Dean, J.: COTS Software Integration: State of the Art (1998) Available at: http://wwwsel.iit.nrc.ca/abstracts/NRC39198.abs
16. Brownsword, L., Oberndorf, P., and Sledge, C.: Developing New Processes for COTS-Based Systems. In: IEEE Software, July/August (2000) 48–55
17. http://www.cebase.org
18. Donald J. R.: Making the Software Business Case. Addison-Wesley, September (2001)
19. Boehm, B., Abts, C., Brown, A. W., Chulani, S., Clark, B. K., Horowitz, E., Madachy, R., Reifer, D., and Steece, B.: Software Cost Estimation with COCOMO II. Prentice Hall PTR, July (2000)
20. Wallnau, K. C., Carney, D., and Pollak, B.: How COTS Software Affects the Design of COTS-Intensive Systems. Available at:
    http://interactive.sei.cmu.edu/Features/1998/june/cots_software/
    Cots_Software.htm
21. Maurizio, M., and Marco, T.: Definition and Classification of COTS: A Proposal. In: First International Conference, ICCBSS 2002, Orlando, FL, USA, February (2002)
22. C. for Software Engineering. Cocots, Technical Report, University of Southern California, Los Angeles, CA, June (1999)
23. COCOTS home page. Available at: http://sunset.usc.edu/research/COCOTS/cocots_main.html
24. Center for Software Engineering, University of Southern California, Los Angeles, CA MBASE home page.
    Available at: http://sunset.usc.edu/research/MBASE/index.html
25. Oberndorf, T.: COTS and Open Systems—An Overview (1997) Available at: http://wei.sei.cmu.edu/str/ descriptions/cots.html#ndi
26. Vidger, M. R., Gentleman, W. M., and Dean. J.: COTS Software Integration: State of the Art (1998) Available at: http://wwwsel.iit.nrc.ca/abstracts/NRC39198.abs
27. Brownsword, L., Oberndorf, T., and Sledge, C. A.: Developing New Processes for COTS-Based Systems. In: IEEE Software, July/August (2000)
28. Fraunhofer IESE. Available at: http://www.iese.fhg.de/Spearmint_EPG/
29. Windows Media Technologies Web Site. Available at:
    http://www.microsoft.com/windows/windowsmedia/download/default.asp
30. Hyperwave AG, Humboldtstraße 10, 85609 Munich-Dornach, Germany Web Site. Available at: http://www.hyperwave.com
31. Microsoft Office Web Site. Available at: http://www.microsoft.com/office/

Defining a Quality Model for Mail Servers[*]

Juan Pablo Carvallo, Xavier Franch, and Carme Quer

Universitat Politècnica de Catalunya (UPC)
c/ Jordi Girona 1-3 (Campus Nord, C6) E-08034 Barcelona (Catalunya, Spain)
{carvallo, franch, cquer}@lsi.upc.es

Abstract. One of the factors that influence the success of COTS product procurement processes is a deep knowledge of the COTS market. The existence of exhaustive and structured descriptions of COTS products belonging to concrete COTS domains may be used as a framework in which particular COTS products could be evaluated and compared to user requirements during the procurement process. Because of its specific characteristics, the domain of mail-related COTS products may benefit from these kind of descriptions. This paper presents an ISO/IEC-based quality model for the mail servers COTS domain, which is built by applying a precise methodology. A general overview of this methodology is presented and its application to the domain is detailed. The use of the mail server quality model is illustrated in some procurement contexts.

1 Introduction

The growing importance of COTS products in software development or company automated support demands the definition of processes, methodologies, models and metrics aimed at supporting the various activities present in this framework. One fundamental activity taking place in this context is COTS[1] procurement [1,2], defined as the process of selecting a particular COTS from the market. For COTS procurement being successful (i.e., reliable and as less time-consuming as possible), many factors should be taken into account, remarkably: a well-defined process [3,4] must be followed; user requirements must be acquired and expressed properly; knowledge about the COTS market must be deep enough. This last issue is addressed in this paper.

Our objective is to provide means to obtain exhaustive and structured COTS descriptions to be used widespread and to serve as a framework in which particular COTS may be evaluated and compared to user requirements during the procurement process. We think that this objective is specially appealing in COTS domains that satisfy two conditions: (1) they are needed by a huge number of companies, and (2) there are lots of COTS available in the market.

---

[*] This work is supported by the Spanish research program CICYT, contract TIC2001-2165.

[1] Throughout this paper, we use the term "COTS" as an abbreviation of "COTS product".

H. Erdogmus and T. Weng (Eds.): ICCBSS 2003, LNCS 2580, pp. 51–61, 2003.

The goal of this paper is the definition of a *quality model* for the mail server COTS domain. The quality model we define is based on the ISO/IEC 9126-1 quality standard [5]. The model is built using a well-defined methodology [6] and results in a taxonomy of quality features and metrics for them. Once built, mail server COTS may be classified in an exhaustive and uniform manner and user requirements may be expressed in terms of the quality concepts therein.

The paper is structured as follows. Section 2 presents the highlights of the ISO/IEC 9126-1 standard. Section 3 sums up the quality model building process. Section 4 describes the domain of mail servers, while Sect. 5 describes the construction of the quality model itself. Section 6 illustrates the use of the quality model for describing COTS and user requirements. Finally, Sect. 7 gives the conclusions.

2   The ISO/IEC 9126-1 Software Quality Model

The original ISO/IEC 9126 standard has been recently replaced by two related multipart standards, ISO/IEC 9126 (software quality) and ISO/IEC 14598 (software product evaluation). The ISO/IEC 9126 now consist of four parts: 9126-1, quality model; 9126-2, external metrics; 9126-3, internal metrics; and 9126-4, quality in use metrics. Although all of these standards (and others related to process quality assurance) influence somehow our proposal, it is the ISO/IEC 9126-1 part [5] the one that specifically addresses to quality models.

The main idea behind this standard is the definition of a quality model and its use as a framework for software evaluation. A *quality model* is defined by means of general *characteristics* of software, which are further refined into *subcharacteristics*, which in turn are decomposed into *attributes*, yielding to a multilevel hierarchy. Intermediate hierarchies of subcharacteristics and attributes may appear making thus the model highly structured (some attributes are suitable for more than one subcharacteristic). At the bottom of the hierarchy, measurable software attributes appear, whose values are computed by using some metric. Throughout the paper, we refer to characteristics, subcharacteristics and attributes as *quality entities*.

The ISO/IEC 9126-1 standard fixes six top level characteristics: functionality, reliability, usability, efficiency, maintainability. It also fixes their further refinement into subcharacteristics but does not elaborate the quality model below this level, making thus the model flexible. The model is to be completed based in the exploration of the particular COTS domain and its application context; because of this, we may say that the standard is very versatile and may be tailored to domains of different nature.

3   An ISO/IEC-Based Methodology for Defining Quality Models

In this section we sketch the methodology used to define the quality model for the mail servers COTS domain, which is described in detail in [6]. It consists of a preliminary stage in which the domain of interest has to be carefully examined and described. Then, six steps can be intertwined or iterated to identify the quality entities conforming the model.

Step 1. *Determining quality subcharacteristics.* The ISO/IEC 9126-1 standard fixes six quality characteristics and their subcharacteristics which may be used as a starting point. The quality team may then add new subcharacteristics specific to the domain, refine the definition of some existing ones, or even eliminate some.

Step 2. *Defining a hierarchy of subcharacteristics.* Subcharacteristics may be further decomposed into new subcharacteristics with respect to some factors.

Step 3. *Decomposing subcharacteristics into attributes.* The abstract subcharacteristics must be decomposed into more concrete concepts, the quality attributes, which keep track of particular observable features of the COTS in the domain.

Step 4. *Decomposing derived attributes into basic ones.* Non-measurable attributes (derived attributes) may still be abstract enough to require further decomposition in terms of others.

Step 5. *Stating relationships between quality entities.* Relationships between attributes are explicitly stated. The model becomes more exhaustive and as an additional benefit, implications of quality user requirements become clearer.

Step 6. *Determining metrics for attributes.* Not only the attributes must be identified, but metrics for all the basic attributes must be selected, as well as metrics for those derived attributes whose definition does not depend on their context of use.

4   A Conceptual Model for the Mail Servers Domain

The basic client-server mailing architecture [7] may be defined as the process of relaying mail from an originator mail user agent (MUA), to a recipient MUA through one (or various) mail servers (named mail transfer agents, MTA). The originator MUA submits mail to a MTA which may then relay it to other(s) MTA. When mail arrives to destination, the final MTA delivers the message to the appropriated mail message store (MS), from where can be accessed by the recipient MUA.

Regardless of the level of detail used to describe the domain in natural language, we felt compelled to represent it using some formal notation, more precisely UML diagrams [8]. In addition to the final product, the diagram construction process itself provided us with a better understanding of the domain, solving many unexpected misunderstandings. We considered necessary the use of two kind of diagrams:

- The first is a UML class diagram that establishes the context of mail servers (see Fig. 1). The purpose of this diagram is to make explicit which other types of COTS interact with mail servers.

- Every class represents a type of COTS available in the market related to the type being described[2]; hierarchies distinguishing particular subtypes are likely to appear. In our case, together with the mail servers themselves (*MTA*), we include mail clients (and remarkably the *MUA* subtype) and message stores (*MS*). Instances of these classes are concrete versions of components of the corresponding COTS types.
- Every association describes types of feasible interactions among COTS of two or more types. So, the *Submission* association states that a *MUA* is able to submit mail to multiple *MTA* and that multiple *MUA* are able to submit mail to a *MTA*. Thus, there will be a Submission instance among concrete *MUA* and *MTA* components just in case the *MUA* is able to submit mail to the *MTA*, which will depend on the types of protocols they support.
- Many associations will be in fact association classes, because they need to maintain some information. This happens with the *Submission* association itself, which has the association class *MailTransferProtocol* bound. In this case, both the attributes and the association itself are defined as derived. The protocols that can be used when a concrete *MUA* submits mail to a particular *MTA* are defined as the intersection of the mail transfer protocols that these *MUA* and *MTA* components support (which are defined as multivalued attributes in the classes).

- The second is another UML class diagram that models the domain of mail servers. Figure 2 includes a partial view of this diagram, which models the structure of the messages that mail servers handle; parts for modelling address books, folders and other concepts also exist. It is important to keep in mind that the aim of this diagram is not the description of a particular mail server, but the description of those elements that are currently accepted as convenient to appear in any mail server and thus present nowadays in most MTA. Standards such as SMTP [9] play an important role in the definition of this diagram.

5   A Quality Model for the Mail Servers Domain

Step 1. Determining Quality Subcharacteristics

The top level hierarchy provided by the ISO/IEC 9126-1 standard is reasonable enough to be used as starting point for the mail server domain quality model. Therefore, we adopted it with just some minor modifications (e.g., the redefinition of the *operability* subcharacteristic to specifically state the configuration of the mail server parameters as a part of the administrator-related operability).

---

[2] As such, these types could also have a quality model defined for them.

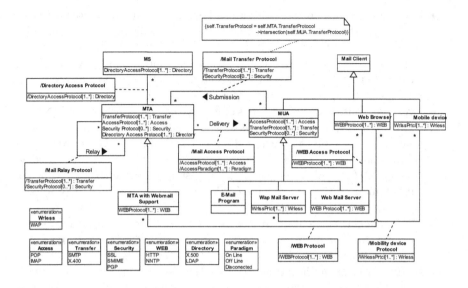

Fig. 1. Mail Server Context Diagram [Some constraints to define derived attributes and associations are not included]

Step 2. Refining a Hierarchy of Subcharacteristics

The ISO/IEC *suitability* subcharacteristic was divided into *mail server suitability* and *additional suitability*. The reason behind this is that many commercial mail servers tend to bind applications that were not originally related to them. For instance, some of the most widely used mail servers include applications which support functionalities such as chat, instant messaging or web workflow processing. Such applications are not usually shipped within the original COTS. They are usually offered separately, as extensions of the original one (most of them are COTS components themselves). But we found that often they were referenced as a constitutive part of the COTS functionality. Many companies may be interested in using them, and so we though that it was important to list them as attributes of a functionality subcharacteristic.

Step 3. Decomposing Subcharacteristics into Attributes

It may not be possible to list all the quality attributes related to a particular COTS domain [10] but it is certainly possible to create a very complete list of the most relevant ones. Complete, independent and reliable information of products is difficult to find. Some of the problems we found are: suppliers are partiality in favor of their products; reports are often unreliable or refuted; evaluations are often based in particular taste rather than technical tests; semantic differences among product characteristics exist. Selection of quality attributes should be

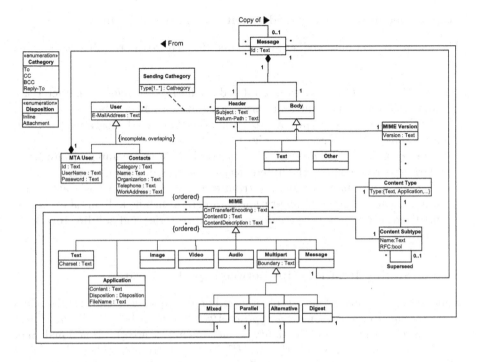

Fig. 2. Mail Server Domain Diagram: an excerpt

made relying on the concepts that are shown (and their possible benefits) instead of the evaluations that manufacturers (or their competitors) give of either themselves, their products or the platforms they require. Some examples follow:

- We searched for the concepts behind the names. *Distribution Lists* and *Group Document in Directory* are different names given by two different leader providers to describe the same concept: the capability of grouping contacts under a single entity which may (for example) be used as a destination mailing address.
- Once we started categorizing attributes, it became obvious that some of them were suited for more than one characteristic. For instance, *Message Tracking and Monitoring* may be seen as a functional attribute that grants accurateness, or else as an analyzability attribute of the maintenance characteristic. Another example is the *Clustering Support* attribute; it can be seen as an attribute that enhance efficiency or as one that improves fault tolerance (making the system more recoverable). Attributes categorized under multiple subcharacteristics may use different metrics for each case depending on the concept they represent under each particular subcharacteristic.

Step 4. Decomposing Derived Attributes into Basic Ones

The quality model obtained so far included derived attributes. Just to name a few:

- The *Choice of Clients* attribute related to the *Interoperability* characteristic was split into three different basic attributes, each one bound to one of the three specific subtypes of *MUA* components (e-mail programs, web mail servers and WAP servers, see Fig. 1).
- The *Open Interfaces and Connectors* attribute was decomposed into basic attributes representing the different types of provided connectors.
- The *Accounts Administration* attribute was factored into basic attributes representing different configuration parameters such as individual or shared mailboxes, user privileges or default user directories and subdirectory hierarchy.

Step 5. Stating Relationships between Quality Entities

Some attributes imply the use of others. For example, if a mail server offers *Secure e-mail Protocols*, some *Encryption Algorithm* must be used, because they are required to grant confidentiality. Other examples are the functional *Sent Multimedia Attachments* and the *MIME Support* attributes, when the SMTP *Message Transfer Protocol* is used. This feature is particularly interesting because once relationships among attributes are identified they may be used to automatically expand requirements and their consequences.

A tabular representation of part of the direct relationships that we found is shown in Table 1. Attributes in rows contribute to attributes in columns, with either a positive (+) or a negative (-) partial support, or just they are required (D), in a similar way as done in [11]. For instance, we visualized that in fact a *Certification System* is required for *Secure e-mail Protocols*, that *Single Copy Store* contributes positively to *Average Response Time* but that this last attribute is damaged by *Online Incremental Backup* policies.

Step 6. Determining Metrics for Attributes

Compared with other experiences we have had on building quality models, the mail server domain is highly representative of what may be expected concerning metrics definition. Some attributes can be evaluated by a simple boolean (i.e., they are or they aren't, such as *Single Copy Store*). Others may be represented by atomic data types such as integer or float values of a particular unit (e.g., the average response time in milliseconds, or the maximum account size in megabytes). A number of attributes require a more complex representation such as fix or open sets (e.g., the list of the default folders which it provides).

Also we found some metrics that were difficult to define. For example *Spammers Thwarting* and *Bulk-Junk Mail Handling* depend on the support of *Filters for Incoming Messages*. *Average Response Time and Message Throughput*

Table 1. Some attribute relationships

CHARACTERISTICS		Functionality	Efficiency
SUBCHARACTERISTICS		**Security**	**Time Behaviour**
ATTRIBUTES		Secure e-mail Protocols	Average response time
Functionality — Security	Certification System	D	-
	Encryption Algorithm	D	-
Reliability — Recoverability	Full or Selective Replication and Synchronization		-
	Single Mailbox Backup & Recovery		+
	Online Incremental Backup		-
	Online Restore		-
	Dynamic Log Rotation		-
	Event Logging		-
	Transaction Logging		-
Efficiency — Res. Behaviour	Concurrent Mail Users per Server		-
	Number of Active Web-mail Clients		-
	Management of Quotas on Message and Mail File Size		+
	Single Copy Store		+

depend on *Hardware Platform* as well as other attributes such as *Number of Concurrent Users* or *Message Sizes*. In this case the metrics have to be defined as functions.

6   Using the Quality Model for COTS Procurement

Once built the model, it can be used in two different contexts related to COTS procurement: precise formulation of quality requirements and description of COTS.

Concerning the first issue, we introduced complete sets of quality requirements that appeared in real mail server selection processes with different characteristics (from a public institution giving service to 50.000 people to a small software consultant and ISP provider company). Some requirements were already presented in a structured way (for example as lists of interconnection-, functionality- and utilization-related requirements) but others not, leading to some extra effort to arrange them.

Rearranging and mapping the quality requirements to quality attributes appearing in the model was not straightforward; some rewriting and reformulation of requirements in terms of attributes in the model was needed but this helped us to discover existing ambiguities and incompleteness. For example, let's consider the requirement: *"Transmission time must be inferior to 1 minute for messages without attachments and for those with attachments it should not exceed 5 minutes per megabyte"*.

The size of a message (even without attachments) is highly variable. To illustrate this situation let's consider two plain text messages, the first one including a short reminder of a meeting and the second one created from resulting output of a medium size company annual accounting report. Because of this variability we concluded that the one-minute-time limit for messages without attachments is not an accurate measure and even worse, it may be (under some situations) *impossible to achieve*. After some analysis and discussion with users the requirement was rewritten as: *"The average response time should not exceed 1 minute and the message throughput rate must be inferior to 5 minutes per megabyte"*. This resulting requirement is closer to reality and may be directly mapped to two of the *Efficiency* quality attributes: *Average Response Time and Message Throughput*.

With respect to the use of the quality model for describing mail server components, basic attributes must be evaluated using the corresponding metrics. Some attribute evaluation requires just very basic hands-on experimentation, but others demand intensive testing and simulation, especially in the presence of dependencies. Two representative examples are the *Average Response Time* and the *Message Throughput* attributes, which depend on others such as *Hardware Platform, Users Concurrency, Logging* and *Backup Mechanisms* or the provided *Encryption Algorithms* (see Table 1).

Once product characteristics were described using the quality model, we were able to compare requirements with COTS characteristics in a more reliable and efficient manner. This allowed us to detect which products were more eligible for each case. The aim of the study was not to name one of the tools as the best for each case, but rather to show that by using the quality model it is possible to detect differences between products as well as determine to what extend they cover the expressed needs. Once we arrived to this point in our experience, we had no doubts about the utility of the quality model as a valuable tool for the description and selection of products.

7   Conclusions

Reliable processing of quality requirements demands precise and complete description of software domains and the components in these domains, especially in the context of COTS selection. Quality models are a specially well-suited means to obtain these descriptions. In this paper we have presented the application of a methodology aimed at building quality models based on the ISO/IEC 9126-1 quality standard to a particular COTS domain, the one of mail servers (the complete model can be found in [12]). The reason for having chosen this particular domain is twofold: a) mail servers need to be present in most companies and organizations worldwide; b) there are a great deal of available components. Both reasons altogether justifies the effort required for building a quality model.

It should be mentioned that the methodology presented here and in [6] has been used in other domains, such as e-learning tools, ERP systems, data structure libraries, etc. Some reflections on reusability of quality models appear in [6].

The observation of this case study agrees with the opinion [10,13] that building the quality model is a complex activity, endangered by many factors: poor description of the domain, lack of ability when identifying the quality entities, inappropriate metrics, etc. However, once available, it becomes a really powerful tool which provides a general framework to get uniform descriptions of the (maybe a great deal of) COTS of the domain. Comparison of these COTS is then favoured. Also, quality requirements can be rewritten in terms of the quality concepts appearing in the model; this reformulation process may help to discover some ambiguities and incompleteness in the requirements and, once solved, the resulting requirements can be more easily compared with the COTS descriptions. Last, quality models can be expressed in a component description language allowing tool support for COTS selection.

Not only the reliability of COTS procurement can be improved with our proposal; also the cost of the very procurement process can. Just consider for a moment the amount of repeated work that is done in the mail server domain. Organisations face exactly the same problems and repeat the same process over and over, wasting human resources and money while doing so. The existence of a quality model for this domain makes mail server procurement a simpler task, since it is not necessary to rediscover which are the factors that influence mail server selection.

In comparison with previous experiences in building quality models, the mail server case study has shown us the additional advantages of using UML class diagrams, because the identification of relationships among quality attributes is ameliorated. This is due to the graphical nature of the diagrams and the characteristics of the modeling process that require its detailed description. Another aspect for which the use of UML class diagrams has proved to be useful is to rearrange the hierarchy of attributes originally listed in the quality model, by identifying new hidden attributes or reordering existing ones. We plan to use other UML diagrams in the future, as use cases and sequence diagrams for stating the interactions between components and their users. Also, agent-oriented models [14] may provide another view of software components when considering components as agents and making explicit their dependencies [15].

References

1. Finkelstein, A., Spanoudakis, G., and Ryan, M.: Software Package Requirements and Procurement. In: Proceedings of the 8th IEEE International Workshop on Software Specification and Design (1996)
2. Ncube, C., and Maiden, N.: Procuring Software Systems: Current Problems and Solutions. In: Proceedings of the 3rd REFSQ, Barcelona, Catalonia, June (1997)
3. Comella-Dorda, S., Dean, J. C., Morris, E., and Oberndorf, P.: A Process for COTS Software Product Evaluation. In: Proceedings of the 1st International Conference on COTS-based Software Systems, LNCS Vol. 2255, Orlando, Florida, USA (2002)

4. Maiden, N., and Ncube, C.: Acquiring Requirements for COTS Selection, In: IEEE Software 15(2) (1998)
5. Software Engineering—Product Quality—Part 1: Quality Model. ISO/IEC Standard 9126-1, June (2001)
6. Franch, X., and Carvallo, J.P.: A Quality-model-based Approach for Describing and Evaluating Software Packages. In: Proceedings of the 10th IEEE Joint Conference on Requirements Engineering, Essen, Germany, September (2002)
7. The Internet Mail Consortium. Available at: http://www.imc.org
8. Unified Modelling Language (UML) 1.4 Specification. OMG document formal/ (formal/2001-09-67), September (2001)
9. RFC 2822. Available at: http://www.imc.org/rfc2822
10. Dromey, R.G.: Cornering the Chimera. In: IEEE Software 20, January (1996)
11. Chung, L., Nixon, B.,Yu, E., and Mylopoulos, J.: Non-Functional Requirements in Software Engineering. Kluwer Academic Publishers (2000)
12. Carvallo, J. P., and Franch, X.: Towards the Definition of a Quality Model for Mail Servers. Technical Report LSI-02-36-R, LSI-Universitat Politècnica de Catalunya (2002)
13. Kitchenham, B., and Pfleeger, S. L.: Software Quality: The Elusive Target. In: IEEE Software 20, January (1996)
14. Yu, E.: Towards Modeling and Reasoning Support for Early-Phase Requirements Engineering. In: Proceedings of the 3rd IEEE ISRE, Annapolis (1997)
15. Franch X., and Maiden N.: Modeling Component Dependencies to Inform Their Selection. In: Proceedings of the 2nd International Conference on COTS-based Software Systems, Ottawa, Canada (2003)

Classifying Interoperability Conflicts*

L. Davis, D. Flagg, R. Gamble, and C. Karatas

Department of Mathematical and Computer Sciences
The University of Tulsa
600 South College Avenue
Tulsa, OK 74104 USA
{davis, flagg, gamble, karatas}@utulsa.edu

Abstract. A common path for application development is to pick the
COTS or legacy products, choose a middleware product, and determine
what additional functionality is needed to make it all work. While this
may seem the most expedient and least costly way to develop an integrated application, unexpected interoperability conflicts can surface
after implementation, deployment and/or evolution of any of the participating components. An interoperability conflict is any factor inhibiting
communication of control or data among components.
Current research has shown that interoperability conflicts can be traced
to the software architecture of the components and integrated application, making this level of abstraction a suitable domain for conflict description. In this paper, we describe and substantiate a set of
architecture-based conflicts that embody the predominant interoperability problems found in software integrations.

1 Introduction

Commercial-off-the-shelf (COTS) components promise implementation short-
cuts to developers that want to employ component-based software engineering
(CBSE) methods. However, application integration, in which COTS, legacy systems, new developments, and data may be all used, often manifest complex
interoperability problems, negating the possible time and cost benefits promised
by CBSE techniques. Interoperability problems are not clearly defined in design,
most are identified by developer instinct as they strive to assess component fit
in an application. Due to the ad hoc nature of conflict descriptions, solutions
to interoperability problems can be overly complex, containing redundant and
non-evolvable functionality. It follows that interoperability conflict description
and understanding can benefit from a principled assessment technique and a
uniform terminology.

* This material is based upon work supported in part by AFOSR (F49620-98-1-0217)
and NSF (CCR-9988320). Any opinions, findings, and conclusions or recommendations expressed in this material are those of the author(s) and do not necessarily
reflect the views of the National Science Foundation or the US government. The
government has certain rights to this material.

H. Erdogmus and T. Weng (Eds.): ICCBSS 2003, LNCS 2580, pp. 62–71, 2003.

Current research has shown that interoperability problems can be traced to the software architecture of the components and integrated application [1,5-7,9-11,14,16,20,22]. Therefore, a description of interoperability problems and the software properties that lead to them can be achieved at this high-level of abstraction. Furthermore, the solutions generated for these problems are guided by an implicit understanding of software architecture. This indicates that integration solutions are intrinsically linked to the conflicts that make them necessary. Due to this, it naturally follows that integration solution identification would be less complex if interoperability problems were uniformly described.

In this paper we define a set of conflicts that embody the predominant interoperability problems found in software integrations. They fall into a limited set of conflicts that are pinpointed through architecture characteristic comparison. They are described using simple definitions that encompass the idea of the problem. Furthermore, they are categorized to make integration assessment easier and solution identification faster.

2   Background

Pre-integration interoperability assessment at the software architecture level relies on software characteristic identification and comparison. The *software architecture* of a system is the blueprint of its computational elements, the means by which they interact, and the structural constraints on their interaction [17,19]. With such abstraction, it is possible to initially focus on important conceptual system issues without becoming entangled in implementation and deployment details. One facet of this description is architectural style, which provides information regarding configuration and coordination constraints on a system's components.

Characteristics defined with respect to architectural styles include those that describe the various types of computational elements and connectors, data issues, control issues, and control/data interaction issues [3-5,11,12,18,20]. These architectural characteristics provide details that further differentiate individual styles, their extensions, and specializations. As a result of characteristic comparison, the phrase *architecture mismatch* was coined to describe certain underlying reasons for interoperability problems among seemingly "open" software components [11]. Other characteristics have been viewed with respect to their potential impact on interoperability [3-5,12,18,20]. These characteristics are used to identify interoperability problems within and between styles [1,20]. However, only subsets based on style constraints have been examined for their role in integration issues [3-5,11,12,18,20]. Nonetheless, all of these cases use characteristic/value comparison to identify interoperability problems.

There are many approaches to interoperability analysis. Some approaches are based on the different viewpoints that come from system specific integration concerns. Barrett et al. [5] focuses on only the event-based architecture style. Thus, they examine only a subset of event-based integration frameworks, i.e., FIELD, POLYLITH, and CORBA. This viewpoint is based upon the integration solution, rather than the component characteristics which lead to the mismatch problems. Other viewpoints, such as Gruhn et al.'s [13] and Hofmeister [21] involve case studies of integration problems and solutions. These cases studies are very informative and represent the current state of practice within industry. However, they offer limited assistance toward developing an encompassing analysis methodology.

Abd-Allah's Architect's Automated Assistant (AAA) system is based on examining style-based differences, focusing on the description of the supposed "encompassing" architectural styles main-subroutine, pipe and filter, distributed processes, and event-based [1,2]. Gacek [10] extends this research to include more architectural styles and more complete evaluations of them in an attempt to cover mismatch occurrences thought missing in Abd-Allah's model. The AAA system requires an in-depth, multi-dimensional description of the entire system prior to analysis. This often requires information from levels of abstraction too low to be available in most products not designed in-house, such as COTS.

DeLine [9] attempts to resolve package mismatch by describing various aspects of each component to be integrated. Properties, such as data representation, data and control transfer, transfer protocol, state persistence, state scope, failure, and connection establishment, are considered. In this approach, control and data transfer mechanisms are tightly coupled. Thus, any control or data problems are assumed related, even though their transfer mechanisms may be independent.

Yakimovich et al. [22] combines both high- and low-level analysis. This approach involves a classification scheme based on the proposed interactions of the components to be integrated. The architectural assumptions that can cause mismatches concern the nature of the components and connectors, the global architectural structure, and the construction process for application. Mixing abstractions, e.g., component-hardware interactions vs. component-software interactions can be confusing, leading to problems during the classification process. Other approaches also mix high- and low-level descriptions, e.g., Abd-Allah and Gacek, but to a lesser degree.

We use the meritorious aspects of the above approaches to establish a conflict set that maintains a uniform viewpoint and granularity. Only limited component detail should be needed to generate this conflict set for COTS integration. We incorporate our research on architecture properties for integration to achieve this objective.

3   The Basis for Conflict

The easiest way to understand a conflict is to define the foundation for its existence. For architecture-based interoperability conflicts, we use architecture characteristics as the foundation. There are many such characteristics, at differing levels of abstraction and viewpoints. Our previous research examined 70 published component architecture properties [3-5,11,12,18,20]. Through extensive empirical analysis and the development of semantic networks relating the properties, we found that with respect to interoperability, these properties are manifested in ten high-level characteristics (Table 1). We refer the reader to [6] for a detailed explanation of the analysis and findings.

We use the characteristics for component-level and application-level descriptions [6,8,15]. *Component-level characteristics* contribute to an understanding of the exposed interfaces of components. In turn, *application-level characteristics* address architectural demands on configuration and coordination of the component systems into a single integrated application to satisfy overall requirements.

The characteristics that we use to describe the conflicts can be seen in Table 1. The name appears in column one. Each characteristic is distinguished in column two by whether it is component-level (C), application-level (A), or both. Definitions and values are in columns three and four, respectively.

Table 1. Application and Component-Level Characteristic

CHARACTERISTICS	TYPE	DEFINITION	VALUES
Blocking	C	Whether or not the thread of control is suspended.	Blocking, Non-Blocking
Control Structure	A, C	The structure that governs the execution in the system.	Single-Thread, Multi-Thread, Concurrent
Control Topology	A, C	The geometric form control flow takes in a system.	Hierarchical, Star, Arbitrary, Linear
Data Format Difference	A	Describes whether or not data being passed within the application is in the same format.	Yes, No
Data Storage Method	C	How data is stored within a system.	Local, Global, Distributed
Data Topology	A, C	The geometric form data flow takes in a system.	Hierarchical, Star, Arbitrary, Linear
Identity of Components	C	Awareness of other components in the system.	Aware, Unaware
Supported Control Transfer	C	The method supported to achieve control transfer.	Explicit, Implicit, None
Supported Data Transfer	C	The method supported to achieve data transfer.	Explicit, Shared, Implicit-Discrete, Implicit-Continuous, None
Synchronization	A	The level of dependency of a module on another module's control state.	Synchronous, Asynchronous

4   Classifying Interoperability Conflicts

In this section, we define and discuss each conflict. References are given where the conflict appears as well as from what properties it is derived. The characteristics in Table 1 are then used to illustrate the architectural basis for the conflict.

It is important to note that interoperability conflicts occur from different comparisons of interactions, some component to component and others application to component.

4.1   Restricted Points of Control Transfer

Transferring control is a major part of integrating the communication between components. DeLine states that in order for two components to transfer control, they must agree on the direction of the transfer [9]. The component passing the control will do so according to its own assumptions about the exchange. However, these assumptions may be erroneous [10]. For instance, one assumption about the interface of the component accepting control is that it is of the same type as the one passing control. A conflict that arises from this assumption is that often the sink has a specific mechanism, port, or interface that receives control that the source does not have.

Example: Hierarchical Control Topology vs. Arbitrary Control Topology. A hierarchical control topology requires call and return control communication but an arbitrary control topology does not expect a fixed entry point. Thus, the control transfer to a hierarchical component cannot occur without an intelligent intermediary knowing the point of exchange.

4.2   Unspecified Control Destination

Direct communication between components is often a necessary form of control transfer. Kazman states that if a component cannot be transferred control, it cannot be reused in an integration as readily as one that can always be called [14]. A component's methods may also be encapsulated and private, making them invisible to the calling component. Furthermore, a component's interface may not be specified until runtime due to dynamic binding [22]. This is problematic, as the dynamically bound component cannot be located consistently by components that wish to communicate with it.

Example: Arbitrary Control Topology vs. Arbitrary Control Topology. An arbitrary control topology may have multiple control destinations. Thus, control exchange is inhibited because the control must match the correct destination.

4.3   Inhibited Rendezvous

To transfer control it is often necessary for the component to rendezvous or handshake for the exchange. Deadlock can occur if the threads of communicating components are blocked or have failed [1]. Rendezvous problems also occur when the components involved in the exchange have different control transfer assumptions [10], such as different calling structures, independent and non-terminating execution that cannot be pre-empted, or several seats of control. In these cases, the communicating components may not be able to synchronize. One example of this is when two components are both blocking.

4.4   Multiple, Unsequenced Control Transfers

Integrating control between components is not just a matter of facilitating the transfer of communications. Preserving the intent of the transfers is also necessary. Mularz stresses the need for management of required sequencing between components [16]. If concurrent, external transfers occur, the receiving component must be equipped to accept them. Thus, should a single-threaded component be transferred concurrent communications from multiple threads, all but one will be refused and there is no guarantee the one allowed entry will be the correct one.

4.5   Restricted Points of Data Transfer

Similar to transferring control, correct transfer of data is essential for a usable integrated system. Mularz highlights the maintenance of data communication transparency as a guiding motivation for integration architectures [16]. Inaccessible data hinders data transfer. Accessibility issues emerge when transfer mechanisms of connectors are different or inactive [9,10].

Example: Explicit Supported Data Transfer vs. Shared Supported Data Transfer. Explicit data exchanges through push and pull message requests are required by a communicating component. However, when a component shares its data, it expects other components to read and write from the shared location. Because a component with a shared data transfer method does not know to direct data transfer to an explicit interface point, any component expecting this behavior will not receive the data.

4.6   Unspecified Data Destination

A direct communication of data is a prevalent data transfer mechanism among components. Kazman asserts that components should have similar assumptions concerning the application environment for correct data exchange [14]. Components must have equivalent knowledge about other components with which they wish to communicate [10]. Problems surface when one component's thread expects to directly pass data to another component but cannot find either a waiting thread or the address of a component's interface [10]. Should the component be dynamically bound, its address is variable and cannot be called using a static address.

Example: Single-Threaded Control Structure vs. Arbitrary Data Topology. Components that exchange data using a single seat of control expect to have direct communication with all components in the application. If the topology of the sink component's data flow is arbitrary, then there is no single-thread specified at the interface to communicate with. Thus, a single-threaded component will not be able to transfer its data directly according to its expectations.

4.7 Unspecified Data Location

Data must to be transferred to complement the buffering mechanisms of the various components to achieve an integrated system. DeLine states that data layouts must be obvious to all components for data transfer [9]. If the communicating components disagree on the transmission method in such a way that the data location is obscured then transmission is impeded. This can occur if a component attempts to access private data. Should a component wish to communicate data to an object whose data store is dynamically bound it will have difficulty locating that buffer [10].

Example: Local Data Storage Method vs. Unaware Identity of Components. A component storing its data locally expects to be passed data directly to the local buffer. However, an unaware component has no knowledge of the other components in the system; hence no knowledge of the component's data storage location.

4.8 Inconsistent Data

A data transfer, if inconsistently communicated, can permute the data content of a communication. Abd-Allah indicates that to exchange data, synchronization of the exchange must be maintained [1]. Data can be corrupted or lost if care is not taken to manage data exchange [16]. Synchronization problems can result from an incorrect handoff, e.g., from a connector process that has failed during transmission [10]. If components access a resource that must be identical over two systems but isn't, dirty reads or lost updates may occur [1].

4.9 Invalid Data

Invalid data is perhaps the most widely recognized conflict. This is because data format transparency is a pre-requisite for integrating data properly. Moreover, translation and marshalling is well understood. If the data formats do not agree, then data received by a component will have no meaning, and all subsequent computations performed on the data will also result in invalid data [1,2,10,16,22].

4.10 Multiple, Unsequenced Data Transfers

It is particularly important that data transfers be accepted in the appropriate sequence by a component in order to guarantee its content. Conflicts occur when the mechanisms for data transfer are disparate [1]. Multi-threaded components that maintain concurrent threads can pass data simultaneously to another component. Data can be lost at a receiving component that does not embody concurrency control. Moreover, there is also no guarantee that the data received by the sink component was the first packet of the sequence of communications.

Example: Concurrent Control Structure vs. Linear Data Topology. A component with a linear data topology supports a single control unit or multiple, synchronized units for data transfer. If it interacts with a concurrent component, multiple, possibly simultaneous data transfers will occur. As the linear data topology will only support synchronous transfers, the sequence of those data transmissions cannot be guaranteed.

4.11   Mismatched Data Transfer Assumptions

The mechanisms by which each component transfers data is what determines the mode of data communication across the integrated system. Abd-Allah states that if these mechanisms are incompatible, then the exchange of data between components will be impeded [1]. These mechanisms tend to conflict as their mode of transfer gets less direct [10]. Specifically, this occurs when a source has an explicit data transfer conflict with those whose mode of transfer is implicit.

4.12   Uninitialized Control Transfer

An integration effort may be hindered by one or multiple components that are unable to exchange control. If control transfer mechanisms are unrecognizable by participating components, control transfer will be obstructed [1]. Furthermore, components wishing to pass control may have no means to do so [10]. Such things as awareness of communication partners and the connectors by which they naturally communicate are factors contributing to this problem. Thus, if a component is implemented such that it cannot push communications to and beyond its interface, control exchange is impossible.

Example: Blocking vs. Unaware Identity Of Components. Because a component is unaware of the presence of other components waiting for it to communicate with them, none of the components can initialize the transfer, causing the possibility of deadlock.

4.13   Unitialized Data Transfer

Sometimes transfer of data cannot occur from one or many components slated for integration. Abd-Allah indicates that transfer mechanisms must be recognizable to the component sending data for a transfer to occur [1,10]. Components that cannot communicate externally also produce this conflict when being integrated [10].

Example: Star Data Topology vs. Unaware Identity Of Components. A component with a star topology expects pointed transfer of data. The unaware component, however, has no knowledge of other components in the system. Therefore, it will be unable to initialize a data transfer to the sink component.

5   Conclusions

COTS integration is becoming more predominant in component-based software engineering, as are the complex interoperability problems COTS integrations manifest. Due to this, pre-integration interoperability assessment techniques can benefit from a principled conflict categorization. Interoperability problems can be normalized across abstraction-levels, benefiting from a foundational approach like software architecture. They can also elucidate solutions, grounding middleware choice via a principled design path. In this paper, we categorize interoperability problems into a set of conflicts that is encompassing and descriptive, yet not complex. We describe the conflicts and exemplify them using architecture characteristic/value comparisons.

As a consequence of the research, we can devise direct solution information to the conflicts. This solution guidance expresses the type of translation, extension, and control needed to resolve each individual conflict [6]. Composition of the solutions forms the foundation for integration functionality. We have performed conflict detection using our comparison process on a number of industrial and model problems, yielding a design solution traceable to component properties. Thus, the conflicts are an integral part of the knowledge needed for this history.

References

1. Abd-Allah, A.: Composing Heterogeneous Software Architectures. Ph. D. Dissertation, Computer Science, University of Southern California (1996)
2. Abd-Allah, A., and Boehm, B.: Models for Composing Heterogeneous Software Architectures. USC-CSE-96-505, University of Southern California (1996)
3. Abowd, G., Allen, R., and Garlan, D.: Formalizing Style to Understand Descriptions of Software Architecture. In: ACM Transactions on Software Engineering and Methodologies 4(4) (1995) 319–364
4. Allen, R.: A Formal Approach to Software Architecture. TR CMU-CS-97-144 (1997)
5. Barret, D., Clarke, L., Tarr, P., and Wise, A.: A Framework for Event-Based Software Integration. In: ACM Transactions on Software Engineering and Methodology 5(4) (1996) 378–421
6. Davis, L., and Gamble, R.: The Impact of Component Architectures on Interoperability. Journal of Systems and Software (2002)
7. Davis, L., Gamble, R., Payton, J., Jonsdottir, G., and Underwood, D.: A Notation for Problematic Architecture Interactions. In: ESEC/FSE, Vienna, Austria (2001)
8. Davis, L., Payton, J., and Gamble, R.: How System Architectures Impede Interoperability. In: 2nd International Workshop On Software and Performance (2000)
9. DeLine, R.: Techniques to Resolve Packaging Mismatch (1999)
10. Gacek, C.: Detecting Architectural Mismatches During Systems Composition. Usc/cse-97-tr-506 (1997)
11. Garlan, D., Allen, A., and Ockerbloom, J.: Architectural Mismatch, or Why it is Hard to Build Systems Out of Existing Parts. In: ICSE, Seattle, WA (1995)
12. Garlan, D., Monroe, R., and Wile, D.: ACME: An Architectural Description Language. In: Cascon (1997)
13. Gruhn, V., and Wellen, U.: Integration of Heterogeneous Software Architectures. Experience Report (1999)
14. Kazman, R., Clements, P., Bass, L., and Abowd, G.: Classifying Architectural Elements as a Foundation for Mechanism Matching. Washington, DC (1997)

15. Kelkar, A., and Gamble, R.: Understanding the Architectural Characteristics Behind Middleware Choices. In: 1st International Conference in Information Reuse and Integration (1999)
16. Mularz, D.: Pattern-based Integration Architectures. In: PLoP (1994)
17. Perry, D., and Wolf, A.: Foundations for the Study of Software Architecture. In: ACM SIGSOFT 17(4) (1992) 40–52.
18. Shaw, M., and Clements, P.: A Field Guide to Boxology: Preliminary Classification of Architectural Styles for Software Systems. In: 1st International Computer Software and Applications Conference, Washington, DC (1997)
19. Shaw, M., and Garlan, D.: Software Architecture: Perspectives on an Emerging Discipline. NJ: Prentice Hall, Englewood Cliffs (1996)
20. Sitaraman, R.: Integration of Software Systems at an Abstract Architectural Level. University of Tulsa (1997)
21. Soni, D., Nord, R., and Hofmeister, C.: Software Architecture in Industrial Applications. In: International Conference on Software Engineering, Seattle, WA (1995)
22. Yakimovich, D., Travassos, G. H., and Basili, V.: A Classification of Software Components Incompatibilities for COTS Integration (2000)

COTS Software Quality Evaluation

Ljerka Beus-Dukic[1] and Jørgen Bøegh[2]

[1] Cavendish School of Computer Science, University of Westminster,
115 New Cavendish Street, London W1W 6UW, United Kingdom
L.Beus-Dukic@wmin.ac.uk
[2] DELTA Danish Electronics, Light & Acoustics, Venlighedsvej 4,
2970 Hørsholm, Denmark
jb@delta.dk

Abstract. Assessment and evaluation of COTS software products has become a compulsory and crucial part of any COTS-based software system lifecycle. A risk of selecting a product with unknown quality properties is no longer acceptable. This paper presents a framework for quality evaluation process of COTS software products. Our approach, based on the latest international standards for software product quality and evaluation, provides acquirers of COTS software with a method to select software products with identified and measured quality characteristics.

1   Introduction

Commercial-off-the-shelf (COTS) software is defined by a market-driven need, is commercially available, and its fitness for use has been demonstrated by a broad spectrum of commercial users [14]. Here, we assume that a COTS software product is a software package, self-contained, independent, and with significant functionality and complexity. Examples are graphics packages, utility programs, and database programs.

COTS-based software systems are being used in a wide variety of application areas and their correct operation is often critical for business success and human safety. Therefore, it is very important to select high quality COTS software products.

Assessment and evaluation of COTS software products has become an obligatory part of any COTS-based software system lifecycle. Software quality evaluation is the systematic examination of the software capability to fulfill specified quality requirements. This paper suggests a framework for quality evaluation process applicable to COTS software products. The framework is based on a set of current international standards for quality and evaluation of software products. Although, some of the standards distinguish between the custom made software packages and COTS software packages there is no separate evaluation process for COTS software product.

1.1   Assessment Approaches

An assessment process has to verify that the actual service exhibited by a software product is a trusted representation of its specified service. Two different types of software assessment exist: process and product assessment. Although different, process and product assessments complement each other. Monitoring products helps to assure the quality of deliverables and in turn, helps in the improvement of the processes that contribute to product realisation [9].

Process assessment. Process assessment is assessing the methods that are used to produce the software. If a high quality software product is to be produced, processes used to design, build, test and control it must be consistent and rigorously scrutinized. The process approach is promoted by the ISO 9001:2000 [11], TickIT scheme in the UK [9], and SEI's Capability Maturity Model [13].

Product assessment. While the process assessment can encompass a large number of different development models, product assessment is usually much easier to perform if the product belongs to a specific product class. Hence, product assessments for a specific product class such as compilers are well established but general product assessment remains to become a widespread practice.

Black-box assessment is based entirely on actual execution of the software product without any reference to its internal workings. This type of assessment is typical for the COTS software and addresses a wide range of application domains. **Specific characteristic assessment** is the assessment of software products towards specific characteristics other than functionality. This kind of assessment already exists for a limited number of characteristics. Examples are: security (Common Criteria for IT Security Evaluation [15]), safety (a number of domain standards—e.g. ISO/IEC 61508 [8]—and harmonized criteria [20]), usability (IBM's common user access standard for graphical user interfaces, Department of the US Air Force's software usability evaluation guide) and maintainability.

1.2   Evaluation

By definition [5], quality evaluation is the systematic examination of the extent to which an entity is capable of fulfilling specified requirements. When a product is developed for unspecified users the requirements are specified by the development organisation. Software product quality can be measured externally (performance) or internally by measures such as compliance with coding standards and program structure.

Currently most independent quality evaluations are performed because they are required by law or public authorities. However, a demand for software evaluations for other reasons is on the increase. A software company may be asked by an acquirer to accept an independent quality evaluation as a part of development contract. Some evaluations are intended for issuing quality marks or seals, with the aim to provide a marketing advantage to good quality software products (e.g., OSE real-time kernel certified by TÜV Nord [19]). Evaluation schemes are also used for comparing similar software products when choosing a software supplier.

2 Standards

A number of international standards which define software quality framework exist or is currently being developed by ISO and IEC. To ensure product quality there are essentially two accepted approaches: 1) assurance of the process by which the product is developed, and 2) the evaluation of the quality of the end product. Process quality contributes to improving product quality. This is recognised in the 2000 issue of ISO 9001 standard which has the requirement for assessing both processes and products.

In parallel with these standards, industries which deal with safety-critical systems (e.g. nuclear, space, railway) developed domain specific standards concerned with a particular quality characteristics or sub-characteristics.

In this paper, we are concerned with the quality evaluation of software products. A brief summary of each of the existing software product quality standards is given in the following section.

2.1 Product Related Standards

ISO/IEC 9126 Software Product Quality. This is the first standard for software product quality. The original ISO/IEC 9126: Software product evaluation—Quality characteristics and guidelines for their use [16] has been replaced by two related standards—ISO/IEC 9126: Software Product Quality and ISO/IEC 14598: Software Product Evaluation.

The ISO/IEC 9126 has four parts.

- Part 1: Quality model—defines a set of quality characteristics and corresponding sub-characteristics which have measurable attributes. These sub-characteristics are manifested externally when the software is used as a part of a computer system, and are a result of internal software attributes [3].
- Part 2 External Metrics—deals with external measurements made when validating the software in a system environment.
- Part 3: Internal metrics—deals with internal measurements made during the development phases.
- Part 4: Quality in-use metrics—deals with user perception and acceptance of the software.

ISO/IEC 12119: Software Packages—Quality Requirements and Testing. This standard [4] establishes quality requirements for software packages and instructions for testing software packages against these requirements by a third party. It deals only with software packages as "offered and delivered" so it is intended for suppliers, acquirers and third-party assessors. ISO/IEC 12119 uses the quality model from ISO/IEC 9126:1991 [16] which has six quality characteristics and attached sub-characteristics: functionality, reliability, usability, efficiency, maintainability, and portability. The standard is currently being updated and the new version will explicitly cover COTS software. It will support COTS suppliers when specifying quality requirements for COTS, when issuing declarations of conformity [17], and when applying for certificates or marks of conformity [18]. The standard also supports testing laboratories and certification bodies when setting up third party certification schemes or schemes for marks of conformity.

ISO/IEC 14598: Software Product Evaluation. The ISO/IEC 14598 series of standards [5] provides guidance and requirements for the software product evaluation process. The standard consists of six parts and provides guidance to a developer, acquirer and evaluator:

- Part 1: General overview—describes general concepts and terminology for evaluation.
- Part 2 Planning and management—covers planning and development of evaluation activities.
- Part 3: Process for developers—covers evaluation process performed concurrently with the development.
- Part 4: Process for acquirers—covers quality assessment and evaluation of pre-developed software products (more details in Sect. 4).
- Part 5: Process for evaluators—covers requirements and recommendations for independent evaluation including third-party evaluation.
- Part 6: Documentation and evaluation modules—describes the structure and content of an evaluation module.

3   Quality

Quality of a software product is the totality of its characteristics. Specification and evaluation of software product quality is a key factor in ensuring adequate quality. This can be achieved by defining appropriate quality characteristics, taking account of the purpose of usage of the software product.

3.1   ISO/IEC 9126 Quality Model

The new version of ISO/IEC 9126 [3] applies three views on quality: internal, external and quality in use.

Internal quality is the totality of characteristics of the software product from an internal view, i.e. during development. Details of software product quality can be improved during code implementation, reviewing and testing, but the fundamental nature of the software product quality represented by internal quality remains unchanged unless redesigned.

External quality is the totality of characteristics of the software product from an external view. It is the quality when the software is executed, which is typically measured and evaluated while testing in a simulated environment with simulated data using external metrics. As it is difficult to correct the software architecture or other fundamental design aspects of the software, the fundamental design usually remains unchanged throughout testing.

Internal and external quality is modeled with six quality characteristics and a number of sub-characteristics as it is shown in Table 1.

Table 1. External and internal quality characteristics of software products

Characteristics	Sub-characteristics
Functionality The capability of the software product to provide functions which meet stated and implied needs when the software is used under specified conditions.	**Suitability** **Accuracy** **Interoperability** **Security** **Functionality compliance**
Reliability The capability of the software product to maintain a specified level of performance when used under specified conditions	**Maturity** **Fault tolerance** **Recoverability** **Reliability compliance**
Usability The capability of the software product to be understood, learned, used and attractive to the user, when used under specified conditions.	**Understandability** **Learnability** **Operability** **Attractiveness** **Usability compliance**
Efficiency The capability of the software product to provide appropriate performance, relative to the amount of resources used, under stated conditions.	**Time behaviour** **Resource utilisation**. **Efficiency compliance**
Maintainability The capability of the software product to be modified. Modifications may include corrections, improvements or adaptation of the software to changes in environment, and in requirements and functional specifications.	**Analysability** **Changeability**. **Stability**. **Testability**. **Maintainability compliance**
Portability The capability of the software product to be transferred from one environment to another.	**Adaptability** **Installability**. **Co-existence** **Replaceability** **Portability compliance**

Quality in use is the user's view of the quality of the software product when it is used in a specific environment and in a specific context of use. It measures the extent to which users can achieve their goals in a particular environment, rather than measuring the properties of the software itself (more details shown in Table 2).

3.2   Quality Measurement

Software product quality can be evaluated by measuring internal attributes (typically static measures of intermediate products) or by measuring external attributes (typically by measuring the behaviour of the code when executed) or by measuring the quality in use attributes. For example, reliability may be measured externally by observing the number of failures in the given period of execution time, and internally by inspecting the detailed specifications and source code to assess the level of fault tolerance. A failure in quality in use (e.g., safety) can be traced to external quality attributes (e.g., time behaviour) and the associated internal attributes which need to be changed.

Table 2. Quality in use characteristics of software products

Characteristics	Sub-characteristics
Quality in use The capability of the software product to enable specified users to achieve specified goals with effectiveness, productivity, safety and satisfaction in specified contexts of use.	**Effectiveness** - The capability of the software product to enable users to achieve specified goals with accuracy and completeness in a specified context of use. **Productivity** - The capability of the software product to enable users to expend appropriate amounts of resources in relation to the effectiveness achieved in a specified context of use. **Safety** - The capability of the software product to achieve acceptable levels of risk of harm to people, business, software, property or the environment in a specified context of use. **Satisfaction** - The capability of the software product to satisfy users in a specified context of use.

It is important that every relevant software quality characteristic is specified and evaluated whenever possible using validated and accepted metrics. Measurement scales for the metrics used for quality requirements are divided into categories corresponding to different degrees of satisfaction of the requirements. For example the scale can be divided into two categories: unsatisfactory and satisfactory.

4   Evaluation Process for COTS Software Acquirers

4.1   Current Quality Evaluation

At present, there is only a limited number of practical evaluation schemes for software packages, based upon standards for quality of software products. From the overview of these schemes given in [2] it is clear that there are even fewer schemes which specifically target COTS software packages. TÜV Nord in Germany evaluates COTS software on the basis of ISO/IEC 12119. In Brasil, the Technological Center for Informatics Foundation (CTI) developed the method MEDE-PROS (based on ISO/IEC 9126, ISO/IEC 12119 and ISO/IEC 14598) with emphasis on functionality and usability of software packages. This evaluation method is applied for awarding the best software product of the year in Brasil. Several hundred software packages have been evaluated under this scheme. The French standardisation body AFNOR also adopted the ISO/IEC 12119 as the base standard for a quality mark called NF Logiciel [12] and are supporting the update of the standard to include COTS software.

MicroScope [2] is an example of a commercial third party software product evaluation scheme based on the ISO/IEC 9126 quality model [3] and the ISO/IEC 14598 evaluation procedure [7]. Until now, about hundred evaluations have been conducted on a commercial basis. The evaluations cover many application areas including: fire alarms, burglar alarms, offshore systems, gas burners, railway signals, process control systems, medical systems, automatic weighting systems, and windmills. Most evaluations have been related to safety-critical applications. With respect to effort almost half of the evaluation time has been spent on offshore systems and almost 25% of time was spent on fire alarms. The MicroScope scheme applies 12 evaluation modules (ISO/IEC 14598-6). They are checklist based and contain more than 1800 questions. The 12 evaluation modules cover all six quality characteristics of ISO/IEC 9126. For a specific evaluation only relevant evaluation modules are applied.

4.2   The Process

The essential parts of software quality evaluation are: a quality model, the method of evaluation, software measurement, and supporting tools.

The requirements for software product quality will generally include internal quality, external quality and quality in use. However, with COTS software products, usually only external quality and quality in use can be assessed.

The ISO/IEC 14598, provides a primary reference for evaluation process during acquisition of COTS products. Clause 6 in Part 4 of this standard focuses on the evaluation process of product quality during acquisition of "off-the-shelf" products. The evaluation process can be broken down into four major steps (see Fig. 1):

- **Step 1: Establish evaluation requirements**. This includes specifying the purpose and scope of the evaluation, and specifying evaluation requirements. The Evaluation Requirements Specification should identify software quality requirements (using the quality model ISO/IEC 9126-1) but also other aspects such as users and their goals, the integrity level of the software application, and supplier services to be assessed.
- **Step 2: Specify the evaluation.** This includes selecting the metrics and the evaluation methods. The quality requirements to be evaluated need to be correlated to external metrics (ISO/IEC 9126-2) and quality in-use metrics (ISO/IEC 9126-4). Example of external quality characteristic is efficiency—for sub-characteristic time behaviour selected external metric can be elapsed time between the start of system action and receipt of system response. ISO/IEC 14598-4 gives detailed guidance for developing the Evaluation Specification which is end result of this step.
- **Step 3: Design the evaluation.** This needs to consider access to product documentation, development tools and personnel, evaluation costs and expertise required, the evaluation schedule, criteria for evaluation decisions, and reporting methods and evaluation tools. The output of this step, Evaluation Plan, can incorporate test plan made on the basis of testing instructions for software packages in ISO/IEC 12219.
- **Step 4: Execute the evaluation**. This includes execution of the evaluation methods and analysis of the evaluation results. The conclusions should state whether the software product is appropriate for use in the intended application.

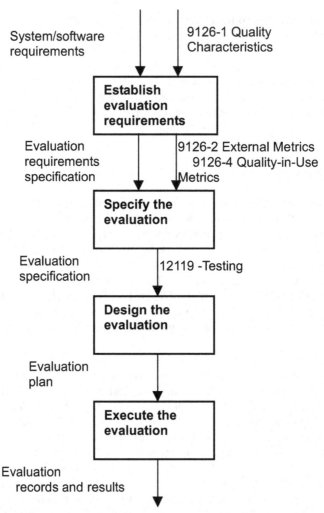

Fig. 1. Evaluation process during acquisition of COTS software products

5   Conclusion

The standards for product quality and evaluation provide ready-made framework for evaluation of COTS software packages. However, majority of COTS software evaluations are still performed without reference to quality or no or little use of the existing standards. In this paper we suggest the evaluation process for COTS software acquirers which is redressing this unbalance This process gives enough flexibility to fit in with the existing practices for evaluation of COTS software products in the organisations which are building COTS-based software systems. It enables structured and methodical assessment of commercially available software products with moderate effort, while providing documented evidence for the future evaluations.

References

1. Bache R., and Bazzana G.: Software Metrics for Product Assessment. McGraw-Hill (1994)
2. Bøegh, J.: Quality Evaluation of Software Products. Software Quality Professional 1(2) (1999)
3. Information Technology—Software Product Quality—Part 1: Quality model. ISO/IEC 9126-1 (2001)
4. Information Technology—Software Packages—Quality Requirements and Testing. ISO/IEC 12119 (1994)
5. Information Technology—Software Product Evaluation—Part 1: General overview. ISO/IEC 14598-1 (1999)
6. Software Engineering—Product Evaluation—Part 4: Process for Acquirers. ISO/IEC 14598-4 (1999)
7. Information technology—Software product evaluation—Part 5: Process for Evaluators. ISO/IEC 14598-5 (1998)
8. Functional Safety of Electrical/Electronic/Programmable Electronic Safety-Related Systems. IEC 61508 (1998)
9. BSI: Getting the measure of TickIT. Available at: http://www.tickit.org/measures.pdf
10. CEC: Information Technology Security Evaluation Criteria (1991)
11. Quality Management Systems—Requirements. EN ISO 9001 (2000)
12. Geyres S.: NF Logiciel: Affordable Certification for all Software Products. In: Achieving Software Product Quality, Uitgeverij Tutein Nolthenius (1997) 125–135
13. Humphrey, W. S.: Managing the Software Process. Addison-Wesley (1989)
14. IDC: The Software Construction Components Market. Available at: http://www.componentsource.com (2000)
15. International Standard (IS) 15408: Common Criteria for Information Technology Security Evaluation Version 2.1 (1999)
16. ISO/IEC 9126: Information Technology—Software Product Evaluation—Quality Characteristics and Guidelines for Their Use (1991)
17. ISO/IEC Guide 22: General Criteria for Supplier's Declaration of Conformity (1996)
18. ISO/IEC Guide 23: Methods of Indicating Conformity with Standards for Third-party Certification Systems (1982)
19. OSE. Available at: http://www.ose.com
20. SQUALE: Dependability Assessment Criteria. ACTS95/AC097, LAAS-CNRS (1998) Available at: http://albion.ncl.ac.uk/squale/index.html.

Modelling Component Dependencies to Inform Their Selection

Xavier Franch[1] and N.A.M. Maiden[2]

[1] Universitat Politècnica de Catalunya (UPC)
c/ Jordi Girona 1-3 (Campus Nord, C6) E-08034 Barcelona (Catalonia, Spain)
franch@lsi.upc.es
[2] Centre for HCI Design, City University
Northampton Square, London EC1V OHB, UK
n.a.m.maiden@city.ac.uk

Abstract. Selecting multiple, interdependent software components to meet complex system requirements is difficult. This paper reports the experimental application of the i^* agent-based system approach to model a system architecture in terms of dependencies between components to achieve goals, satisfy soft goals, complete tasks and provide and consume resources. It describes two treatments, at the architecture and component levels, that can be applied to these architecture models to determine important system properties that inform multiple component selection. The modelling approach and treatments are demonstrated throughout using the example of a meeting scheduler system.

1 Introduction

Most reported component selection processes [2,9] and techniques [7,11] support the selection of individual and independent software components. However, in real-world applications, the decision to select one component is rarely so simple and depends on which other components will be selected [1]. This paper reports preliminary research, using a simple case study, which investigates the feasibility and potential utility of modeling dependencies between software components to inform component selection.

This paper reports two innovations. The first is to apply advanced agent-oriented system modeling techniques, and in particular i^* goal modeling [14], to software component selection. The i^* approach was originally developed to model information systems, and in particular the dependencies between human and technological actors in a more software-oriented system architecture. In our work, we apply i^* SD models to model software architectures, not in terms of connectors and pipes (e.g. [13]), but in terms of actor dependencies to achieve goals, satisfy soft goals, use and consume resources, and undertake tasks.

This has two major advantages for software component selection. Firstly, the focus on goal and soft goal dependencies means that the selection process relies less on pre-emptive decisions about the architectural design or component selection—decisions that you should postpone for as long as possible. Secondly the architecture is expressed in terms of the problem domain rather than

H. Erdogmus and T. Weng (Eds.): ICCBSS 2003, LNCS 2580, pp. 81–91, 2003.

the machine [5], thus enabling more effective participation of stakeholders in a requirement-driven selection process.

The second innovation is to analyse these models to infer properties about the system architecture that impact on the satisfaction of non-functional requirements such as reliability and security, in order to assess the impact of selecting one component over another on requirement satisfaction. We present these properties as easy-to-use treatments of i^* models, and demonstrate their role using the selection of a meeting scheduler component. This part of our work fits well with the ATAM method for evaluating architecture-level designs taking into account simultaneously various non-functional requirements, although the study of tradeoffs and the iterative nature of the process is not considered in this paper.

The remainder of the paper is in 6 sections. Section 2 presents a simple case study—selecting meeting scheduler software. Section 3 introduces the i^* goal modeling approach and applies it to the case study. Section 4 describes some relevant characteristics of COTS products to be used in the case study. Section 5 delivers an architecture-level analysis of the system using an i^* model of the meeting scheduler system, then Sect. 6 delivers a component-level analysis of the same system model. The paper ends with a discussion of the results from the case study and posits a research agenda for scaleable component selection processes.

2   A Case Study

Scheduling meetings is an activity that takes place in companies and organizations worldwide. Computer support is helpful for improving the effectiveness of meeting arrangement—consequently many COTS products exist in the market for this purpose. Most incorporate mail facilities that allow participants to communicate whilst others offer features ranging from meeting management to the detection of conflicts that then necessitate resolution with conventional e-mail components. Furthermore, some existing e-mail components incorporate time-specific functions for managing calendars and agendas that may be used for scheduling meetings.

We are defining a COTS-based system for managing a meeting scheduler that shall send notifications to prospective participants and manage address books and distribution lists. We consider the following non-functional requirements based on the definition of non-functional characteristics [4]:

- *Reliability:* capability of the system to maintain its level of performance.
- *Security:* prevention of unauthorised access to the data such as personal addresses and meeting information that is managed by the system.
- *Usability:* how usable the system is to undertake tasks.
- *Interoperability:* ability to interact with other systems. In particular, the system is required to interact with a particular spreadsheet COTS component to load timetables.

Functional requirements include:

- The system shall maintain all the meeting information sent to or received from meeting participants.
- The system shall send messages to schedule meeting participants.
- The system shall read messages to get participants' feedback and confirmations.
- The system shall handle address books and distribution lists.
- The system shall warn prospective participants in case of meeting clashes.

These and other similar requirements provide the foundations for selecting software components on the basis of individual compliance with these requirements [1,9]. The next sections extend these approaches by applying the i^* approach to model component dependencies in terms of these requirements and other concepts.

3 Actor System Models

We apply Yu's (1993) i^* approach to model complex systems and their requirements, and in particular its Strategic Dependency (SD) model for modeling networks of dependency relationships among actors in a system. Opportunities available to actors are explored by matching a *depender*, which is the actor that "wants", and a *dependee* which has the "ability" to give what the depender wants. Since the *dependee's* abilities can match the *depender's* requests, a high-level dependency model of a system can be developed. The i^* approach was originally developed for socio-technical systems that involve different software, human and organisational actors. Our innovation is to exploit i^*'s modeling of goal-based dependencies between actors to model software-based system architectures as dependencies between different candidate software components.

SD models express dependencies using four main types of dependency link. For goal dependencies the *depender* depends upon the *dependee* to bring about a certain state in the world. A *goal* represents a condition or state of the world that can be achieved or not. For task dependencies, the *depender* depends upon the *dependee* to carry out an task. A *task* represents one particular way of attaining a goal. It can be considered as a detailed description of how to accomplish a goal. For resource dependencies, the *depender* depends upon a *dependee* for the availability of an entity. *Resources* can be physical or informational, and considered as the availability of some entity or even the finished product of some action, process or a task. For soft goal dependencies, the *depender* depends upon the *dependee* to perform some task that meets the soft goal or non-functional requirement, or to perform the task in a particular way.

Figure 1 shows an i^* SD model that represents a high-level architecture for our meeting scheduler system. It shows 6 actors, 4 software (*mail client, server, meeting scheduler* and *MS Office*) and 2 human (*user* and *meeting participant*). It also shows dependencies between these actors. For example, the mail client depends on the server to achieve the goal *e-mail is read* (indicated in i^* by a lozenge shape). The mail server also depends on the server to obtain the resource *secure protocols* (indicated by a rectangle). Elsewhere the meeting scheduler depends on the mail client to be reliable in scheduling meetings (indicated by a flag shape).

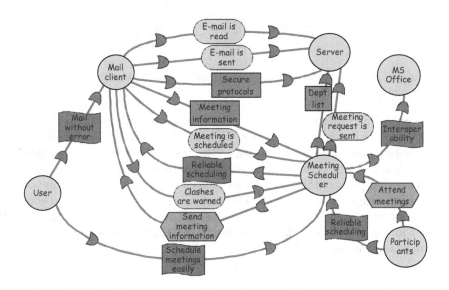

Fig. 1. *i** SD model for the meeting scheduler system [A useful mnemonic for the dependency link is to check the direction of the half-circles of the dependency. Consider each as a letter "D"—the direction that the D faces denotes the direction of the dependency. As the letter "D" is read, on the left is the depender and on the right is the dependee]

We have also used *i** Strategic Rationale (SR) models for modeling the intentionality associated with each actor. Figure 2 shows a simple SR model that describes and decomposes the soft goal *whole system is reliable*. The satisfaction of the soft goals *mail client is reliable* and *server is reliable*, and the goals *scheduled goals sent on time* and *new function added* all contribute positively to the higher-level soft goal. As such we use SR models to decompose and make testable soft goals that are dependent on actors modeled in the SD model.

4   Some Candidate COTS Components

Many current mail client components include both basic and advanced calendar and scheduling services. Most meeting scheduling components offer built-in mail notification facilities, which may be implemented either as a proprietary service or with an external mail client. These components also offer address books and distribution list management, which can be shared or synchronized with external

Fig. 2. i^* SR model showing the refinement of the soft goal whole system is reliable

resources of the same kind, although this restricts supplier selection. Although mail clients and servers are different components some suppliers provide both, sometimes as part of a larger package. Mail clients and servers from different suppliers must often be integrated using standard protocols (STMP-based).

For the purposes of this paper we have invented 6 example COTS components with different combinations of these features. Figure 3 outlines their behaviour with respect to some goals, dependencies and resources expressed in the SD model in Fig. 1. We use these characteristic COTS components later in the example selection process.

| Product | Covered agent | | | Characteristics |
	MS	MC	S	
MS1	x			Requires MC1 to send and receive messages Fails on sharing group lists
MS2	x	x		Requires MC2 to share group lists with external mail client Not satisfices the usability soft goal *schedule meetings easily*
MC1	x	x		Fails to remove corrupted attachments Does not work on S2
MC2		x		Fails to remove corrupted attachments Does not send messages when quota is exceeded
S1			x	Sends and reads mails. Provides distribution lists. Does not use secure protocols.
S2			x	Sends and reads mails. Provides distribution lists. Uses secure protocols.

Fig. 3. Description of some components (MS: Meeting Scheduler; MC: Mail Client; S: Server) ['x' indicates that the component has the characteristic in the indicated covered agent]

5   Architecture-Level Analysis of the System

To inform the selection of the meeting scheduler component the selection team must analyse how the concrete assignment of component types to system actors can affect the behaviour of the overall system using architecture properties that indicate feasible system architectures with respect to non-functional requirements. In this treatment, when one actor is implemented by more than one component, dependencies involving the actor are duplicated, i.e. we obtain *multiple dependencies*. We consider this a kind of *agent instantiation* in the model that affects the dependencies. Multiple dependencies must be taken into account in the definition of the properties and their metrics in terms of *instance dependencies* instead of *model dependencies*.

5.1   Derivable System Properties

Next we enumerate 6 system properties derivable from the soft goals that appear in the meeting scheduler $i*$ SD architecture model:

- *Diversity:* Having services and data replicated in more than one COTS component makes the system more robust with respect to temporal failure or the unavailability of one component [8]. If an actor is duplicated, others that depend on it are more reliable since the dependencies can be satisfied in more than one way.
- *Vulnerability:* Actor dependencies indicate the potential impact of the failure of one component on the system as a whole—the more a failed component is a dependee (that is, other components depend on it), the fewer goals are achieved, soft goals satisfied, tasks completed and resources delivered. Vulnerability is a transitive property—if A depends on B depends on C, then A is vulnerable to the failure of C.
- *Packaging.* Delivering more services with one large COTS component means that dependencies between actors implemented with this component are often implicitly satisfied.
- *Self-containment.* The flow of information from one component, shown using resource dependencies, exposes data to potential security breaches.
- *Uniformity.* Users can use a system more easily when they interact with fewer different COTS components with different communication styles and interfaces (Nielsen 1993). A few dependencies with a high number of interacting components will lessen the usability of the system.
- *Connectivity.* The same as before, but regarding external actors instead of user ones. Connectivity is damaged when the number of system components interacting with external ones (the *MS-Office* actor in our case) grows.

Figure 4 summarizes this information and provides concrete formulae that define the metric bound to each property. The metrics are defined in terms of the cardinality of the following sets of dependencies: Model Dependencies (MD); Non-Duplicated Model Dependencies for component c (NDMDc); Instance Dependencies (ID); Hidden Instance Dependencies (HID, means number of instance dependencies between those agents covered by the same component); Instance Resource Dependencies (IRD); Hidden Instance Resource dependencies (HIR); (stemming from) User Agents Instance Dependencies (UAID); Components that interact with User Agents (CUA); External Agents Instance Dependencies (EAID); Components that interact with External Agents (CEA).

Property	Definition	Softgoal	Metric
Diversity	Ability of the system to survive to failure of one component.	Reliability	$\dfrac{ID - MD}{ID}$
Vulnerability	Impact of failure of one component in the system.	Reliability	$\min\limits_{c \in C} \dfrac{MD - NDMD_c}{MD}$
Packaging	Grouping of system characteristics into components.	Reliability	$\dfrac{HID}{ID}$
Self-containment	Containment of data inside components.	Security	$\dfrac{HIR}{IRD}$
Uniformity	Avoiding different interface styles.	Usability	$\dfrac{UAID - CUA}{UAID}$
Connectivity	Ease of interconnection with other tools.	Interoperability	$\dfrac{EAID - CEA}{EAID}$

Fig. 4. Six properties of a system architecture [each with a definitions and metric]

5.2   Properties of the Meeting Scheduler Architecture

We can determine 3 possible basic architectures for the meeting scheduler system based on different configurations of actors to software components, independent of the individual software components selected:

- **Arch1.** A different COTS component for each of the 3 actors—a typical legacy architecture in which the mail client does not provide adequate scheduling services and the meeting scheduler does not provide built-in mail facilities.
- **Arch2.** A single COTS component is assigned to the mail client and meeting scheduler actors, so that, from the architecture point of view, it is not important whether the COTS component is primarily a mail client or a meeting scheduler.
- **Arch3.** The same as Arch2 but another instance of a COTS component is kept on the system. This architecture arises primarily when the meeting scheduler provides built-in mail facilities but also allows connection to an external mail client.

Figure 5 shows the values of the architecture-related-property metrics for these 3 different architectures. Results reveal that no single architecture is the best selection with respect to all of its non-functional properties. Arch3 has some potential *diversity* due to duplicated mail facilities. Arch2 and Arch3, which rely on larger COTS components, have higher *packaging* scores in their favour. Likewise, the use of larger COTS components increases the *uniformity* scores for Arch2 and Arch3.

6   Component-Level Analysis of the System

To inform the selection of the *meeting scheduler* component the team must also investigate concrete COTS products and dependencies for a chosen architecture.

Property	Arch1	Arch2	Arch3
Diversity	0	0	0.20
Vulnerability	0.60	0.47	0.60
Packaging	0	0.33	0.28
Self-containment	0	0.33	0.33
Uniformity	0.50	0.75	0.60
Connectivity	0	0	0

Fig. 5. Application of the 6 architecture property metrics to the 3 meeting scheduler system architectures (Arch1, Arch2, Arch3) and the system model in Fig. 1

We propose 3 complementary treatments to assist this investigation, first to determine feasible candidate architecture instances using component dependencies, then to explore the consequences of selecting a COTS component with respect to the system architecture and dependencies, and finally to investigate groups of system dependencies. The first 2 are reported in this paper.

6.1 Determining Feasible Instances of Candidate Architectures

Once an architecture has been chosen the first step is to determine which concrete COTS components can be implemented using this architecture. Component dependencies are crucial in this analysis. These dependencies state that a component A requires component B to attain its results, or else that A does not work together with other component B. These dependencies are also modelled as i^* dependencies, considering A and B as agents and putting the right type of dependency links. For instance, the component dependency *MS1 requires MC1 to achieve the goals e-mails sent and received* (see Fig. 3) yields to 2 goal dependency links from *MS1* to *MC1*. The left-hand side of Fig. 6 summarizes the 3 component dependencies that appear in the description of the components that instantiate actors in Fig. 3.

Let us assume that architecture *Arch1* has been chosen. Figure 6, right, shows how, from the 8 possible architecture instances bound to *Arch1* (all combinations of the products presented in Sect. 4), 5 of them are discarded because of the component dependencies.

6.2 Analysis of the Impact of Component Selection

The previous kind of analysis is useful when the context of the system forces a particular kind of architecture to be selected. Other treatments are needed when selecting individual COTS components when some components in the system have already been selected and implemented. We call this treatment *component anchoring*.

In our meeting scheduler system, it is likely that the company needing the new component has been using mail server and client components before the

Component dependency	Component			Feasibility
	MS	MC	S	
D1. MS1 requires MC1	MS1	MC1	S1	Accepted
	MS1	MC1	S2	Discarded by D3
D2. MS2 requires MC2	MS1	MC2	S1	Discarded by D1
	MS1	MC2	S2	Discarded by D1
D3. MC1 does not work on S2	MS2	MC1	S1	Discarded by D2
	MS2	MC1	S2	Discarded by D3
	MS2	MC2	S1	Accepted
	MS2	MC2	S2	Accepted

Fig. 6. Determining feasible instance architectures for Arch1

selection process takes place—assume that it is currently using server S1 and mail client MC1. The selection process begins by anchoring these components in the SD model. If we add all the *i** component dependencies involving MC1 and S1 to the SD architecture model, we can observe that both Arch1 and Arch2 are valid candidate architectures as both have one architecture instance using MC1 and S1 that satisfies all dependencies. In the case of Arch1, MS1 shall be plugged into the system (see first row in Fig. 6), while with respect to Arch2, the current two components form a complete system.

However, the component anchoring analysis can be more sophisticated if we implement the notion of heavy and light component anchors. Light anchors represent components that could be replaced in the system. In our example, the mail server is clearly a heavy anchor while the mail client can be defined as a light one. Component dependencies on light anchors are used to make suggestions about component substitutions. For example if we define MC1 as a light anchor we can substitute MC1 with MC2 to produce a second candidate instance architecture, with MS2 as meeting scheduler component. Figure 7 summarises this situation.

Architecture	Component combination	Light anchor management
Arch1	MS1, MC1, S1	None
	MS2, MC2, S1	MC1 substituted by MC2
Arch2	MC1, S1	None
Arch3	MS2, MC2, S1	MC1 substituted by MC2

Fig. 7. Feasible architecture instances considering MC1 as light anchor and S1 as heavy anchor

Definition of light anchors is especially useful when model and component dependencies reveal that no possible instance architectures are possible.

7 Conclusions

This paper reports an informal experiment to apply the i^* approach (Yu 1993) to model dependencies between components in a software architecture and to analyse these models for properties that inform the selection of COTS components. This innovative approach differs from more traditional system architecture modeling approaches [13] in that it does not require pre-emptive decision making about system architectures prior to COTS component selection. Specific contributions include:

- Highlighting the role of dependencies among types of COTS components during selection with the introduction of a framework that allows a team to model them and explore them deterministically. The framework is also well suited to obtain the characteristics that should be analysed in COTS candidates.
- Separating functionality from COTS components using agents that encapsulate functionality, so that assignment of functions to components is systematic by exploring dependencies between agents using some architectural properties.
- Integrating model dependencies among COTS components. Consequently, the universe of discourse for architectures and components is the same. We may thus reason about the result of the selection in a flexible way, ranking the feasible architecture instances, then exploring consequences of choosing one of them by fixing and removing particular components, and so on.

Our next step is to extend our REDEPEND prototype for i^* modeling and multicriteria decision-making to implement and evaluate model checking features that automate detection of the architecture- and component-level properties reported in this paper. This tool implementation will enable us to integrate component architecture modeling into the wider BANKSEC component selection environment [10] that we are currently experimenting with in trials with European banks on component selection projects. At the same time we will extend, formalise and evaluate the current prototype set of model properties that are useful during component selection.

References

1. Burgués, X., Estay, C., Franch, X., Pastor, J. A., and Quer, C.: Combined Selection of COTS Components. In: Proceedings of the 1st International Conference on COTS-based Software Systems, LNCS Vol. 2255, Orlando, Florida, USA (2002)
2. Comella-Dorda, S., Dean, J. C., Morris, E., and Oberndorf. P.: A Process for COTS Software Product Evaluation. In: Proceedings of the 1st International Conference on COTS-based Software Systems, LNCS Vol. 2255, Orlando, Florida, USA (2002)
3. Chung, L., Nixon, B., Yu, E., and Mylopoulos, J.: Non-Functional Requirements in Software Engineering. Kluwer Academic Publishers (2000)
4. Software Engineering—Product Quality—Part 1: Quality Model. ISO/IEC Standard 9126-1, June (2001)

5. Jackson M.A.: Software Requirements and Specifications. Addison-Wesley (1995)
6. Kazman, R., Klein, M., Barbacci, M., Longstaff, T., Lipson, H., and Carriere, J.: The Architecture Tradeoff Analysis Method. CMU/SEI-98-TR-008, July (1998)
7. Kontio J.: A Case Study in Applying a Systematic Method for COTS Selection. In: Proceedings 18th International Conference on Software Engineering, IEEE Computer Society Press (1996)
8. Littlewood, B., Popov, P., and Strigini, L.: Assessing the Reliability of Diverse Fault-tolerant Software-based Systems. In: Safety Science 40, Pergamon (2002) 781–796
9. Maiden, N., and Ncube, C.: Acquiring Requirements for COTS Selection. In: IEEE Software 15(2) (1998) 46–56
10. Maiden N. A. M., Kim H., and Ncube C.: Rethinking Process Guidance for Software Component Selection. In: Proceedings 1st International Conference on COTS-Based Software Systems, LNCS Vol. 2255, Springer-Verlag (2002) 151–164
11. Ncube C., and Dean J. C.: The Limitations of Current Decision—Making Techniques in the Procurement of COTS Software Components. In: Proceedings 1st International Conference on COTS-Based Software Systems, LNCS Vol. 2255, Springer-Verlag (2002) 176–187
12. Nielsen J.: Usability Engineering. Morgan-Kauffman, San Francisco (1993)
13. Shaw M.: Heterogeneous Design Idioms for Software Architecture. In: Proc. Sixth International Workshop on Software Specification and Design, IEEE Computer Society Press (1991) 158–165
14. Yu E. S. Y.: Modeling Organisations for Information Systems Requirements Engineering. In: Proceedings 1st IEEE International Symposium on Requirements Engineering, IEEE Computer Society Press (1993) 34–41

The Space Shuttle and GPS: A Safety-Critical Navigation Upgrade

John L. Goodman

United Space Alliance,
LLC, 600 Gemini Avenue, Houston, TX, USA 77058-2777
`john.l.goodman@usahq.unitedspacealliance.com`

Abstract. In 1993, the Space Shuttle Program selected an off-the-shelf Global Positioning System (GPS) receiver to eventually replace the three Tactical Air Navigation units on each space shuttle orbiter. A proven, large production base GPS receiver was believed to be the key to reducing integration, certification, and maintenance costs. More GPS firmware changes, shuttle flight software changes, and flight and ground testing were required than anticipated. This resulted in a 3-year slip in the shuttle GPS certification date. A close relationship with the GPS vendor, open communication among team members, Independent Verification and Validation of source code, and GPS receiver design insight were keys to successful certification of GPS for operational use by the space shuttle.

1   Introduction

In the early 1990s, Tactical Air Navigation (TACAN) ground stations were scheduled for gradual phase-out starting in the year 2000 due to the introduction of Global Positioning System (GPS) navigation. The five-channel Miniaturized Airborne GPS Receiver (MAGR) was chosen in 1993 to eventually replace the three TACAN units on each shuttle orbiter [1]. A preproduction MAGR (the "3M") flew seven times on Endeavor from December 1993 to May 1996. Test flights of a single MAGR/Shuttle (MAGR/S) began in September of 1996 on STS-79. Certification of the MAGR/S for TACAN replacement and the first all-GPS, no-TACAN flight was scheduled for 1999. By mid-1998, the three TACAN units had been removed from the orbiter Atlantis and three MAGR/S units were installed. However, MAGR/S and shuttle computer issues that surfaced during the flight of STS-91 (June 1998) resulted in a delay in MAGR/S certification. Additional flights and ground tests, along with additional MAGR/S firmware changes, were mandated. Changes were made to the project to enhance communication among participants, increase insight into the MAGR/S design, and fully integrate the MAGR/S vendor into the project. Three TACAN units were re-installed in Atlantis and one MAGR/S remained on board for data gathering. By the spring of 2002, all four shuttle orbiters were equipped with one MAGR/S, and certification for TACAN replacement occurred in August of that year. Due to the slip in the predicted start of TACAN ground station phase-out to 2010 [2], it is expected that the shuttle orbiters will fly with three TACANs and one GPS receiver for some time.

H. Erdogmus and T. Weng (Eds.): ICCBSS 2003, LNCS 2580, pp. 92–100, 2003.

2   Communicate Early, Communicate often

Cost and schedule concerns can lead to restrictions on communication among both management and technical personnel. Attempts to avoid discussing issues that are "out-of-scope" of the contract can lead to reluctance to discuss topics that are "in scope." Restricting technical discussions to a small group, in the interest of meeting a success-oriented schedule, can result in problems later in the project. This is particularly critical in the requirements definition phase. Requirements and technical issues must be identified and resolved early in a project to avoid negative impact to cost and schedule later in the project [3]. Multiple layers of management and contractors further degrade open, accurate communication, particularly among technical personnel. Lack of communication can lead to misunderstanding of requirements, software design and unit operating procedures, as well as a failure to recognize, properly diagnose, and resolve technical issues. Cost, schedule, and technical problems caused by poor communication may create adversarial relationships at both the organizational and individual levels.

In the wake of the GPS and shuttle computer problems encountered on STS-91, weekly participation in the MAGR/S Problem Resolution Team teleconferences was expanded to include all civil service and contractor organizations on the shuttle GPS team, including the vendor. Face-to-face meetings were held two to four times a year at the Johnson Space Center. Good interpersonal relationships and team building created an environment in which different points of view could be expressed and issues could be resolved in a manner that satisfied the concerns of project members. Special teams that included representatives from various contractor and civil servant organizations were formed to address specific technical issues. Accurate and detailed records of meetings, issues, issue resolution, and design rationale were kept. This allowed participants to stay informed on issues within the project and provided a record for engineers that will work with the MAGR/S in the future.

3   Establish a Close Relationship with the Vendor

Use of software intensive products in high-visibility, high-risk, and safety-related applications requires a higher level of vendor participation than other applications. Many vendors have little or no insight into how their products are integrated and used. The vendor can provide valuable information that should be factored into system and software-level requirements definition, flight and lab testing, issue identification, and issue resolution. Vendor involvement can permit timely identification of problems before cost and schedule are negatively impacted. Advice from the vendor is particularly important if the intended application of the product is significantly different from the application for which it was originally designed.

Integrators and users must maintain enough "in-house" expertise to define integration architecture, perform testing, identify and resolve problems, avoid false diagnosis of healthy units that are perceived to be malfunctioning, define test and operating procedures, and provide management with advice concerning which products are best for an integration. The use of a COTS device should not be used to justify "buying" technical expertise as a COTS product. Vendors in competitive markets may not want key technical personnel assigned to one project for long periods.

Initially, contact with the MAGR/S vendor was limited to a small group of personnel. Information obtained from the vendor was not passed on to other project participants, and the vendor was not consulted enough on integration and performance issues. After STS-91, the MAGR/S vendor was fully integrated into the GPS project team. The vendor was interested in learning how the Space Shuttle Program differed from previous users of their product. Observing shuttle ascent and entry from Mission Control, flying landings in a shuttle simulator, and participating in MAGR/S testing at Space Shuttle Program facilities enabled the vendor to become familiar with the shuttle flight regime, crew and Mission Control procedures, flight rules, and aspects of shuttle mission design. The vendor provided advice that improved ground and flight-testing, issue identification, and issue resolution. Interaction with project participants during weekly teleconferences and face-to-face meetings enabled the vendor to understand concerns and various points of view expressed by project members, enabling them to propose solutions that were agreeable to all parties.

4   Design Insight May Be Necessary

Design insight is required for high-risk, safety-related applications for the COTS integration to be successful. Users of COTS units usually have little or no insight into firmware design, design rationale, and operation. Available documentation may not contain accurate, pertinent information that would aid an integrator in designing integration architecture, defining interface and software requirements, test and operational procedures, and issue identification and resolution. A vendor supplied Interface Control Document (ICD) may not contain enough information to permit host system interface software requirements creation. Many devices, such as GPS receivers, contain legacy code, some of which may be one or more decades old. Vendor engineers may not have participated in the original development of the product. Over time, "corporate knowledge loss" concerning design rationale occurs due to retirements, employee attrition, office clean-ups, and corporate takeovers. This will make it difficult for the vendor to answer integrator and user questions. Vendor answers to questions may be limited to "how" a device operates, but not "why" it was designed to operate that way. If a vendor is not forthcoming concerning design insight, consultants and other users of the product may be able to provide information.

The STS-91 incident revealed that the shuttle computer software that interfaced with the MAGR/S was designed with an inadequate understanding of MAGR/S operation. The shuttle software was later modified to handle known and unknown receiver anomalies. Expanded vendor involvement after STS-91 brought much needed design insight to the project, which greatly aided issue identification and resolution. In hindsight, some aspects of the MAGR/S interface and integration might have been done differently if the vendor had been involved when the shuttle computer software requirements to support GPS were initially defined.

The vendor provided much needed education concerning the challenges of GPS design and operation in the flight environment for which MAGR was originally designed. A formal "questions for the vendor" list was maintained and answers were recorded.

Insight into test equipment design and operation is critical. Like vendors of GPS receivers, vendors of test equipment may not understand the applications that their equipment supports. Many issues that arose during MAGR/S ground testing concerned GPS signal generators. These issues had an impact on test results, cost, and schedule. Insight into GPS signal generator design and operation was a challenge throughout the project.

5 Define Realistic Schedule, Budget, and Requirements

A key question to be answered is, "Will the proposed use of the product differ greatly from the original application for which it was designed?" This question must be answered in order to create a realistic budget and schedule. If the proposed application is the same or very similar to that for which the product was originally designed, it may be possible to treat it as a "plug and play" project. However, if modifications must be made to accommodate operation in a different environment, the project is really a development project, and a fixed-price contract should be avoided. Fixed-price contracts often result in inflated initial cost estimates and remove the incentive for the vendor to pursue and resolve technical problems.

Technical risk must be taken into account when defining budget and schedule. Traditionally, navigation unit integration has revolved around hardware integration and testing (such as shock, vibration, thermal, radiation). However, with the increasing use of embedded computers, software development, maintenance, and testing must be budgeted for as well.

If extensive modifications and operation in a different environment are required, more testing will have to be performed. Provision for interim firmware versions should be provided in the budget. The vendor will have to be more involved than on "plug and play" integrations. Understanding the design rationale and original user requirements is important, and provision for discussing this with the vendor should be included.

Lessons learned from users of the same or similar products should be considered, particularly when defining requirements for the COTS item. "Loose" requirements may be easily met with little or no budget impact. However, they could permit problems to go unnoticed and unresolved and could impact future use of the device. Such requirements result in a "let's see what we can get by with" attitude rather than a "let's do what is right for the application" approach.

Some GPS receivers used on NASA spacecraft have a specified rate of receiver resets to recover from software anomalies [4] of less than one per day. Such a requirement, along with a maximum allowable solution outage time, will help motivate a vendor to pursue software issues.

6   Plan for Enough Testing and Code Audits

A number of spacecraft failures have resulted from a lack of comprehensive, end-to-end testing [5]. A limited amount of flight and ground testing to ensure that the unit "meets specifications" may not exercise enough of the software to uncover software issues. If the new application is different from that for which the product was designed, and modifications have been made, the amount and scope of testing will have to go beyond that needed to verify that the unit meets contract specifications. Both off-line and integrated testing of interface software in units that interact with the COTS product are required.

The shuttle/GPS integration architecture allowed a single GPS receiver to be flown for data collection while the baseline, certified legacy shuttle navigation system operated. Shuttle software that interfaced with and processed MAGR/S data was exercised in flight. For operational flexibility, shuttle software was designed to support three different vehicle configurations: three TACANs and no GPS, three TACANs and one GPS, or three GPS units and no TACANs.

Flight or lab testing will not find all software issues, nor will it enable verification of all software modifications. GPS signal generators will not exactly duplicate the radio-frequency environment present during a flight, nor will such lab testing exercise all possible logic paths in the GPS receiver software. After STS-91, the role of NASA's Independent Verification and Validation (IV&V) contractor was expanded to include an audit of the MAGR/S source code, which had been developed at government expense [6]. IV&V personnel possessed prior experience with the MAGR on aircraft integrations. The IV&V contractor played a valuable role in identifying, assessing the criticality of, and assisting with the resolution of software issues. IV&V audits and access to source code may be required for high-risk applications where human safety is a concern. The trend to use non-developmental item products containing proprietary software may be a safety risk in these applications.

Vendors of products such as GPS receivers often state that users do not provide enough data and hardware configuration information when a problem with a unit is reported. The performance of GPS receivers and other software intensive units is a function of a variety of factors. The cause of a suspected software or hardware issue cannot be diagnosed with only position and velocity data. Other parameters characterizing receiver performance should be supplied, in digital form, along with hardware configuration and procedures used. Before contacting the vendor, users should confirm that the suspect performance is not the result of user error.

7   Unrealistic Expectations Lead to COTS Disappointment

The success of inexpensive and easily available GPS technology has led some to believe that applying GPS technology is relatively straightforward, with low risk and low cost. Not understanding the complexity of GPS technology will lead to unrealistic budget, schedule, and technical success expectations. Assuming "cheap and easy" terrestrial GPS means applying such technology to spacecraft will be "cheap and easy" has prevented the maturation of GPS units for use on spacecraft [7].

"COTS disappointment" results from a failure to meet overly optimistic budget and schedule goals (i.e., the number of technical issues encountered exceeded expectations). COTS disappointment will lead to suspicion of the technology in the COTS product and reluctance to work with the technology in the future. The issue is not with "technology," but with unrealistic expectations attached to use of the COTS device. These unrealistic expectations arise from a failure to appropriately investigate and plan for the use of a COTS product when defining schedule, budget, and requirements.

8   Firmware Quality Is Important

Over the last 40 years, integration of off-the-shelf systems had changed from being primarily hardware integration to software integration. This presents new challenges for users of off-the-shelf systems. Developers of such systems must compete in a market that demands short time-to-market and low overhead. This results in short development and test cycles, less rigorous requirements definition and documentation, and a small group of programmers; and it can lead to a higher probability of software errors. Some products contain "legacy code" that may be decades old, and proper coding standards may not have been adhered to. Vendors often maintain a library of common software modules used in a variety of products. Cost and schedule concerns may lead the vendor, integrator, or user to judge a software issue to be "no impact" and not fix it. However, this can lead to propagation of software problems throughout a product line, and it could negatively impact users whose applications of the product in question are different from the original user.

Historically, navigation unit problems and failures in the legacy shuttle navigation system tended to be of a hardware nature. However, problems encountered with GPS have concerned software. GPS receivers contain tens or hundreds of thousands of lines of code. Code errors may not always manifest in a predictable or easily observable manner and may lie dormant for years until the proper set of conditions permits them to become visible. Software errors that do not manifest in an aircraft application of a GPS receiver may be an impact in orbit, where vehicle dynamics, satellite visibility, and flight times are very different.

Much attention has been paid to detecting and mitigating the impact of GPS satellite malfunctions on GPS receivers through the use of ground station monitoring (such as the U.S. Wide Area Augmentation System or the European Geostationary Navigation Overlay System) or suspect measurement detection and isolation (Receiver Autonomous Integrity Monitoring) within the receiver itself. A recent study [8] of stand-alone aviation GPS receivers that meet Federal Aviation Administration TSO C-129 requirements found that the probability of a receiver outage from a software issue was higher than a signal in space problem from a malfunctioning GPS satellite. The study concluded that more attention should be paid to improving GPS receiver software quality and characterizing GPS receiver failure probability and failure modes. Test flights of GPS receivers on the space shuttle have led shuttle navigation personnel to the same conclusions.

9   Provide Guidelines for COTS Use and Application of Faster-Better-Cheaper Principles

Recent analyses indicate that a lack of guidance on the application of COTS and faster-better-cheaper principles leads to projects that exceed cost and schedule estimates, and, in some cases, resulted in project failure [9,10]. Policies governing COTS and faster-better-cheaper approaches must be defined to permit clear and consistent application and to mitigate risk to budget and schedule [11-19].

Trade studies of COTS products involving "must meet," "highly desirable," and "nice to have" requirements will help determine what product to choose, what requirements it must meet, and if a custom approach should be taken instead. Any addition to or relaxation of requirements must be identified. A need for new requirements may not become visible until testing and implementation of the product is underway. The impact of COTS driven hardware and software changes to an integrated system must be assessed.

A certification plan must take into account how much vendor certification can be relied on and if additional testing beyond what the vendor performs is needed. Vendor certification for both hardware and software should be studied to determine if it is adequate. Vendor support required for testing, integration, and maintenance over the life cycle of the product must be defined. If white box testing (rather than black box testing) must be performed, design insight from the vendor will be required and proprietary agreements must be negotiated. The vendor may possess information on problems other users have encountered, which will be useful during integration and over the life cycle of the product.

Guidelines for use of COTS or Modified Off-The-Shelf (MOTS) software based on the criticality of the application in question were developed by the Space Shuttle Program in the wake of the GPS integration effort [20].

10   Summary

The Space Shuttle Program has successfully integrated and certified an off-the-shelf GPS receiver into the space shuttle avionics system. However, the time and effort required to certify the integration exceeded expectations. Integration and use of software intensive, off-the-shelf units into safety-related applications for which they were not originally designed requires vendor support and design insight above that required for other off-the-shelf integrations.

References

1. Goodman, J. L.: Space Shuttle Navigation: in the GPS Era. In: Proceedings of the National Technical Meeting 2001, Institute of Navigation, Fairfax, VA, January (2001) 709–724
2. Federal Radionavigation Plan-2001. U. S. Departments of Defense and Transportation (2002)
3. Rosenberg, D., Linda, H. et al.: Generating High Quality Requirements. In: Proceedings of the AIAA Space 2001 Conference and Exposition, AIAA Paper 2001–4524, American Institute of Aeronautics and Astronautics, Reston, VA, August (2001)
4. Bertiger, W. et al.: Precise Orbit Determination For The Shuttle Radar Topography Mission Using a New Generation Of GPS Receiver. In: Proceedings of ION GPS 2000, Institute of Navigation, Fairfax, VA, September (2000)
5. Newman, J. S.: Failure-Space: A Systems Engineering Look At 50 Space System Failures. In: Acta Astronautica, Elsevier Science Ltd. 48(5–12) (2001) 517–527
6. Beims, M. A., and Dabney, J. B.: Reliable Tailored—COTS Via Independent Verification and Validation. In: Proceedings of NATO Commercial Off-The-Shelf Products in Defense Applications Symposium, Brussels, Belgium, April (2000)
7. Bauer, F. H. et al.: Spaceborne GPS Current Status and Future Visions. In: Proceedings of ION GPS-98, Institute Of Navigation, Fairfax, VA, September (1998) 1493–1508
8. Nisner, P. D., and Johannessen, R.: Ten Million Data Points from TSO Approved Aviation GPS Receivers: Results of Analysis and Applications to Design and Use in Aviation. In: Navigation: Journal of the Institute of Navigation 47(1), Institute Of Navigation, Fairfax, VA (2000) 43–50
9. Anderson, C. et al.: Lewis Spacecraft Mission Failure Investigation Board Final Report. February (1998)
10. Gross, R. L.: Faster, Better, Cheaper: Policy, Strategic Planning, And Human Resource Alignment. Report Number IG-01-009, NASA Office Of The Inspector General, March (2001)
11. Adams, R. J., and Suellen, E.: Lessons Learned from Using COTS Software on Space Systems. In: The Journal Of Defense Software Engineering, U.S. Department of Defense, June (2001)
12. Brownsword, L., Carney, D., and Oberndorf, T.: The Opportunities and Complexities of Applying Commercial-Off-the-Shelf Components. In: The Journal Of Defense Software Engineering, U.S. Department of Defense, April (1998)
13. Carney, D. J., and Oberndorf, P. A.: OSD—Commandments of COTS: In Search of the Promised Land. In: The Journal Of Defense Software Engineering, U.S. Department of Defense, May (1997)
14. Carney, D.: Quotations from Chairman David—A Little Red Book of Truths to Enlighten and Guide on the Long March Toward the COTS Revolution. Carnegie Mellon University Software Engineering Institute, Pittsburgh, PA (1998)
15. Dean, J., and Gravel, A. (ed): COTS-based Software Systems. In: Proceedings of the First International Conference on COTS-based Software Systems, LNCS Vol. 2255, Springer-Verlag, Heidelberg, Germany (2002)
16. Lipson, H. F., Mead, N. R., and Moore, A. P.: Can We Ever Build Survivable Systems from COTS Components? CMU/SEI-2001-TN-030, Carnegie Mellon Software Engineering Institute, Pittsburgh, PA, December (2001)

17. Meyers, B. C., and Oberndorf, P.: Managing Software Acquisition: Open Systems and COTS Products. In: The SEI Series in Software Engineering, ISBN 0-201-70454-4, Addison-Wesley, Boston, MA (2001)
18. Oberndorf, P.: COTS and Open Systems. Carnegie Mellon University Software Engineering Institute, Pittsburgh, PA, February (1998)
19. Place, P. R. H.: Guidance on Commercial-based and Open Systems for Program Managers. CMU/SEI-2001-SR-008, Carnegie Mellon Software Engineering Institute, Pittsburgh, PA, April (2001)
20. Dittemore, R. D.: Commercial Off-the-Shelf (COTS), Modified Off-the-Shelf (MOTS) Software Policy. In: Space Shuttle Program Structure And Responsibilities, Book 2, Space Shuttle Program Directives, NSTS 07700. NASA Johnson Space Center, April (2001)

A Model for Recording Early-Stage Proposals and Decisions on Using COTS Components in Architecture

Tuomas Ihme

VTT Electronics
P. O. Box 1100, FIN-90571 Oulu, Finland
Tuomas.Ihme@vtt.fi

Abstract. Large networked systems can include the whole technological spectrum of embedded systems from deeply embedded application-specific systems to software intensive applications including COTS component intensive subsystems. Significant up-front and early-stage architectural design is required for COTS component acquisition and evaluation. COTS related architectural decisions, constraints and knowledge must be communicated from design processes to component acquisition and business processes and vice versa. This paper describes a model for identifying and recording constraints, possibilities and needs for COTS components in architecture. The decision model associates COTS component needs with elements in the first part of the software architecture to be designed. Decisions related to a specific architectural model are listed in a table form. A decision includes a reference to the related architectural model element or to a separate variation point model that describes relationships between architectural elements and the results of the decision.

1 Introduction

Large networked scientific mission systems as well as large networked telecommunication and automation systems can include the whole technological spectrum of embedded software and hardware from deeply embedded application-specific systems to software intensive applications including commercial system infrastructures. A need for the technological spectrum of systems arises from the spectrum of system requirements from maximizing performance and reliability with limited software and hardware resources to maximizing reusability and functionality with flexible software and hardware constraints. The whole spectrum of components, in-house software, custom components, modified off-the-shelf (MOTS) [9] components and commercial off-the-shelf (COTS) [9] components, is usually needed to build a commercial application. One important development goal of the software intensive subsystems has been to maximize software reuse for reducing time-to-market and minimizing software development costs.

H. Erdogmus and T. Weng (Eds.): ICCBSS 2003, LNCS 2580, pp. 101–111, 2003.

Product-line approaches [5] develop reuse infrastructures for achieving these goals in families of products. Modeling the commonality and variability of components in a product line has received an increasing attention over the past few years [2,4]. Component-based software engineering [7] supports the development and reuse software components and nowadays also COTS components for reaching similar goals. The integration of product-line and component-based software engineering approaches help to achieve architectures that can be managed even when accommodating changes in the component market. However, the architectural ideas of component-based methods and product-line approaches need to be evolved because COTS components differ from in-house components in that they are black box components intentionally hiding the details of their internal state. Findings from the actual COTS-based software processes [12] indicate that COTS components are identified, evaluated and selected in several decision steps during the requirements analysis phase. These decisions have often resulted in deteriorated architectures because the role of the integrator's software architecture has been far too small. The role is of utmost importance, but difficult because of changes in the evolving component market [14,15].

A high level architecture that captures essential static properties of software architecture is needed as early as in the requirements analysis phase for analyzing integration effort and incompatibilities and dependencies between the product line architecture [5] and COTS components and among COTS components. Conceptual configuration from the conceptual view [3,8] is an architecture of that kind because the engineering concerns of the conceptual view include the issues of how the COTS components are to be integrated and how they should interact with the rest of the system [8]. The conceptual architecture is the first part of the software architecture to be designed for a single software system. A domain-specific architecture, a reference architecture or a product-line architecture can be used as a starting point for the conceptual architecture of a product or products if they use modeling terms that are consistent with the conceptual architecture [8].

The second section of this paper presents an example of a high-level conceptual configuration. The third section describes a COTS component decision model for identifying and recording constraints, possibilities and needs for COTS components in architecture. The fourth section discusses how to get a balance between COTS component concerns and other important development goals in the example network of systems. System-specific COTS component decisions will be addressed in the fifth section considering the high level decisions of the previous section. The sixth section discusses some interesting issues concerning the proposed COTS decision model. Finally, conclusions will be drawn in the last section.

2   Conceptual Configuration from the Conceptual View

A high-level conceptual configuration with the UML-RT structure (collaboration) diagram notation [13] for networked space mission systems is depicted in

Fig. 1. The conceptual structural model shows not only data flow connections but also control connections. The networked system is decomposed into conceptual systems in the top-level decomposition model. The conceptual systems include conceptual subsystems that are decomposed into conceptual components. An important goal of the decomposition is to allow adding, removing or modifying conceptual elements according to evolution needs and reuse opportunities.

Figure 1 illustrates the distribution of roentgen-gamma-ray measurement software in the overall conceptual architecture. The Measurement subsystem is a conceptual subsystem of the Spectrometer system [11]. Measurement Control, Data Acquisition Control and Data Management are the conceptual components of the Measurement subsystem. The Measurement Control component controls the Data Acquisition Control and Data Management components in a predefined sequence. The Data Acquisition Control component provides interfaces for controlling the data acquisition and hides data acquisition details. The Data Management component provides interfaces for storing data chunks and hides data storing details. It transmits the stored science data to the Instrument Remote Control subsystem in the Mission Control System by request, via Satellite Computer and Ground Station Equipment (during the mission) or via Ground Station Equipment (during testing phases before the mission). Measurement commands are transmitted from the Instrument Remote Control subsystem to the Measurement Control component in reverse direction.

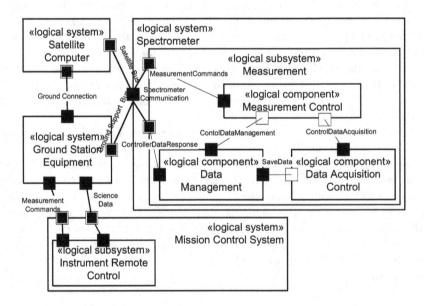

Fig. 1. Conceptual configuration for networked space mission systems from the point of view of roentgen-gamma-ray measurement software components

3   COTS Component Decision Model

The existing architectural descriptions [10] should be augmented by new COTS
component related stakeholders and concerns such as 'What constraints, possibilities and needs are there for COTS components in the architecture?', 'How
to describe the product line architecture for COTS component acquisition and
evaluation?' and 'How to open the product line architecture for COTS suppliers?'. A COTS component decision model is used for identifying and recording
constraints, possibilities and needs for COTS components in the architecture.
The decision model associates COTS component needs with elements in the architectural models. Decisions are listed in a table form as shown in Table 1. A
decision includes

- ID. Each decision can be identified by the name of the related architectural
  model or model element and the ID number of the decision.
- Concern. The concern is a COTS (or other commercial component) issue or
  a list of issues which this decision addresses. Concerns are stated in the form
  of questions.
- Variation point or Subject. The variation point identifies a place or places
  for COTS components in architecture. It refers to the related architectural
  model element or to a separate variation point model that describes relationships between architectural elements and the results of the decision.
  Subjects for decisions replace variation points when decisions are related
  to design styles and component roles and do not identify places for COTS
  components in architecture directly.
- Resolutions. The resolutions are answers to the decision's concern.
- Dependence. The dependence captures the dependence of the decision on
  other decisions in the decision model.
- Rationale. Risks and rationale of the decision.

Due to space limitations, the Rationale column has to be omitted from the
decision tables in this paper. COTS component concerns and related decisions
can be inter-related at different levels of detail and abstraction. The dependence
structure of decisions is acyclic. The decision table examples of this paper are
classified according to the decomposition of the conceptual configuration for the
networked space mission systems.

4   The Roles of Systems in the Use of COTS Components

Table 1 lists the component acquisition decisions related to the systems in the
conceptual configuration in Fig. 1. The decision 1 concerns the use of COTS
software in the communication between the systems. The decision 1 has two
possible resolutions: Yes, or No.

Systems in this kind of system of systems can be classified into the following
main categories by the particular quality attributes that they have to optimize:
deeply embedded systems (e.g., Spectrometer in Fig. 1), real-time systems (e.g.,

Ground Station Equipment), and COTS-intensive systems (e.g., the Mission Control System). The most important development goal of highly embedded systems is to maximize operational qualities like performance, reliability and availability. Soft real-time goals and particularly a set of hard real-time goals drive the system and software architecture of real-time systems. One of the main development goals of COTS-intensive systems is to maximize the use of COTS components and other commercial components. Functionality is allocated to COTS-intensive systems whenever realistic. The logical systems in Fig. 1 do not match exactly with the above system stereotypes but they have characteristics from several system stereotypes. However, it is important to identify the main architectural drivers and constraints for each system.

Table 1. Component acquisition decisions concerning the roles of the systems in the conceptual configuration

ID	Concern	Subject	Resolutions	Dependence
	Conceptual configuration for networked space mission systems			
1	Is it possible to use COTS in communication between systems?	The connectors between the systems in Fig. 1	Yes	
			No	
2	Does each system support COTS or MOTS use?	The Spectrometer and Satellite Computer systems in Fig. 1	Restrictedly	
			No	
3		The Ground Station Equipment in Fig. 1	To some degree	
			No	
4		The Mission Control System Fig. 1	Yes	
			No	

Deeply embedded systems typically include application-specific hardware for maximizing hardware performance. Often, only processor-specific software tools and languages are available due to the used special processors. The needs for optimizing software lead to application-specific software architecture and infrastructure and, often, to the use of assembly language in implementation, although a high-level language is available. The Spectrometer and Satellite Computer systems are deeply embedded systems with application-specific software and hardware. They can support the use of COTS or MOTS components only restrictedly (Decision 2 in Table 1).

Real-time systems often have to fulfil real-time-specific technological requirements such as the use of real-time-specific development tools, processors, software infrastructures and components. In addition, deeply embedded systems and real-time systems often have to fulfil company or domain-specific technological requirements such as the use of domain-specific development tools, processors and operating systems. It is likely that the requirements constrain software reuse within the specific technology domains. Real-time systems in the Ground Station Equipment can support the use of COTS or MOTS components to some degree (Decision 3 in Table 1).

The key technologies of COTS-intensive systems are open standards, vendor independent software and hardware infrastructures and platforms, standard design and programming languages that support component-oriented development, and standard component models. The Mission Control System in Fig. 1 is itself a distributed system, whose structure is not shown in the figure. The system includes subsystems, whose strategic development aims emphasize the following properties: easy and cost-effective to customize, vendor independent, and easy to augment with COTS components (Decision 4 in Table 1).

5   System-Specific COTS Component Concerns

The decision 1 in Table 2 concerns the use of MOTS protocols in communications from and to the Spectrometer system via the Spectrometer Communication port (Fig. 1 and 2). It has three possible disjoint resolutions (variants) for each protocol type: MOTS Protocol, Optimized MOTS Protocol and self-made protocol. The possible protocol types are RS-232 or Ethernet for the Ground Support Bus, and a special protocol for the Satellite Bus. The Measurement subsystem is isolated from the protocol types by its interface ports.

The protocol-specific variation point classes RS-232 Protocol, Ethernet Protocol and Satellite Bus Protocol inherit from the abstract Spectrometer Communication Protocol class. The Binding Time describes the last possible time, design, when the decision can be taken. The Multiplicity attribute of the Ground Support Bus variation point specifies that it is possible to select the RS-232 or Ethernet bus or both for the desired product. The Multiplicity attribute of the Spectrometer Communication Protocol variation point specifies that only one protocol variant of each protocol type can be used in a product. The Dependence column in Table 2 describes how the decisions 1 and 2 depend on the Restrictedly or No resolutions of the decision 2 in Table 1.

The decision 2 in Table 2 concerns the use of a COTS operating system in the Spectrometer system and the Measurement subsystem. The requirement specification of the systems emphasizes the capability of handling worst case event bursts from hardware sensors, strict timing of event responses, highly speed-optimized reading of the scientific data sensors, very limited front end scientific data processing, and optimized use of hardware such as processors, disks and communication buses. The decision 2 has two possible resolutions: COTS operating system, or No.

The decision 1 in Table 3 has two possible resolutions on the use of a MOTS Product Line Asset Base in the Mission Control System: Yes, or No. The decision 2 has three possible resolutions on the use of a COTS database in the

Table 2. Component acquisition decisions concerning the Spectrometer system in the conceptual configuration

ID	Concern	Variation point	Resolutions	Dependence
Conceptual configuration, Spectrometer				
1	Is it possible to use a MOTS Protocol that includes a COTS kernel?	See Fig. 2	Variant MOTS Protocol	Decision 1 in Table 1: Yes Decision 2 in Table 1: Restrictedly
			Variant Optimized MOTS Protocol	Decision 1 in Table 1: Yes Decision 2 in Table 1: Restrictedly
			Self-made protocol	Decision 1 in Table 1: No Decision 2 in Table 1: No
2	Is it possible to use a COTS operating system?	The Spectrometer system and the Measurement subsystem in Fig. 1	COTS operating system	Decision 2 in Table 1: Restrictedly
			No	Decision 2 in Table 1: No

Table 3. Component acquisition decisions concerning the Mission Control System in the conceptual configuration

ID	Concern	Subject	Resolutions	Dependence
Conceptual configuration, Mission Control System				
1	Is it possible to use a MOTS Product Line Asset Base?	The Mission Control System in Fig. 1	Yes.	Decision 4 in Table 1: Yes
			No	
2	Is it possible to use a COTS Database?	The Instrument Remote Control in Fig. 1	Acquired with the Product Line Asset Base	Decision 1: Yes
			Acquired separately	
			No	

Instrument Remote Control subsystem: Acquired with the Product Line Asset Base, Acquired separately, and No. The resolution 'Acquired with the Product Line Asset Base' requires the resolution of the decision 1 to be Yes.

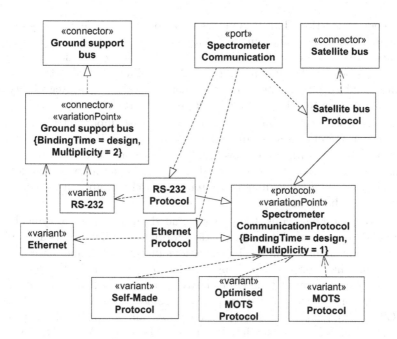

Fig. 2. Variation points for the decision on the use of MOTS protocols in the realization of the Spectrometer Communication port

6   Discussion

The proposed approach supports making and communicating early-stage draft resolutions on the use of heterogeneous technologies and styles of COTS components in heterogeneous networked systems. High-level architectural visions can be ensured and over-hasty commitment to specific technologies and solution architectures can be avoided by using conceptual architecture models in identifying possibilities and needs for COTS components. These models augmented by COTS decision tables and variation point models can be used as architectural basis for starting the acquisition and evaluation processes of COTS components.

Conceptual architecture may include several views such as the structural, functional, behavioral, concurrency and deployment views [3]. The conceptual configuration from the structural view is the most important for identifying COTS component needs and possibilities in architecture; however, models from the other views may provide useful additional information. The structural elements, i.e. components, connectors and ports, of the conceptual configuration in Fig. 1 can be modeled using UML [13], but the more compact UML-RT structure diagram form was used. The elements are similar to the conceptual configuration in [8], with the exception of connectors that are passive conduits and not connector classes or types as in [8]. UML-RT provides a seamless modeling paradigm for components and connectors from conceptual models to executable designs and target code generation. This also allows for a continuous refinement of decisions on using COTS components in the architecture of a system or a product line. Interface ports and protocols of UML-RT capsules allow one to standardize component interfaces so that it is possible to connect different candidates or variants of commercial software in the architecture for evaluating their integrability using the Rational Rose RealTime tool that supports UML-RT.

The proposed decision model associates the most important COST component decision factors using a table form. The proposed decision table structure follows the architectural decomposition of the system. The dependence factor will have an important role when the dependence structure will include COTS component decisions concerning also later-stage architectures and all conceptual systems and subsystems.

Due to space limitations, the paper included few examples of typical COTS component questions and decisions, little information about factors and only one variation point model example. The questions in Tables 1, 2 and 3 are necessary because they have been and will be asked in real-life, implicitly or explicitly. Explicit questions are necessary for clarifying the role software architecture in the COTS component acquisition process. Some decisions concerned the use of MOTS components that may play an important wrapper role in providing tailoring capabilities for associated COTS components. A MOTS component may include or be associated with COTS components, e.g. the MOTS protocol and the MOTS Product Line Asset Base in this paper.

The proposed approach supports opening a product line architecture for COTS suppliers. For example, the decision 1 in Table 2 and Fig. 2 capture adequate architectural information for starting the COTS component acquisition process and negotiations with COTS suppliers. There is no need to deliver or reveal the architecture in Fig. 1 or the inside of the Measurement subsystem.

The KobrA decision model [2] describes the existing variabilities identified in the models of products in a product line while the proposed decision model describes proposals for the variabilities. The proposed decision tables can be utilized when constructing KobrA decision tables for the realized variabilities of components that were proposed earlier in the development process by using the decision model of this paper. The decision tables of the two approaches have several similarities.

The modeling elements of the variation point model in Fig. 2 are similar to UML extensions for variability in [4]. However, Fig. 2 shows potential realization variants for protocols associated with three elements of the conceptual configuration in Fig. 1 but not variants of the elements themselves. Therefore the "realize" relationship of UML has been used between the elements and the variation points. In addition, Clauss [4] does not use abstract variation point classes. The Binding Time and Multiplicity attributes of the variation point stereotype have been derived from [4].

A design framework (e.g., the ROOM framework [11] for the Measurement subsystem and the IRC framework [1] for the Instrument Remote Control subsystem) and a product line asset base (e.g., the Control Channel Toolkit [5] or SCOS-2000 [6] for the Mission Control System) can define the operational context of COTS components in the final selection phase. The proposed component decision model can be also applied to final COST component selections. The proposed approach allows these components to be composed into systems in a combination of an architecture-centric (top-down) and component-centric (bottom-up) process.

7   Conclusions

The long-lasting acquisition of COTS components is usually based on the information available during the requirements analysis phase where architectural information is scarce in traditional development methods whereupon component selections have often resulted in deteriorated architectures. On the other hand, current architectures have not adequately allowed the utilization of COTS components in large networked embedded systems. Architectural models should be available in early development stages and they should make it possible to address COTS component related concerns.

The proposed decision model supports capturing information about the architecture of a system or a product line for COTS component acquisition and evaluation as well as for COTS suppliers. It supports identifying and recording constraints, possibilities and needs for COTS components from the conceptual configuration that is one of the first software architectural models to be designed. Variation point models are used to describe relationships between the elements of the conceptual configuration and the results of the decisions. Decisions can be inter-related at different levels of detail and abstraction. The proposed decision model allows the communication about COTS related architectural decisions, constraints and knowledge from design processes to component acquisition and business processes and vice versa. Future work will concentrate on COTS component decisions related to other architectural models and later-stage software architectures as well as on the process and tool support for the decisions.

Acknowledgements. This work was done in the Minttu project (Software component products of the electronics and telecommunication field) funded by the Technology Development Centre of Finland (TEKES), Finnish industry, and VTT Electronics.

References

1. Ames, T., Koons, L., Sall, K., and Warsaw, C.: Using XML and Java for Astronomical Instrumentation Control. In: Proceedings of the Sixth International SpaceOps Symposium, Toulouse, France (2000)
2. Atkinson, C., Bayer, J., Bunse, C., Kamsties, E., Laitenberger, O., Laqua, R., Muthig, D., Paech, B., Wust, J., and Zettel, J.: Component-based Product Line Engineering with UML. Addison-Wesley, New York (2001)

3. Bachmann, F., Bass, L., Chastek, G., Donohoe, P., and Peruzzi, F.: The Architecture Based Design Method. CMU/SEI-2000-TR-0001, Carnegie Mellon University, Software Engineering Institute, Pittsburgh, PA (2000)
4. Clauss, M.: Generic Modeling using UML Extensions for Variability. In: Proceedings of the OOPSLA 2001 Workshop on Domain Specific Visual Languages, Tampa Bay, Florida (2001) 11–18
5. Clements, P., and Northrop, L.: Software Product Lines: Practices and Patterns. Addison-Wesley, New York (2001)
6. Di Girolamo, G., Maldari, P., Croce, F., and Albeti, M.: INTEGRAL Mission Control System (IMCS): Technology and Integrated Solutions for Supporting a Complex Scientific Mission. In: Proceedings of 27th EUROMICRO Conference, IEEE Computer Society, Warsaw, Poland (2001) 154–161
7. Heineman, G. and Councill, W.: Component-based Software Engineering. Addison-Wesley, New York (2001)
8. Hofmeister, C., Nord, R., and Soni, D.: Applied Software Architecture. Addison Wesley, Massachusetts (1999)
9. IEEE Recommended Practice for Software Acquisition. IEEE Std-1062, 1998 Edition, The Institute of Electrical and Electronics Engineers, Inc., New York (1998)
10. IEEE Recommended Practice for Architectural Descriptions of Software-Intensive Systems. IEEE-Std-1471, The Institute of Electrical and Electronics Engineers, New York (2000)
11. Ihme, T.: A ROOM Framework for the Spectrometer Controller Product Line. In: Proceedings of the Workshop on Object Technology for Product Line Architecture, ESI-199-TR-034, European Software Institute, Lisbon, Portugal (1999) 119–128
12. Morisio, M., Seaman, C., Parra, A., Basili, V., Kraft, S., and Condon, S.: Investigating and Improving a COTS-based Software Development. In: Proceedings of 22nd International Conference on Software Engineering, ACM Press, Limerick, Ireland (2000) 32–41
13. Selic, B., and Rumbaugh, J.: Using UML for Modeling Complex Real-Time Systems. Rational Software. Cupertino, CA (1998)
14. Szyperski, C.: Component Software: Beyond Object-oriented Programming. Addison Wesley, Harlow, England (1998)
15. Wallnau, K., Hissam, S., and Seacord, R.: Building Systems from Commercial Components. Addison-Wesley, New York (2001)

Designing Secure Integration Architectures*

G. Jonsdottir, L. Davis, and R. Gamble

Department of Mathematical and Computer Sciences
The University of Tulsa
600 South College Avenue
Tulsa, OK 74104 USA
{gogsi,davis,gamble}@utulsa.edu

Abstract. Security has become a paramount concern due to dramatic advances of network technologies and a wide variety of new business opportunities. These advances have also brought the need for integration of computers systems to the surface, mainly for real-time, information sharing. As these systems are network-based, COTS products are predominantly used in these types of integration efforts. Since security is still a relatively new concern, it is often addressed as an afterthought in software development. Unfortunately, to ensure a high degree of security, it is imperative to address the concerns in a principled manner. Software architectures provide a unique opportunity to assess and structure the security as part of integration solution design. In this paper, we describe an approach to constructing secure integration architectures— architectural solutions to component interoperability that both satisfy known functional security policies and that specify the functionality of security mechanisms used to fulfill them.

1 Introduction

Due to frequent mergers, acquisitions or business restructuring, legacy systems that previously depended on mere physical security are now left vulnerable to intra- and inter-net attacks. However, securing individual, implemented systems is a complex and error-prone process. It is also a well-known fact that addressing security after implementation often forces developers to awkwardly shoehorn security mechanisms into the application [6]. Thus, development of techniques to address security throughout the development lifecycle is a growing focus for researchers.

COTS products offer reliable systems for integration efforts while reducing deployment time. However, an internally secure COTS product does not ensure the overall security of integrated applications that include that secure

* This material is based upon work supported in part by AFOSR (F49620-98-1-0217) and NSF (CCR-9988320). Any opinions, findings, and conclusions or recommendations expressed in this material are those of the author(s) and do not necessarily reflect the views of the National Science Foundation or the US government. The government has certain rights to this material.

H. Erdogmus and T. Weng (Eds.): ICCBSS 2003, LNCS 2580, pp. 112–122, 2003.

COTS product. Current advocates of secure COTS integration stress assessing the security levels of the COTS themselves and how the security levels can be mismatched [14].

Software engineering approaches to ensuring secure integrated systems treat security as a non-functional requirement. Some attention has been paid to characterizing non-functional requirements to assess mismatch [8,11]. Frameworks have also been proposed to construct software architectures that incorporate non-functional concerns [19]. However, security, particularly secure integration of COTS, is not being approached as an independent concern in software architecture. Thus, separating security issues as an independent issue with its own exclusive assessment is necessary.

The most compelling reason to assess security issues early and with a more intense focus is due to the continued acceptance of patching and spaghetti-code in software development and integration. Such rushed and extemporized implementation will have devastating consequences for the security of government and business information. If security concerns are addressed at the design level, violations will be at least minimized, and if design considerations are taken seriously, the concerns at implementation time may be non-existent.

We start with the software architecture of the overall application: the highest level of abstraction that provides meaningful information. This abstraction provides key information to an initial security assessment. The software architecture of a system is the blueprint of its computational elements, the means by which they interact, and the structural constraints on their interaction [7,17,22].

In this paper, we illustrate how security can be analyzed effectively and incorporated into an integration solution during design, resulting in secure integration architectures. Section 2 presents research that is directly relevant to this topic. In Sect. 3, we present an example that will be used throughout the paper. In Sect. 4, we analyze the example with respect to authentication, and refine the integration solution to fulfill the security requirements. Finally, Sect. 5 concludes with final results and future work.

2   Background

In this section, we discuss security issues including definitions and current high-level work in security to form the foundation for its consideration in integration solution design. Software architecture research and its relation to the techniques used in our research are also discussed.

2.1   Defining Security Issues

Top management usually supports high-level *security policies*, which state the overall direction that the company takes to protect its assets. Security policies are the rules and procedures (e.g., manuals) set by the authority governing the use and provision of security services and facilities [24]. There are many types of security policies currently in use, e.g., most companies have a "General Organization Security Policy" in place. A policy might state that appropriate steps must be implemented to protect the organization's assets from a variety of threats, such as error, disclosure violation, terrorism, etc. [21].

Functional security policies are implementation specific policies. They state the general functional requirement for certain security mechanisms [21]. These policies are directly related to specific computer systems. Not all companies have these policies documented, but they are usually implicitly known for each application in the organization by the development team. These policies can apply to *security mechanisms* such as authentication, access control, message protection, and audit. Security mechanisms are the actual implementations (i.e., code) of the functionality that provides protection to an application. Correct implementation of security mechanisms should fulfill the requirements set forth by the security policies [24].

2.2   Security and Software Architecture

Software engineering researchers are recognizing the need for an architectural perspective on security [6]. Research has attempted to incrementally add security mechanisms, such as Kerberos, to generic communication mechanisms (e.g., RPC) [23]. Architectural mismatch and component security, when assessed individually often produce redundant or overly complex functionality for the overall integration solution. Only when the solutions are modeled uniformly can the redundancy and complexity be seen and then eliminated in their composition. However, most security solutions do not take architectural issues into consideration.

Architectural assessment is effective in illuminating behavioral conflicts among components in an integrated application. The phrase *architecture mismatch* was coined to describe certain underlying reasons for interoperability problems among seemingly "open" software components [7]. As a result, researchers began to examine architectural characteristics to locate potential interoperability problems. These characteristics are defined with respect to architectural styles and their various types of computational elements and connectors, data issues, control issues, and control/data interaction issues [1,3].

Comparing characteristics across interoperating components identifies problematic architecture interactions [4,9]. These conflicts are described as patterns, which facilitate the construction of composite integration architectures from Extender-Translator-Controller (ETC) integration elements [5]. ETC integration elements are minimal functional units that resolve architectural conflicts [12,13]. Security policy mediation and its composition with integration architectures highlight the need for further design research [16]. Having an initial integration architecture allows us to analyze its configuration to determine restrictions that must be imposed on the integration architecture so that it can become secure.

Integration architectures [12,13,15] describe the strategies and patterns for an integration solution. Software architecture provides a unique viewpoint with which a developer can locate and structure security correctly in an integrated application. By assessing the security issues of a system using its components, connectors and their interaction assumptions, potential violations and restrictions that must be imposed on the integration architecture before it can be considered secure can be pinpointed without considering implementation details [22]. We define secure integration architectures as integration architectures that satisfy known functional security policies and that specify the functionality of the security mechanisms used to fulfill them.

3 Motivating Example

We use a simple, industrial example to demonstrate our approach toward designing secure integration architectures. In this example, a local telecommunication company seeks to integrate a Provisioning system with a Workflow system (both COTS) using TIBCO Rendezvous (middleware product). We highlight the relevant parts of the initial integration architecture in Fig. 1[1] [20]. The Provisioning and Workflow Integration (PWI), eliminates all "manual" communication (e.g., email, ftp, hand-carry) between those two systems, allowing orders to be transferred as workflow commands to the Workflow system from the Provisioning system.

Because the Provisioning system has no calling facilities but offers a CORBA API (ORB) to access its internal data and functions, an Observer is implemented external to both the component and middleware. The Observer queries the ORB for new transactions and forwards them to TIBCO Rendezvous. This is possible because the Provisioning system is configured to write a limited entry key to a log file. The Observer reads the log file to determine which requisitions are new and then queries Provisioning for information relating to these new transactions.

During requirements engineering, the development team generates a set of use cases that include functional security scenarios for the PWI system. These functional security use cases abide by the General Organizational Security Policy of the company. For purposes of brevity, the approach we discuss in this paper would address only those use cases related to authentication (see Sect. 4). Thus, a secure integration architecture for the PWI system must fulfill the authentication requirement set forth by the policy without altering the system's original functionality.

4 Securing the Integration Architecture

To design truly secure integration architectures, all aspects of security (authentication, access control, message protection, and audit) must be assessed and implemented correctly. The objective is to perform this assessment such that the path from its results to a correct implementation is direct. The difference

---

[1] There is actually another Observer and Translator that front Workflow, but its impact on the solution is minimal, so for brevity we do not include it.

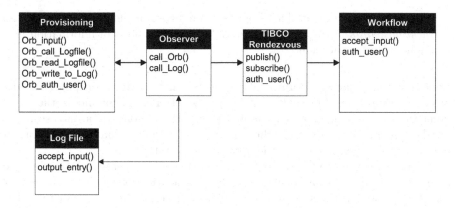

Fig. 1. Provisioning and Workflow Integration

between this type of analysis and component interoperability analysis is that security must permeate the integrated application. It is not just a control/data exchange behavior issue among specified components. Therefore, if an implementation patch is used to prevent improper use of one component, there is no guarantee that this prevention will be propagated to all components.

For this paper, we focus on authentication. Authentication can be specified in a number of different ways. The most common type is password protection where a subject must identify itself with the correct password. There are challenge-response systems where a subject is authenticated by providing the correct answer to a shared secret. A shared key, used to shield communicated data, is the basis for encryption authentication techniques. Appending an encrypted version of the data as a signature can also authenticate a subject. In all of these cases a buffer or registry of identification information (password, shared secret, shared key) is necessary. A decision component that can use the information and input to validate the identity of a subject is also essential.

When discussing the example, we refer to the log file and the ORB as part of the Provisioning system. In addition, we assume that all internal functionality of TIBCO Rendezvous is encapsulated. Thus, we are not concerned with the internal processing of this product in our assessment. We are mainly concerned with external actions of the product, such as information entering and exiting.

4.1 Assessing the Integration Architecture

Creating secure integration architectures requires careful examination of the initial integration architecture that results from resolving component behavior mismatch. The application can't be secured without this architecture solution in place. In fact, it is advantageous to understand as much about the application architecture as possible, e.g. the middleware planned for and evolution expectations. This realistically grounds the refinements needed to address security.

Selected refinements are based on: (1) an analysis of the position of *security verification points* in the architecture, and (2) the topology of information flow throughout the application.

Security Verification Points. We define security verification points as any place in the architecture that must be protected. This is commonly the entry point into a component, a consolidated group of components, a data store, or middleware process. However, they may also be found along communication paths between components, as the application dictates.

Correctly implemented authentication ensures that a subject accessing the application is really what it claims to be. Authentication must be present at the appropriate locations in an integrated application to eliminate any unauthorized access that would compromise the confidentiality and integrity of the entire application. In this example, the two systems have relatively similar authentication mechanisms in place. However, for the PWI example, an unauthorized party should not have the means to gain entry into the integrated application. Hence, all direct access should be guarded.

Focusing on authentication, we find the initial set of security verification points by looking at the authentication that is in place, the component interfaces, the middleware properties, and the application constraints. When integrating legacy systems and/or COTS components, it is reasonable to assume that many of them have some authentication in place. For instance, Provisioning is equipped with an ORB (see Provisioning's interface functions in Fig. 1), which by default provides basic security services that can be used to fulfill the authentication requirements. Workflow also has an authentication mechanism in place. Finally, TIBCO Rendezvous authenticates components wishing to transfer data over the message bus.

Figure 1 depicts the bidirectional information flow present in the system between Provisioning and the Observer. The Observer can also call and receive messages from the Log File. The Observer forwards all of the transactions it gathers to TIBCO, which then passes them to Workflow. Table 1 shows the security verification points and their associated component(s).

Table 1. PWI Security Verification Points

Security Verification Points	Associated Components
ORB authentication	Provisioning
Log file authentication	Provisioning
TIBCO authentication	TIBCO Rendezvous
Observer authentication	Observer
Workflow authentication	Workflow

Examining Information Flow. The communication interchange among components through security verification points reveals important information about potential security violations. We examine this, along with the propagation of identification information, to determine the problem, and formulate the requirements for its resolution. This identification is what a user/component needs to pass for entry.

Potential problems are indicated at the security verification points when components provide no authentication or component interactions bypass verification points. In the PWI example, when the Observer queries Provisioning, the query is intercepted by the authentication service of the ORB, and is therefore checked for the appropriate identification information. Figure 1 depicts this through the Orb interface function Orb_auth_user (). ORB authentication might seem like enough. However, there is a problem at the Log file security verification point. The Observer can call the Log File directly, bypassing Provisioning's authentication mechanism in the ORB. This indicates that additional authentication is needed to protect the Log file from unauthorized access.

It is also clear in Fig. 1 that the Observer does not have an authentication mechanism. Therefore, it cannot detect transactions from unauthorized entities or store user identification information. An additional problem occurs at the TIBCO verification point as a consequence of the Observer verification point problem.

When the Observer forwards the query result to the Message Bus, it is neither authenticated nor is it appended with identification information from the Observer. Therefore, though TIBCO has identification information from Provisioning, it does not have an entry for the Observer. Thus, the communication would get authenticated, but a malicious intruder could compromise the communication any time between Provisioning and TIBCO without being detected. TIBCO could also be implemented such that it expects identification information from the Observer. Thus, TIBCO would not supply this information, and the application would be deadlocked. Though the latter scenario does not cause a breach of security, it does illustrate how security concerns manifest interoperability problems. Finally, the Workflow verification point, like Provisioning's verification point, does not have an authentication violation. Given that communication reaches Workflow's interface, TIBCO's authentication functionality provides the correct identification information to be authenticated.

4.2   Refinement

The security verification points and the violations indicated by examining the information flow dictate the need and type of architectural refinement. This refinement must be controlled to ensure that the initial functionality of the integration architecture is maintained.

Given that Provisioning already has acceptable authentication functionality in place, the PWI application must be required to route all Observer requests for data (log file keys and workflow commands) through the security verification point of the ORB. To do this, we modify the Observer such that it sends its request to read the log file through the ORB. However, further requirements are needed to secure the integration. An understanding of the interaction among the components, as well as authentication mechanisms, clarifies the additional requirements [2,6,18].

The log file should be protected from unauthorized access. This requires a controller (LogController) that intercepts all incoming requests and makes a decision whether the request should be granted or not. All requests *not* coming from the ORB or the Provisioning system itself are routed to the ORB for authentication. Only requests coming from the ORB will be allowed access to the log file. This authentication/redirection mechanism can be seen in Fig. 2.

The Observer requires the addition of an authentication mechanism. As discussed early in Sect. 4, this requires a small data store for the information to signify a valid response to a specific request. We call this StoreExtender. Thus, when a request is sent to Provisioning, StoreExtender stores information based on the request. The incoming response is routed through AuthController, which queries StoreExtender for details responding to the outgoing request. AuthController compares the request to the incoming answer and verifies that Provisioning actually sent the response.

Modeling the specific authentication requirement using a uniform model can be beneficial. The models resulting from the assessment could then be mapped to specific, reusable solutions. This would clearly depict the needed functionality for developers to implement the security mechanisms themselves.

4.3   Change Control

After security measures have been successfully merged into the system, it becomes important to ensure that none of the previously implemented functionality has been compromised. The initial integration architecture was constructed to facilitate component interoperability and communication. Therefore, it must be maintained within the confines of the secure integration depicted in Fig. 2. Moreover, the integration must still fulfill the initial application requirements.

In the PWI example, the only significant restrictions imposed on the architecture are the redirection of the Observer's log file requests and the addition of the log file and Observer's authentication mechanism. This does not hinder any of the initially defined coordination or communication requirements of the integration architecture.

It is important to ensure all identification information is propagated correctly. With the addition of the AuthController and LogController, Provisioning's identification information is propagated to the Observer. However, without an additional piece of functionality, the Observer cannot communicate its identification information to TIBCO, resulting in deadlock. Thus, an IDTranslator (see Fig. 2) is inserted which appends the Observers identification information.

Guaranteeing that this information can still be passed provides a reasonable assurance the architecture has not been compromised. However, whether the identification information reaches its destination often depends on other nonfunctional properties such as reliability. Encryption of identification information

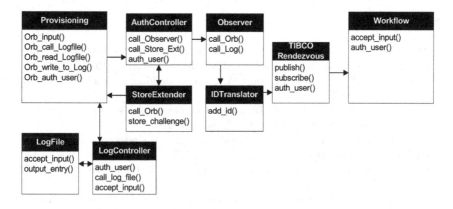

Fig. 2. Authentication Integration Elements

must also be taken into consideration, however that requires some the consideration of key management issues and requires further research.

5 Discussion and Conclusions

Assessing security at the software architecture level provides a unique opportunity to tightly weave security mechanisms into an integrated application design. This affords developers with the ability to create secure integration architectures instead of awkwardly forcing security into the application after implementation. Information gathered about design decisions can prove valuable during maintenance or incremental additions to the system [10].

Gleaning requirements for authentication mechanisms at the architectural level highlights the coordination constraints often imposed on a security mechanism. One goal would be to taxonomize different security mechanisms using a pattern-like approach to identify distinguishing characteristics and functionality. This future research would streamline their incorporation into integration architectures.

Our general approach is, at present, somewhat ad hoc. It does fulfill our main goal, illustrating the importance of architecture information to security issues in an integration setting. In future work we plan to improve our model by developing a more rigorous and methodical process. This will afford a more general method to securing integrations at the design level. While our approach lays out a secure integration architecture, security will always partially depend on the actual implementation of security mechanisms that are used. We recognize that certain security breeches, such as buffer overflows, must still be handled at the implementation level. While this is only the first step on the road to a secure system, it is an important step to establish the framework.

References

1. Abd-Allah, A.: Composing Heterogeneous Software Architectures. Ph. D. Dissertation, Computer Science, University of Southern California (1996)
2. Anderson, R.: Security Engineering—A Guide to Building Dependable Distributed Systems. John Wiley & Sons, Inc. (2001)
3. Davis, L., and Gamble, R.: The Impact of Component Architectures on Interoperability. In: Journal of Systems and Software (2002)
4. Davis, L., Gamble, R., Payton, J., Jonsdottir, G., and Underwood, D.: A Notation for Problematic Architecture Interactions. In: ESEC/FSE, Vienna, Austria (2001)
5. Davis, L., Gamble, R., and Underwood, D.: Conflict Patterns: Toward Identifying Suitable Middleware (2000)
6. Devanbu, P., and Stubblebine, S.: Software Engineering for Security: a Roadmap. In: The Future of Software Engineering, Special Volume published in conjunction with ICSE, Limerick, Ireland (2000)
7. Garlan, D., Allen, A., and Ockerbloom, J.: Architectural Mismatch, or Why it is Hard to Build Systems out of Existing Parts. In: ICSE, Seattle, WA (1995)
8. Han, J., and Zheng, Y.: Security Characterisation and Integrity Assurance for Component-based Software. In: International Conference on Software Methods and Tools, IEEE Computer Society Press, Wollongong, Australia (2000)
9. Jonsdottir, G.: Notating Problematic Architecture Interactions. M.S. Thesis, Department of Mathematical and Computer Sciences, The University of Tulsa (2002)
10. Jónsdóttir, G., Flagg, D., Davis, L., and Gamble, R.: Integrating Components Incrementally for Composite Application Development. SEAT-UTULSA-2001-19, Department of Mathematical and Computer Sciences, The University of Tulsa (2001)
11. Kazman, R., Klein, M., and Clements, P.: ATAM: Method for Architecture Evaluation (2000)
12. Keshav, R.: Architecture Integration Elements: Connectors that Form Middleware. M.S. Thesis, Department of Mathematical and Computer Sciences, University of Tulsa (1999)
13. Keshav, R., and Gamble, R.: Towards a Taxonomy of Architecture Integration Strategies. In: 3rd International Software Architecture Workshop (1998)
14. Lindqvist, U., and Jonsson, E.: A map of Security Risks Associated with Using COTS. In: IEEE Computer 31(6), (1998) 60–66
15. Mularz, D.: Pattern-based Integration Architectures. In: PLoP (1994)
16. Payton, J., Jónsdóttir, G., Flagg, D., and Gamble, R.F.: Merging Integration Solutions for Architecture and Security Mismatch. In: International Conference on COTS-Based Software Systems, Springer-Verlag, Orlando, Florida (2002)
17. Perry, D., and Wolf, A.: Foundations for the Study of Software Architecture. In: ACM SIGSOFT 17(4) (1992) 40–52
18. Pfleeger, C.: Security in Computing. NJ: Prentice-Hall Inc., Upper Saddle River (1997)
19. Rosa, N., Justo, G., and Cunha, P.: A Framework for Building Non-Functional Architectures. In: 16th ACM Symposium on Applied Computing, Las Vegas (2001)
20. Sellers, C., Gamble, R., Jónsdóttir, G., Flagg, D., and Davis, L.: Middleware Properties: Essential Pieces to the Component Integration Puzzle. SEAT-UTULSA-2001-18, Department of Mathematical and Computer Sciences, The University of Tulsa (2001)

21. Shaurette,K.: Enterprise Security Management (2001)
    Available at: http://www.softmart.com/connected/Spring2001/enterprise.htm.
22. Shaw, M., and Garlan, D.: Software Architecture: Perspectives on an Emerging
    Discipline. NJ: Prentice Hall, Englewood Cliffs (1996)
23. Spitznagel, B., and Garlan, D.: A Compositional Approach for Constructing Con-
    nectors. In: The Working IEEE/IFIP Conference on Software Architecture, Ams-
    terdam , The Netherlands (2001)
24. Wheeler, A., and Wheeler, L.: Security Taxonomy & Glossary (2001) Available at:
    http://www.garlic.com/~lynn/secgloss.htm.

Coordination in COTS-Based Development

Moshe Krieger[1], Mark Vigder[1], John C. Dean[1], and Muddassir Siddiqui[2]

[1] Building M-50 Montreal Road, National Research Council Canada,
Ottawa, Ontario, Canada, K1A 0R6
{Moshe.Krieger,Mark.Vigder,John.Dean}@nrc.ca
[2] School of Information Technology and Engineering, University of Ottawa,
Ottawa, Ontario, Canada, K1N 6NS
Mudi@rogers.com

Abstract. This paper introduces the basic concepts of coordination based design and addresses three important issues of COTS-based systems: meeting user needs, selection of proper COTS software and meeting non-functional requirements. It shows that established engineering practices that deal with these issues may be imposed during the development cycle by separating coordination from execution. By integrating COTS software using a coordinator, designers can address these issues up front.

1 Introduction

The idea of coordination is a very general concept that is applicable both for handling complexity and to provide disciplined integration [1]. This paper outlines the applicability of coordination as a general development environment that allows for a methodical design of COTS-based systems. In more detail, after briefly outlining coordination-based design (CBD) [2], this paper describes how the methodology can be used for COTS-based design by showing the following:

- The development of user-centric COTS-based systems by providing direct user involvement in requirements specification.
- The selection of the COTS software needed to implement the system.
- Satisfaction of the non-functional requirements typically encountered in COTS-based systems.

In Sect. 2 we briefly describe coordination-based design while Sect. 3 shows how requirements are acquired and provides some tools for this process. Section 4 contains a discussion of selection of COTS software. Section 5 establishes the link between the non-functional requirements and coordination-based design. Finally, in Sect. 6 we present our conclusions.

2 Coordination-Based Design

Coordination based design (CBD) [3] is a general methodology for the design complex systems, that considers a computer based system as a set of assignable

H. Erdogmus and T. Weng (Eds.): ICCBSS 2003, LNCS 2580, pp. 123–133, 2003.
© Springer-Verlag Berlin Heidelberg 2003

resources, for example, software modules, hardware components, interfaces allocated to execute the required system responses. It considers system requirements as work to be executed in response to user requests. Furthermore, it assumes that all work has two components: the various activities (units of work) that have to be executed and the coordination of these activities. Since most environments are dynamic (widely varying user demands and changing conditions), the system to be realized is considered as a set of assignable resources that are coordinated to meet varying working conditions.

The basic premise of coordination is that the only way to handle the complexity of real systems is by managing it—a well known and accepted engineering, industrial and societal principle. The idea of coordination fits well with an event-driven or behavioural view of systems, that is, specifying system behaviour in terms of event responses, each corresponding to a set of activities (units of work) that have to be executed in a given precedence relation.

The fundamental proposition behind the development environment of coordination-based design is the coordination based system architecture [4]. This architecture views the system as one or more coordinators that specify the sequence of activities which has to be initiated in response to an event, and a number of execution units or executors that execute the different activities. Note this view of systems as coordinators/executors, anthropomorphically is equivalent to the various levels of managers/workers of complex industrial or governmental institutions. This coordination-based architecture provides a separation of concern by separating execution (what it has to be done, the execution of units of work) from coordination (when to do it, managing work).

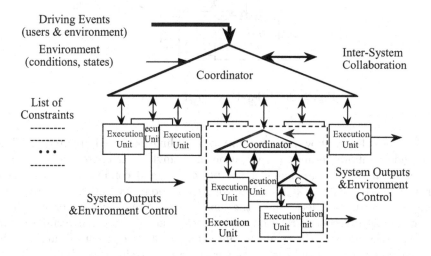

Fig. 1. Coordinator Organization

In the organization shown in Fig. 1 only the upper level coordinator receives driving events from the environment and it transmits events to the lower level coordinators as required. Lower level coordinators may also receive environment conditions or states (local inputs, not driving events). Lower level coordinators are viewed as execution units by the upper level coordinator.

In the literature the term coordination can also includes collaboration. Here we distinguish between these terms as follows:

- The coordinator is the equivalent of a manager that considers all the units in the layer below it as execution units—workers. Between the coordinator and executors there is a command, or a master/slave, relationship.
- Collaboration is considered as a passive or semi-passive integration medium that facilitates cooperation between relatively independent system elements. In other words, collaboration between these systems is done between their highest level coordinators in a peer-to-peer relationship (one may say "no" to a request).

We focus on the coordination aspects rather than collaboration.

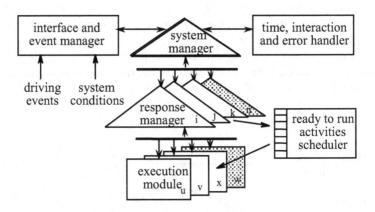

Fig. 2. Single level coordination organization

To more clearly show the simplicity of coordination based architecture, Fig. 2 provides a more detailed organization of a single level coordination. In this organization the system manager accepts events and conditions, checks them for authenticity and awakens the appropriate response manager. Each response manager continually determines the next ready to run activity or activities, based on the precedence relations of the activities of the given response. The specific assignment of the ready to run activities to free execution units is the responsibility of the scheduler, using various predetermined scheduling schemes (such as priority-based, first-come first-served, shortest activities first). The system manager controls all communications. The response managers communicate with each other and with the environment through the system manager.

When considering COTS-based systems, the COTS software takes the role of execution modules while the coordinator becomes the integration framework for the system. Selection of COTS modules will be discussed in detail in Sect. 4. The coordinator, in its simplest form, could correspond to a graph traversal algorithm that invokes the different COTS software as dictated by the responses. The coordinator can also include additional features in order to meet the nonfunctional requirements discussed in Sect. 5.

3   Requirements Specification

A first step in CBD is the requirement specification of the system as a set of event responses represented as event response diagrams. These diagrams are a precedence graph that specifies the order of execution of the associated activities and the interaction between the event responses. These response diagrams only define the relations between the different activities, and not the activities themselves, using a few basic connectives, such as sequence, concurrence and alternation. The activities (units of work), and communications (interactions or notifications) can be expressed in any language; in the case of COTS-based systems the activities correspond to the basic responses that can be directly performed by the COTS software.

Requirement acquisition starts with the system developer/architect asking the user to outline system requirements as a set of behaviours, by narrating[1] the expected system responses to user actions and/or environmental conditions. For example, in a business environment in which a user can request a document for update, the event response narrative can be expressed in tabular format as in Fig. 3. Note that each system response must have a single well-defined start and end.

To "formalize" these behaviours, the developer translates the above tables into event response diagrams using the elements shown in Fig. 4.

The order of execution of the different activities, that define system behaviour, is specified using the following connectives (Fig. 5):

- Sequence: to execute a set of activities one after another until all are completed.
- Concurrence: to execute activities in any order, in parallel, depending on the availability of resources, until all are completed.
- Alternation: like concurrence except that it is completed when the first activity is finished; all others that were started are discarded.

---

[1] The narrative approach is used here because humans are story-telling animals. There is the Talmudic saying: "If you have trouble explaining something tell its story". Relating to requirement acquisition, this can be modified to: "The best way to explain something is to tell its complete story: what it does, how it does it, why it is needed, and where it fits in (its limitations)."

User Action Events	System Response Activities
Start User ID & doc. #	
	Check user ID
	Check access right to doc.#
	Fetch and display doc.
Update xxx	
	Enter update
	Display updated doc.
Save doc. #	
	Store updated doc. End

Fig. 3. Sample event response narration

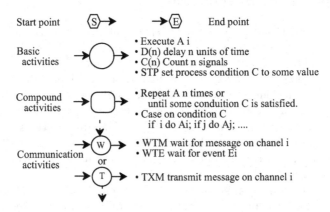

Fig. 4. Event response elements

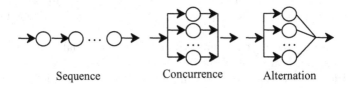

Sequence   Concurrence   Alternation

Fig. 5. Representation of Activity Connectives

The elements and connectives are the basic entities of a high level event response diagram. Domain specific systems may include additional domain specific activities and/or connectives. The system remains extensible as long as one assumes activities that terminate and one defines single-input single-output connectives.

Figure 6 corresponds to a response in which, after waiting for the starting event S, the system executes two sequences concurrently. The first sequence corresponds to the execution of activity A1 followed by the execution of activity B twice, after which it has to transmit a message. The second sequence starts

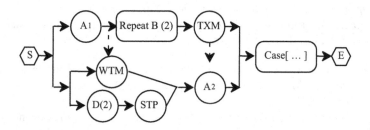

Fig. 6. Sample event response diagram

with an alternation which states that one waits for a message for two units of time and a system condition is set if it does not arrive within this time. If the message arrives in time the system condition is not changed. The second sequence is completed after the execution of activity A2. After both of these sequences are executed a Case on some condition completes the response. We have found that with small amounts of practice most users become easily familiar with this notation.

To finalize requirements acquisition the following steps must be completed:

– The system developer/architect and user(s) refine the event response diagrams via a number of "review meetings". To maintain "understandability" of the high level event response diagrams, as a rough guideline, they should not include more than twenty-five activities and connectives.
– The accepted event responses are used to define a requirement prototype for user(s) experimentation to help in reaching the final decisions.
– These accepted behavioural requirements are next annotated with additional nonfunctional constraints that may be pertinent such as execution times, resources to be used, reliability considerations, etc. One can also include the required system instrumentation and the run-time management scheme that is to be employed as discussed in Sect. 5.
– Finally the various deliverables, the initial and consecutive system deployments are agreed upon.

The well-formed nature of the event response diagrams[2] allows both for step-wise refinement (by expressing complex activities as sub responses) and the straightforward implementation of a requirements prototype. We have implemented a tool that converts the XML directly to a prototype. A snapshot of the prototype is shown in Fig. 7.

– The specified event responses are transcribed as XML files using DTD (Document Type Definition) syntax.

---

[2] In developing the CBD we have defined a unified easily mastered notation [2], the process activity language (PAL) similar to event response diagrams, for capturing requirements, for reasoning, for decision making, and for communication between the various stakeholders.

– Using Java's DOM (Document Object Model) for XML API (Application Programming Interface), the event responses are represented visually in an easily understood tree like format.

A GUI application was written using Swing (part of the Java Foundation Classes) API for Java that forms a requirement prototype that can be exercised by the user to make final decisions.

Using the requirement prototype the user can select various events to start specific event responses, which are shown as responses trees. In the response trees, the currently executing activities are highlighted, as indicated in Fig. 7.

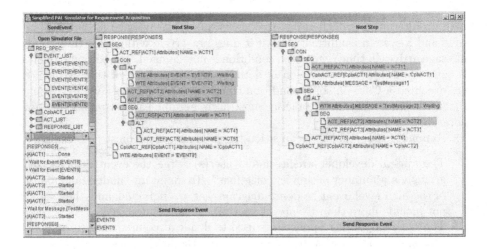

Fig. 7. Snapshot of Requirement Prototype

Furthermore the user can select any activity, or group of activities, by selecting the encapsulating construct, and then select "next step" to determine the activities that will execute after these are finished. It is important to note the similarity of this structure to scenarios and use cases.

4   Selection of COTS Software

Once the requirements specification is finalized as a set of event responses, the activities of the responses are grouped into related response subsets that correspond to those requirements that are directly executable by a single (or an ensemble[3] of) COTS software. Potential COTS candidate products are then evaluated against the groupings and are selected based on their fit to the response criteria. Should there not be a good component match the developer

---

[3] An ensemble of COTS software is a group of products that operate together, i.e. although separate they are treated as one component.[5]

either negotiate with the user to restate the event responses, or repartition the event responses, to more clearly match the available functionality of the components.

The negotiation with the user requires that the user revisit the response narrations originally supplied to determine if there is any flexibility in the way a particular set of activities might be accomplished, or, in the extreme case, if there is some way to eliminate that particular activity. The repartitioning of event responses will normally be undertaken as a result of the developer gaining a greater understanding of the available functionality supplied by the COTS products under consideration.

In either case there will remain a subset of the event responses that cannot be fulfilled by the selected COTS products. This situation can be handled in one of two ways:

1. The developer writes custom code to supplement the functionality of the selected products.
2. For that subset repeat the selection process with COTS software that can fulfill all or part of the remaining event responses.

Note that this is a cyclical process that corresponds very nicely to the Spiral development model of Boehm [6]. The termination condition for this process is where the developer determines that the return on investment of the selection process is subsumed by the cost of constructing a custom solution to satisfy the remaining event response subset.

As can be seen this successive repartitioning will result in the creation of a new requirements prototype for each cycle of the selection process. Throughout this discussion we have assumed that there will be COTS products available that can supply the majority of the required functionality. However the same process can be applied, even if COTS software fulfills only a limited portion of the functionality.

5   Assessing the Coordination Architecture

Software architecture should be driven by requirements, both functional and non-functional. Functional requirements are described in previous sections. The non-functional requirements for COTS-based systems differ from custom built systems due to the processes required to build and maintain systems constructed from black-box commercial components that are under ownership and control of commercial vendors. The major non-functional requirements for COTS-based systems that are different from commercial systems are the following:

– Reconfigurability. A common activity for maintaining and evolving COTS-based systems is to replace software products with newer versions of the product as they become available, or to replace a product from one vendor with a competing product from another vendor.

- Visibility. Visibility is the ability to observe the internal behaviour of the system. This is particularly important for COTS-based systems, as there may be little visibility into the individual COTS software products.
- Testability. Integration testing for COTS-based systems is complicated by the fact that the COTS software are generally black-box and no tests can be done based on the internal structure of these products. Since the integration architecture is under control of the designers, they must design the system to allow for the testing of the integration.
- Tailorability and configurability. The COTS products provide much of the generic functionality for a system. The business processes specific to the organization, however, are generally supplied by tailoring and configuring the system. These business processes are highly volatile and must be quickly evolved as the business needs of the organization change and are better understood. Since source code of COTS products is not available, the architecture of the system must allow this rapid business process evolution to take place.
- Reliability and security. Although all systems require reliability and security, the issue that arises with COTS-based systems is how to build reliable and secure systems with COTS products for which the reliability and security characteristics are unknown. With COTS products quality and test data may not be available from the vendor.

A set of architectural properties has been identified that improves a systems' ability to meet the non-functional requirements of COTS-based systems [7]. Coordination based design satisfies a number of these architectural design properties. Using COTS products as the execution modules, when glued together with a custom built coordinator, satisfies many COTS-based system design criteria, as outlined in [8].

Primary among the design principles of CBD that support COTS integration is the encapsulation of the component interactions. The encapsulation of COTS product interactions within a controller helps to satisfy many of the nonfunctional requirements. Some examples are:

- Minimal direct coupling between the COTS software facilitates reconfiguration.
- The coordinator provides a central location where instrumentation code can be added to improve the visibility and testability of the system.
- Each COTS software can be tested separately by exercising its' calls. For integration one checks response managers to verify the correct sequencing of COTS invocations. This provides integration testability [9].
- Much of the tailorability for COTS-based systems involves modifying the execution control of functionality provided by COTS software. Encapsulating the control within a coordinator provides a single entity that must be altered in order to tailor system behaviour.
- Security and reliability can be addressed by providing adequate checks within the coordinator. The coordinator can verify events and responses being

passed between the execution units, and can introduce access checks to control unauthorized access.

There are a number of other design principles included in [7] that apply to COTS integration that, although they are not directly addressed by CBD, can be included without contradicting any of the CBD properties.

6 Conclusions

We have described how the coordination based architecture and the requirements prototype can be applied to the development of COTS-based systems. This approach has significance in solving the problem of collaboration between architecturally disjoint COTS software. Furthermore when analyzing complex systems, one can see that they include coordination in one form or another—it is a natural way to integrate. The main difference is that here we have outlined a methodology that uses coordination directly—up front.

This approach results in better systems by properly meeting functional requirements. First, it implements systems that more closely correspond to user needs. Secondly, it provides controlled collaboration between architecturally disjoint COTS software. The coordination architecture also allows for better designed systems by meeting the main non-functional requirements of COTS-based systems such as: reconfigurability, tailorability, tailorability, visibility reliability and testability.

Our experience in using this methodology for developing tailorable component based systems [10,11] indicates that applying it to COTS-based systems should be straightforward. In addition the use of CBD allows for better visibility of design decisions relating to:

– System evolvability. Behavioural specification allows for partial initial specification and the inclusion of new details, new responses, interactions, and refinements as one uncovers them during design and use.
– System manageability. By instrumenting the system, placing counters and watchdogs at the interface of the coordinators and executors, one can detect unacceptable delays in responses and/or executor overloading. This run time system monitoring allows for proactive management by reallocating resources to meet changes in demand.
– System scalability. The executors can be looked upon as resources that can be plugged in (added) as needed. This resource view also fits well with the component view; one can equate the resources at various levels as the different levels of component abstractions.
– System reliability. By introducing checks (for lack of and/or improper response) between the coordinators and executors one can detect faulty executors and replace them or reallocate their activities to other executors.
– System security. By introducing proper access checks in the coordinator, unauthorized system accesses can be detected and blocked.

References

1. Malone, T. W. and Crowston, K.: The Interdisciplinary Study of Coordination. In: ACM Computing Surveys 26(1), March (1994) 87–119
2. Krieger, M.: Multiactivity Paradigm for the Design and Coordination of FMS's. In: Computer-Integrated Manufacturing Systems 6(3), August (1993) 195–203
3. Krieger, M.: Coordination-Based Design: An Engineering Approach to Software Development. In: Institute of Information Technology Colloquium Series 97–98 Season, National Research Council of Canada, Ottawa Montreal Road Campus, March (1998)
4. Coifan, G.: Coordination Oriented Architecture for Large Software Systems. M.A.Sc. Thesis, University of Ottawa, May (1999)
5. Wallnau, K., Hissam, S., and Seacord, R.: Building Systems from Commercial Components. Addison Wesley (2001)
6. Boehm, B.: A Spiral Model of Software Development and Enhancement. In: ACM SIGSOFT Software Engineering Notes, August (1986)
7. Vigder, M. and Dean, J.: Building Maintainable COTS Based Systems. International Conference on Software Maintenance (ICSM 1998), Washington DC (1998) 132–138
8. Vigder, M.: The Evolution, Maintenance and Management of Component-based Systems. In: Component Based Software Engineering: Putting the Pieces Together, Addison Wesley (2001)
9. Krieger, M. and Lemire, S.: Restricted Object Based Design of Event Driven Commercial Software. In: CASCON'94 Integrated Solutions, Toronto, Ontario, November (1994)
10. Cox, C.: Coordination-based Design for Tailorable Busines Software: A Computerized Maintenance Management System Example. M.A.Sc. Thesis, University of Ottawa, November (1998)
11. Au-Yang, R.: Coordination-Based Design: Towards Component-based Software Design. M.Eng Project, Carleton University, Ottawa, January (1998)

COTS Integration in Safety Critical Systems Using RTCA/DO-178B Guidelines

Burke Maxey

Sensor Systems, Goodrich Corporation
14300 Judicial Road, Burnsville MN 55306 USA
Burke.Maxey@Goodrich.com

Abstract. This paper examines the usage of commercial off-the-shelf (COTS) software embedded in sensor products for avionics applications. Usage of the guidelines of RTCA/DO-178B including consideration of independence, software criticality level and structural coverage is addressed. A comparison is made between development considerations for implementation of different software safety criticality levels.

1 Embedded Avionics Applications

Integration of Commercial Off-The-Shelf (COTS) software in safety critical systems is a task to be approached with diligence and care. The sensor development organization described herein has many years of experience developing systems that are critical to the flight of commercial and military aircraft. Examples of products include air data computers, video surveillance systems, stall warning systems and ice detectors. These systems have traditionally been completely developed in house with no COTS software embedded. Only in the last few years have sensor developers seriously considered the use of embedded components from commercial sources in military and commercial aircraft. The integration of COTS software in avionics systems would not be possible without a means to accept the systems by the certification authorities. The accepted means of certification of flight critical software for commercial aircraft is development per the document Software Considerations in Airborne Systems and Equipment Certification[1] (RTCA/DO-178B). Since the majority of sensor systems developed by Goodrich Corporation are for commercial aircraft application, the documented Sensor Systems software methodology became RTCA/DO-178B based. As the military standards were de-emphasized, multiple military sensor systems have been developed to the Sensor Systems RTCA/DO-178B based methods. For additional background on RTCA/DO-178B, see the article "DO-178B, Software Considerations in Airborne Systems and Equipment Certification"[2]

---

[1] Document RTCA DO-178B, RTCA Inc. December 1992, Washington DC USA

[2] DO-178B, "Software Considerations in Airborne Systems and Equipment Certification", Leslie A. (Schad) Johnson, Crosstalk, October 1998, Hill AFB, USA, www.stsc.hill.af.mil/crosstalk/oct/schad.asp

H. Erdogmus and T. Weng (Eds.): ICCBSS 2003, LNCS 2580, pp. 134–142, 2003.

2   RTCA/DO-178B and COTS Software

RTCA/DO-178B addresses COTS software by stating that "COTS software included in airborne systems or equipment should satisfy the objectives of this document" In addition "If deficiencies exist in the software life cycle data of COTS software, the data should be augmented to satisfy the objectives of this document". The objectives and outputs of RTCA/DO-178B are provided in Annex A of RTCA/DO-178B. Objectives are defined for ten software development processes. For each objective the annex defines:

- The applicability by software safety level.
- Independent verification needed by software safety level.
- The data item the objective should be documented in.
- The category of configuration management control needed per software safety level.

Software safety levels correspond to failure conditions as defined in the FAA and JAA applicable regulations and are defined in Table 1.

Table 1. SW Safety Levels

SW Safety Level	Failure Condition	Description
A	Catastrophic	Prevents continued safe flight and landing.
B	Hazardous/Severe-Major	Large reduction in safety margins.
C	Major	Significant reduction in safety margins.
D	Minor	Slight reduction in safety margins.
E	No Effect	No change in safety margins.

A system safety analysis is performed which identifies the software safety level dependent on whether the software could cause or contribute to a corresponding failure condition. If the software safety level is determined to be E, the RTCA/DO-178B guidelines do not apply and COTS can be integrated readily. If the software level is determined to be B, C or D, the guidelines are varied to be less encompassing then level A. This paper will describe the implementation of a COTS component, a Real-Time Operating System (RTOS), implemented at software level A and provide a comparison with a level D implementation of the same component.

3   Selection of COTS Component

Traditionally products had been developed at Sensor Systems using an infinite loop running in the background to process the real-time data whose acquisition is

signaled by the foreground interrupt service routines. A trade study was initiated
to select a RTOS that would work in a hard real-time environment and was
adaptable to the level A implementation methods. The following attributes were
considered by the trade study:

- Languages supported.
- Memory requirements.
- Multi-tasking strategy.
- Typical context switch time.
- Semaphore capable.
- Mailbox and queue processing.
- Debugger or other tools provided.
- Debugger interface supported.
- Source code available.
- RTCA/DO-178B certified and certification package available for level A.
- RTCA/DO-178B adaptability
- Development platforms supported.
- Purchase price.
- Royalty fees.
- Support fees.
- Target processors supported.

At the time this trade study was performed, there were no commercially available RTOS certification packages available. This limited the selection to easily
modifiable RTOS packages (sometimes called Modified Off-the-Shelf (MOTS)).
Today there are a number of RTOS venders that provide software packages that
are RTCA/DO-178B Level A certification ready. The trade study analysis resulted in the selection of the • C/OS[3] RTOS.

4   RTOS Integration

The development of an air data computer for helicopter and tilt-rotor applications with embedded RTOS based software included the following processes.

4.1   Project Planning

Planning documentation identified the RTOS as COTS software but stated that
RTCA/DO-178B processes would be followed for the COTS component the same
as for the application development code. For level A development all seven objectives of RTCA/DO-178B in the planning process were satisfied.

1. Software development and integral processes are defined.
2. Transition criteria, inter-relationships and sequencing among processes are
   defined.

---

[3] μC/OS, The Real-Time Kernel, R&D Books Miller Freeman Inc., 1993, Lawrence
Kansas USA

3. Software life cycle environment is defined.
4. Additional certification considerations are addressed.
5. Software development standards are defined.
6. Software plans comply with RTCA/DO-178B.
7. Software plans are coordinated.

For a level D development, only objectives 1 and 4 would need to be satisfied. For both level A and level D, no independent verification is needed for planning processes.

4.2 Requirements Definition

The requirements analysis for RTOS took the direction of defining the functions that would be implemented for the project. Functions to be implemented were identified as requirements in a specification and non-essential or non-deterministic functions were eliminated. Verification activities included inspections and reviews of the documentation. Table 2 identifies the functionality eliminated.

Table 2. RTOS Functional Limitations

Function	Description
No dynamic task creation allowed.	All tasks are created prior to starting the operating system. The RTOS will not allow tasks to be created after the RTOS is started.
No task deletion allowed.	The RTOS will not provide a service to delete a task.
No dynamic priorities allowed.	The RTOS will not provide a function to change the priority level of a task.

A trace of software requirements to system requirements, design, code and testing was provided by assigning requirement ID numbers and embedding the IDs in code, design and test artifacts. Table 3 identifies the requirements and IDs.

The verification of the outputs of the requirements process demonstrated the following RTCA/DO-178B objectives were met.

1. Software requirements comply with system requirements.
2. Software requirements are accurate and consistent.
3. Software requirements are compatible with the target computer.
4. Software requirements are verifiable.
5. Software requirements conform to standards.
6. Software requirements are traceable to system requirements.
7. Algorithms are accurate.

Items 1, 2 and 7 above were satisfied with independent verification. For a software safety level D development, only items 1, 2 and 6 need to be satisfied and independent verification is not needed.

Table 3. Requirement Trace IDs

Requirement ID	Title
OS-1100	Task priority level
OS-1200	Task delay
OS-1300	Task stack
OS-1400	Task control block
OS-1410	Task control block list
OS-1500	Task creation
OS-1600	Idle task
OS-2100	Context switch
OS-2110	Deterministic context switch
OS-2200	Context switch on interrupt return
OS-2210	Track nested interrupts
OS-2300	RTOS tick
OS-2310	Update task delay time
OS-2320	Update elapsed time
OS-3050	Mailbox create
OS-3100	Pend on mailbox with timeout
OS-3110	Full mailbox returns message on pend
OS-3120	Empty mailbox context switch on pend
OS-3130	Pend returns message
OS-3140	Pend timeout
OS-3200	Post to mailbox
OS-3210	Post to mailbox and return
OS-3220	Post to mailbox and pending task ready
OS-3230	Post to mailbox and context switch
OS-4100	No interrupts in critical code section
OS-4300	Initialize RTOS

4.3 Design Process

The design of the functions was captured in flow charts and traced to requirements as depicted in Fig. 1.

Verification activities include design inspections and, review and approval of design documentation. Test cases are identified based on the requirements. Through these techniques the following RTCA/DO-178B objectives were satisfied.

1. Design requirements comply with software requirements from the requirements process.
2. Design requirements are accurate and consistent.
3. Design requirements are compatible with the target computer.
4. Design requirements are verifiable.
5. Design requirements conform to standards.
6. Design requirements are traceable to software requirements from the requirements process.
7. Algorithms are accurate.

OSTimeDly()

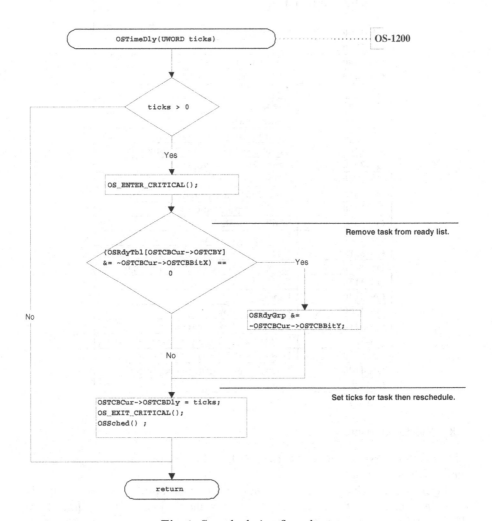

Fig. 1. Sample design flow chart

8. Software architecture is compatible with software requirements from the requirements process.

9. Software architecture is consistent.

10. Software architecture is compatible with target computer, verifiable and conforms to standards.

11. Software partitioning is confirmed. This was not applicable to the RTOS development since all RTOS and application code was developed to level A.

Items 1, 2, 7, 8, 9, and 11 were satisfied with independent verification for level A development. For a level D development, only item 11 needs to be satisfied and independent verification is not needed.

4.4   Coding and Integration Process

Since the code existed off the shelf, the coding process consisted of tailoring existing code to project requirements and integrating the functions. The coded functions were reviewed and inspected in conjunction with the application code. Requirement ID numbers were included as comments in the code of the appropriate module providing the trace of requirements to code. As the application and RTOS functions were integrated, requirements-based tests were developed. Dry runs of the test procedures that consisted primarily of emulator scripts were started. The following RTCA/DO-178B objectives of the coding and integration processes were satisfied.

1. Source code complies with design requirements.
2. Source code complies with software architecture.
3. Source code is verifiable, conforms to standards and is traceable to design requirements.
4. Source code is accurate and consistent.
5. Output of the software integration process is complete and correct.

Items 1, 2, and 4 were performed with independent verification. None of these items are needed at level D.

4.5   Verification Process

Verification of the RTOS was sub-contracted to an independent verification organization[4]. This organization generated and performed requirements-based tests. The coverage of the tests was measured and if portions of the software structure were not tested, additional requirements or tests were generated until 100% of the structural coverage was attained. The following RTCA/DO-178B test objectives were satisfied by the verification organization.

1. Test procedures are correct.
2. Test results are correct and discrepancies explained.
3. Test coverage of software requirements from the requirements process is achieved.
4. Test coverage of design requirements is achieved.
5. Test coverage of the software structure is achieved including modified condition/decision coverage, decision coverage, statement coverage, and data and control coupling.
6. Executable object code complies with software requirements from the requirements process.

---

[4] AVISTA Incorporated, Platteville, Wisconsin, USA, www.avistainc.com

7. Executable object code is robust with software requirements from the requirements process.
8. Executable object code complies with design requirements.
9. Executable object code is robust with design requirements.
10. Executable object code is compatible with target computer.

At level A items 6, 7 and 10 did not need to be satisfied with independent verification. Items 3, 6, 7 and 10 above need to be satisfied at level D and without independent verification.

5   Conclusions

Integration of the RTOS software at level A was accomplished using the identical processes as for the application software. This included:

1. Including RTOS in development, certification, verification, configuration management and quality assurance planning.
2. Developing and verifying RTOS requirements and design.
3. Tracing requirements from the system level to requirements, design, code and test artifacts.
4. Providing independent verification including integration, functional and structural testing.

Once the RTOS is certified in a level A system, the use on succeeding level A or lower systems will consist of submission of the existing certification package with only changes in functionality needing re-certification. The RTOS has been implemented on one product and is in development on two others, including an application on a different processor. The RTCA/DO-178B process guidelines define a graduated methodology for implementing COTS in safety critical applications with defined objectives based on the safety level of the software and the methodology has been successfully adopted as the Sensor Systems development process. Candidate COTS packages for implementation in sensor systems include communication drivers, math packages and application algorithms.

5.1   Future Investigation

Integrating the RTOS in a Level A system using RTCA/DO-178B criteria involved a considerable effort for the developers and the verification team. As shown in Table 3 there were 26 software level requirements associated with the RTOS functionality. Each requirement had design and verification effort associated with it. Less than half as many requirements are typically associated with using an infinite control loop executive. However each system that develops an infinite control loop executive must demonstrate compliance to RTCA/DO-178B guidelines, which results in redundant effort across systems. The level A certified RTOS provides a re-useable base that potentially can reduce the development effort of future systems. The disadvantage is that because of the integration effort involved, there will be a tendency to not move beyond the RTOS that is integrated. The original intent of the developers was for all future systems to take advantage of the RTOS integration effort. However, at least one customer has recommended not using an RTOS because the added overhead could affect the application. Future trade studies will need to re-address application overhead issues, commercially available RTOS certification packages and advancement in RTOS capabilities.

References

1. Document RTCA DO-178B: RTCA/EUROCAE DO-178/ED-12, Revision B, RTCA Inc. Washington DC, December (1992)
2. Johnson, L. A.: DO-178B: Software Considerations in Airborne Systems and Equipment Certification. In: Crosstalk, October (1998) Hill AFB. Available at: http://www.stsc.hill.af.mil/crosstalk/oct/schad.asp
3. μC/OS: μC/OS, The Real-Time Kernel, R&D Books Miller Freeman Inc., Lawrence, Kansas (1993)
4. AVISTA Incorporated, Platteville, Wisconsin, USA.
   Available at: http://www.avistainc.com

Techniques for Embedding Executable Specifications in Software Component Interfaces

Ross McKegney[1] and Terry Shepard[2]

[1] Queen's University & IBM Canada, Toronto, Ontario Canada
mckegney@cs.queensu.ca
[2] Royal Military College of Canada, Kingston, Ontario Canada
shepard@rmc.ca

Abstract. In this paper, we consider interface contracts as a possible mechanism for improving semantic integrity in component-based systems. A contract is essentially a formal specification interleaved with code and allowing a component or object to unambiguously specify its behaviour. The existing techniques that we survey are predominantly designed for object-oriented systems; we therefore investigate the extent to which they can be scaled up to the level of components, and embedded in interface specifications rather than code. We conclude that interleaved specifications are viable and useful at the level of components, but that future work is required to develop languages that can express the constraints that are important at this level of granularity.

1 Introduction

Software components are typically used/reused based on their syntactic interface descriptions and informal documentation of behaviour made available either embedded as comments or in a separate document. We view composition on this basis as being inherently problematic, because the informal descriptions are likely ambiguous and there is no mechanism to ensure that the implementation and its description remain consistent. If we formalize the external documentation then we alleviate the first problem, but formal specification is difficult and expensive [13]. Instead, we view as most promising those techniques that support interleaving formal specifications with source code, where the notation is a slight extension to the language(s) of development. It should be feasible to apply such techniques to component interface descriptions, allowing for the verification of conformance between implementation and specification using static or dynamic analysis.

This paper surveys techniques for embedding formal specifications in software component interfaces. We discuss two classes of techniques: Design by Contract based approaches, and Behavioural Interface Specification Languages. Both provide means for interleaving an executable specification of the abstract behaviour of a component with its syntactic interface description.

H. Erdogmus and T. Weng (Eds.): ICCBSS 2003, LNCS 2580, pp. 143–156, 2003.

2   Components and Composition

We define the term software component as an executable unit of deployment and composition. The implication is that systems are built by composing components built by different groups of developers, based on interface descriptions and external documentation. Component technologies, including Corba, Enterprise JavaBeans^{TM}, and COM greatly simplify the composition process, by providing generic services and enforcing common communication protocols. Unfortunately, although component technologies have made the composition process much easier, they are limited to enforcement of the syntactic aspects of the interactions, and do little to aid with resolving semantic inconsistencies.

In order to ensure that components use each other in the way(s) in which they were intended (what is sometimes referred to as semantic integrity [3]) we need some mechanism to unambiguously specify component behaviour. Essentially, this amounts to understanding the assumptions made by the component developer and providing a mechanism whereby these assumptions can be conveyed to clients wishing to use the component. The range of assumptions that may be of interest is very broad, and would be a worthwhile research area in its own right, but we can state some of the common ones: type and range of parameters and return values; exception semantics; types and versions of dependencies; valid protocols of interaction; effects of operations on internal state; performance assumptions; concurrency assumptions; valid customization/parameterization; control assumptions; security assumptions; data structure semantics. These assumptions are all relevant to the correctness of the component; that is to say that if a client violates one of these assumptions then we cannot guarantee that the component will behave correctly.

Most software processes begin with some form of requirements document, which forms the basis for some design document, which is realized with some implementation, and tested against the requirements. This approach can be applied using informal notations (e.g. UML [4]) or formal notations (e.g. Z [31]). If formal notations are used, then we can sometimes apply a refinement calculus to the specifications as they are iteratively refined to code, verifying at each step that the properties which have been proved of the specification are not violated. The downside is that formal specification, proof, and refinement are all complex activities requiring significant training, knowledge, and experience. There is also the issue of the semantic gap between specification language and language of implementation, it is often non-trivial to map an implementation back to its specification. Finally, the formal specification is yet another work product that must be maintained throughout the development lifecycle, if benefits beyond simply aiding in reasoning about the system's design are to be realized.

An alternative approach, also relying on external formal specification of behaviour, is to use an executable specification language and run the model concurrently with the implementation to verify conformance. This is the approach taken by Microsoft for runtime verification using the Abstract State Machine Language [1] and by Bastide et. al. [2] for verifying a model of the Corba Event Service specified using Petri-Nets. As with the approaches that we will discuss in this paper, these both provide mechanisms for unambiguously specifying component behaviour, and for verifying conformance between specification and implementation.

We have selected to further investigate techniques for behavioural specification of components by interleaving executable formal specifications with source code. Ideally, such techniques would also work in conjunction with standard component technologies.

3   Design by Contract

The first techniques that we will discuss are based on Design by Contract^{TM}, as introduced by Meyer in [26], and implemented in the Eiffel programming language [27]. Design by Contract can be viewed as a merger of abstract data type theory and Hoare logic [15]. Classes are specified using contracts interleaved with source code, consisting of internal consistency conditions that the class will maintain (invariants) and, for each operation, the correctness conditions that are the responsibility of the client (pre-conditions) and those which the operation promises to establish on return (post-conditions). Because these conditions are to be expressed in the language of development, and interleaved with source code, they can be mechanically checked at runtime.

Design by Contract is typically implemented in terms of assertions, but it provides far more than this. Contracts represent a specification of the system that, through tool support, can be extracted and viewed as a separate artifact. The differentiation between pre-conditions, post-conditions and invariants allows for selective checking at runtime, based on the development phase. Specifications in terms of contracts can be used as the basis for unit test generation. Finally, contracts can be inherited from parent to child class, and refined.

In the remainder of this section, we further elaborate the Design by Contract programming style as implemented in Eiffel, followed by brief summaries of Design by Contract implementations for other programming languages.

3.1   Eiffel

Systems in Eiffel are modeled as a set of 'clusters', logical components (there is no physical construct for clusters in Eiffel, they are implemented as a group of related classes) with their specifications interleaved with the code. These clusters can be sequentially or concurrently engineered, using a micro-process of analysis, design, implementation, verification & validation, and generalization (this final step is similar to refactoring, and involves evaluating and preparing the cluster for general reuse). Throughout the process, all work is performed on a single product—the cluster source code—producing at the end a self-describing software component. Maintaining a high level of reliability from the outset is considered a core principle (above functionality); error handling and assertions are put in first, followed by the implementation of the methods.

Eiffel is a fully object-oriented language, with several interesting features that we will not discuss here (for a good introduction to the language itself, see [25]). What we will elaborate further is the implementation of Design by Contract as a core feature. We mentioned above that in Eiffel there is only one work product—the source code—and that Eiffel supports features for expressing the other work products that we would normally expect (requirements documents, design documents, etc.). The approach taken by Eiffel is to express this information in terms of contracts between collaborating components, unambiguously specifying each party's expectations and guarantees in terms of pre-conditions, post-conditions, and invariants on the services provided. Contracts permit the specification of semantic aspects of an object or component's functionality beyond what can be achieved through method signatures alone. Additionally, the executable nature of contracts assists in testing, since errors in the code may cause localizable contract violations rather than a failure later on. From a development perspective, contracts mean that servers do not have to check the values of inputs as they are received from clients (assuming that the server has properly specified its pre-conditions), and likewise the clients do not have to check the output values returned (assuming that the server has properly specified its post-conditions). The implication is that the specification defines what values are valid, and the underlying implementation can assume that it will always be working on valid data. If an error does occur, then it means either that there is a problem with the specification or that one of the components/objects has violated its contract. The downside of the approach is that the extra code for contract checking may slow down the system; as a result, Eiffel supports a variety of compiler options for the amount of contract code to generate. It is recommended that contracts be turned on to the highest level (all assertions) during development and testing, then switching to a lower level (no assertions or preconditions only) when the system is released.

In Eiffel, child classes automatically inherit not only the attributes and methods of the parent class—but also the parent's contracts. Just as Eiffel supports refining or extending the parent's class functionality, so does it support extending the contracts, using the require else (for weakening the original pre-condition) and ensure then (for strengthening the original post-conditions) clauses. As the level of nesting increases, the contracts can become complex—because they are spread across many classes. The solution provided by the Eiffel environment is to allow the viewing of a flat form and a flat contract form of a class. The flat form of a class is simply a view of the class augmented with everything inherited from its ancestors. The flat contract form is a contract version of this class. As with the contract form described earlier, these techniques allow various views of the system.

Despite some nice features that greatly aid in ensuring semantic integrity between components, the Eiffel programming language is unfortunately not widely used. It is object-oriented with support for distributed object computing, just like other more popular programming languages; its relative obscurity can possibly be attributed to relatively poor performance, and lack of support for the standard distributed object platforms.

3.2 DbC for Java^{TM}

iContract [19] is a prototype tool developed by Reliable Systems Inc. for embedding Eiffel-style contracts in Java code. Developers specify contracts using javadoc-style comment tags (@pre for pre-conditions, @post for post-conditions, and @invariant for invariants) on methods of classes or interfaces, and elaborate the contracts using an executable subset of the Object Constraint Language (OCL) [32]. The iContract tool is implemented as a source code preprocessor that instruments the code based on the contracts specified, creating assertions that can be checked at runtime.

Karaorman's jContractor [18] uses the reflective capabilities of Java and the Factory Method design pattern [14] to support the addition of contracts. When objects are instantiated through a special factory class, the factory adds to the new instance the instrumentation code. This approach uses only existing, standard Java constructs and calls. It also provides for retrying a method that throws an exception, and rolling back variables to earlier values. However, the user must specify as distinct private Boolean methods each precondition, postcondition, invariant, and exception handler, leading to a great proliferation of class members.

Biscotti [6], targets the Java Remote Method Invocation (RMI) distributed object infrastructure, and is implemented as an extension of the Java language and modifications to the Java compiler and Java Virtual Machine (JVM). Biscotti introduces six new Java keywords: invariant, requires, ensures, then, old, and result. These keywords can be used to describe pre-conditions and post-conditions on methods, and class and instance invariants on classes and interfaces. Biscotti also introduces assertion reflection, an extension to the standard reflection capabilities of Java so that contract information can be queried. Through the methods getInvariant(), getPrecondition(), and getPostcondition(), it is possible to find out the instance invariants, pre-conditions and post-conditions before making a method call on a distributed object. This is particularly useful when the intention is to leave contracts turned on even in deployed systems. The authors of Biscotti argue that it is unrealistic to rely on well-behaved clients in a distributed object system—which is justification not only for adding assertion reflection, but also for the general approach of requiring a proprietary compiler and JVM to compile and run programs with Biscotti contracts embedded. The downside of this design decision is that components written using Biscotti extensions can only be compiled and executed using the proprietary Biscotti compiler and JVM, and that there is currently no supported mechanism for turning the contracts off—which is often desirable once the component has been thoroughly tested.

3.3 DbC for Other Programming Languages

There have been a variety of research and industrial projects to bring the concepts of design by contract to other, more widely used languages. These include implementations for Ada (e.g. ANNotated Ada [23]), C++ (e.g. A++ [9,10]), Python [28], SmallTalk [5], and Lisp [16].

4   Behavioural Interface Specification Languages

Similar in spirit to the design by contract methodology is the work on behavioural interface specification languages (BISLs), proposed by Wing [33] as a mechanism for assigning formal behaviour models to interfaces. BISLs consist of two tiers, a mathematical tier where 'traits' (e.g. mathematical models of Sets, Bags, etc.) are defined, and an upper tier implemented as an extension to the language of development. These languages do not appear to be widely used in industry, but they are the subject of considerable academic research.

BISLs go beyond simply allowing the specification of valid and invalid behaviour, they also allow for the specification of exceptional behaviour. That is, the developer can specify under which conditions a method will terminate normally, which conditions the method will terminate with a particular exception, and under which conditions no guarantees are made on the implementation. BISLs also typically include the notion of a frame condition, stating which of the model variables the methods can update.

In this section we discuss two BISLs proposed for adding semantics to OMG IDL (Larch/Corba and IDL++), followed by a discussion of the Java Modeling Language, a BISL for Java.

4.1   Larch/Corba

Larch [12] is a formal specification language whose distinguishing feature is that it uses two "tiers" (or layers) [33]. The top tier is a behavioral interface specification language (BISL), used to specify the behaviour of software modules using pre-/post-conditions, and tailored to a specific programming language. The bottom tier is the Larch Shared Language (LSL), which is used to describe the mathematical vocabulary used in the pre- and post-condition specifications. Therefore, LSL specifies a domain model and the mathematical vocabulary, while the BISL specifies the interface and behaviour of program modules. BISLs have been written for a variety of programming languages, including Larch/CLU, Larch/Ada, LCL for ANSI-C, LM3 for Modula-3, Larch/Smalltalk, Larch/C++, Larch/ML, and VSPEC for VHDL (see [20] for pointers to the latest list of implementations). Each BISL uses the declaration syntax of the programming language for which it is tailored, and adds annotations to specify behavior. These annotations typically consist of pre- and post-conditions (typically using the keywords requires and ensures), some way to state a frame axiom (typically using the keyword modifies), and some way to indicate what LSL traits are used to provide the mathematical vocabulary (a trait in Larch is simply a theorem that can be checked with a prover, e.g. a trait used in post-condition might be that result $\bullet$ 0).

In his doctoral dissertation [30], Sivraprasad proposed Larch/Corba, a BISL for OMG IDL. A prototype implementation was produced, allowing for the specification of pre-/post-conditions, invariants, and concurrency in IDL interfaces. Larch/Corba is interesting for our evaluation because it combines a widely used interface definition language with formal specification techniques. Although we found this technique much more complex than the design by contract languages, it is also much more precise than some of the others—particularly because of the ability to specify concurrency and exception conditions.

4.2   IDL++

D'Souza & Wills propose the framework for a behavioural specification extension to OMG IDL in [10]. Their approach is similar in spirit to Larch/Corba; although their emphasis is on the ability to integrate the semantic specifications of objects with OOA/D tools. Their proposal comes as a response to a request for information (RFI) made by the OMG on adding semantics to IDL, and suggests making the behavioural specification of component interfaces as part of a larger process. Design by contract has similar ambitions, with the contracts being a work product that takes the place of design documentation and that aids in every phase of development, but the IDL++ approach takes this a step further by suggesting a customizable formal infrastructure on which components can be built.

As in Larch, semantics are divided into multiple tiers (or layers), but this time instead of two layers there are four. The lowest layer in the IDL++ model is called the 'Traits and Theories' layer, which is analogous to the Larch LSL tier and provides the mathematical foundation on which the remaining layers rest. This layer is given in terms of traits and theories, where a trait is a parameterizable specification fragment (e.g. result • 0) while a theory is a collection of related traits (e.g. the set of traits required to describe the commit/rollback behaviours of a transaction scheme). The second layer is called the 'Fundamental Object Model', and provides mechanisms for specifying objects and their design. It consists of formal models of objects and actions, where an object is a theory giving the generic behaviour of objects, including a list of queries that can be performed on the object and a mapping from an object identity to a state, while an action is simply a message or sequence of messages that causes some change to the object. In this sense, queries abstract away the internal structure of a design while actions abstract away the details of the dialogue.

The top two layers are the ones that developers will use, and include the 'Methodology Constructs' layer and the 'End-User Models' layer. The methodology constructs layer is important in this design because of the emphasis on integration with OOA/D and CASE tools. It should be possible to work on a design using diagrams that have a formal basis allowing for translation to lower-level constructs (e.g. code) for further refinement. The end-user models represent the top layer of the semantics model; this is where analysts and designers will apply the models formalized in the lower layers to the classes and interactions in their designs. Unlike other approaches to semantic extensions to interfaces, IDL++ allows for the specification of both incoming and outgoing invocations for each interface that an object supports, and even for the specification of protocols of interaction. Using these techniques, developers can formally specify patterns or frameworks, which can be reused throughout the system.

Using the proposed approach, developers would model their systems using graphical tools, and the IDL++ interfaces would be generated automatically. These specifications would be machine processable so that design tools would be able to search for, interrogate, select, and appropriately couple components at run time based upon their specifications. Although this is an interesting proposal, and successfully merges ideas from software process and formal specification, it has not been implemented to date.

4.3   JML

The Java Modeling Language (JML) [22] is a behavioural interface specification language (BISL) [33] developed as a collaborative effort between Compaq Research, the University of Nijmegen, and Iowa State University. Self-described as being more expressive than Eiffel, and easier to use than other BISLs such as Larch [12] or VDM [17]; JML uses a slight extension of the Java syntax to allow developers to embed specifications in Java classes and interfaces. The suite of tools surrounding JML is constantly evolving, and currently consists of tools for static analysis, verification, automated document generation, and run-time debugging (see JML website [21] for current tool list).

Like Larch, JML uses a two-tiered approach to specification, a lower level specifying the mathematical notation to be used in specifications and a domain model, and an upper level used to specify interfaces to components in terms of pre-/post-conditions and invariants. A fundamental difference, however, is that both layers are described in terms of the language of implementation (Java).

We found JML to be a much richer language for specifying contracts than the design by contract languages. In particular, the ability to specify not only constraints on valid behaviour, but also constraints on exceptional behaviour was very useful. As with the other BISLs, the ability to describe whether a method call affects the underlying model, and if so what changes are made, is tremendously useful when trying to determine valid ways of using the component. Although we found this technique very useful, we are concerned about issues of scale, as the complexity of the abstract representation of the component becomes greater.

5   Discussion and Opportunities

5.1   Contracts, the Ideal Formal Method?

The first test of the techniques investigated in this paper will be to compare them against the 10 ideal criteria set forth by Clarke and Wing in [7] for practical formal methods.

The first ideal is that developers should get 'early payback'; they should see benefits of using the approach soon after beginning to use the new technology. Techniques for interleaving formal specifications with code achieve this objective in two respects: first, the process of formal specification itself is a worthwhile endeavor; second, by using these techniques the developer is relieved from writing code within the classes to check that input is valid. The second ideal is "incremental gain for incremental effort"; as developers become increasingly proficient with the tool, they should find increasing value. This is certainly true from the perspective that someone with experience writing formal specifications will be able to write them in a more elegant fashion than a novice. However, there are limits to what can be expressed through the techniques discussed in this paper, and complex conditions on concurrency, for example, cannot be expressed. The third ideal states that the method should support "multiple uses"; it should aid in multiple phases of the development cycle. This is one of the greatest benefits of DbC and BISLs, they not only aid in specifying the requirements of a system, they also aid in development (by formally specifying the components that are being assembled), unit testing (through tools that can automatically generate test cases from specifications), integration testing (by turning on contracts and verifying that none of the interactions in the system violate the contracts), maintenance (specifications are embedded in the code, and as such are less likely to become outdated), and reuse (components can be reused on the basis of their specifications rather than their implementations).

The fourth ideal is "integrated use"; methods and tools should work together and with common languages/techniques, with little requirement to buy into new technologies. DbC and BISL implementations exist for a variety of programming languages, meaning that it should be possible to find one to fit with the technologies being used. On the other hand, none of the tools integrate well with any common development environment, and few are suitable for production grade development. These technologies also carry with them a particular methodology, which must be bought into. The fifth ideal is "ease of use". Because these techniques are all implemented as slight extensions to the language of development, the learning curve to their effective use is minimal. However, tool support for most of these techniques is often poor and can be difficult to install and use. The sixth ideal is "efficiency"; tools should make efficient use of developers' time, turnaround time with an interactive tool is acceptable. As currently implemented, the tools are primarily run in batch mode and are not significantly less efficient compiling or executing test suites. If we want to build static checking capabilities on top of these notations that may change, but as currently implemented there is no efficiency penalty in this sense.

The seventh ideal is "ease of learning." With the exception of Larch/Corba, all of these techniques were easy to learn. The Larch Shared Language that underlies Larch/Corba and all of the other Larch BISLs is complex and requires training. The eighth ideal is "error detection oriented"; methods/tools oriented toward finding errors rather than proving correctness. This is precisely what these techniques are good for, aiding in finding bugs in programs before they manifest themselves as faults. The ninth ideal is "focused analysis"; methods/tools good at analyzing at least one aspect of a system well. This is at once a strength and a weakness of these approaches. These techniques are good at describing functional attributes of a system, but cannot easily be extended to describe other attributes of interest. The last ideal is "evolutionary development";

allow partial specifications that can be refined/elaborated. The only technique that explicitly supported refinement was JML. All of the techniques support partial description of systems.

5.2   Contracts for Components?

Contract-based design is generally perceived as being good practice, and is even a fundamental part of some object-oriented [26] and component-based development processes [11]. Nonetheless, given its purpose as a technique for improving semantic integrity between objects, it is worth discussing whether it can realistically be applied to components—which are not only at a different level of abstraction, but also possess some significant differentiating characteristics.

Unfortunately, although software contracts can be used to facilitate interface conformance checking (both on the part of the supplier of a service and the client, at compile-time and at runtime), alone they do not have the power and flexibility to resolve semantic integrity. Component-based systems are typically heterogeneous and distributed, meaning that a runtime contract evaluation tool will probably not be able to check all of the components. Further, since the goal in many component-based systems is to reuse, outsource, or purchase components off-the-shelf, it is unrealistic to expect that all of the interfaces in the system will be described in terms of the same contract technology (if at all). A potential solution is to use the wrapper design pattern [14] to wrap all components with contract-extended interfaces. The tradeoff to be considered in this case is homogeneity and the benefits of contracts vs. performance. An approach such as this would be particularly useful if the contract-extended interfaces included a reflection capability, such as is supported by Biscotti, which would enable components to inquire about the contracts of other components at runtime. Particularly if the system is composed dynamically, keeping the contracts active even for a final deployment may be an effective strategy.

Next is the issue of component granularity, which can vary significantly within and across applications. Contracts rely on being able to model the abstract type of a component or object, which may become infeasible as components increase in size and complexity. In the worst case, contracts may become unfeasible for everything except range and possibly type checking of parameters and return values.

The next issue is that components typically exhibit more complex interaction mechanisms than objects. Whereas it is reasonable to restrict the specification of protocols between objects to method calls, components often employ mechanisms such as event broadcasting and callbacks—which cannot be modeled succinctly using existing contract languages.

A final issue that must be reiterated is that techniques for embedding contracts in component interfaces typically do not consider non-functional attributes such as performance or security. Given that we are seeking to analyze component-based systems to ensure that assumptions made by a component's developers are not violated by other components, and that these assumptions may include these non-functional attributes, it is clear that contracts alone are insufficient.

The Real-time Corba specification [29] is the only mechanism we have found for quality of service contracts, allowing for the propagation of process priorities across a system and the specification of resource requirements, but this technique unfortunately makes assumptions about the configuration that are not realistic for most systems (e.g. that every host will be running a real-time Corba orb on a fixed priority real-time operating system). On the other hand, because contracts do allow us to express safety constraints, we can use them to check if two components are functionally equivalent—and if so select one or the other based on some non-functional quality attribute.

One of the other interesting properties of components is that they are often designed with some capability for customization and parameterization. We see the behavioural subtyping techniques as a promising mechanism for defining the inherent behaviour of a component, and for evaluating a given customized/parameterized version of the component for conformance. The one caveat is that we are not convinced that behavioural subtyping techniques will scale to large granularity components, for the same reason that design by contract techniques may not scale as the abstract type of the object becomes larger and more complex.

Our position at this stage is that component interface-level contracts are an important starting point for ensuring semantic integrity, but they must be either used in conjunction with other techniques (such as formal specifications or architectural description languages), or extended to support the types of constraints that arise when composing software from components.

5.3   Where Do We Go from Here?

We believe that the relationship between the contract techniques discussed here and some of the established techniques of software architecture description and formal methods could be very interesting. For example, to describe a system in terms of a formal specification or architecture description language then generate component interfaces with embedded semantics, then to implement components for the specification and use constraint checking to ensure that the implementation and interface are consistent. Inversely, given a component contract language that expresses the constraints that we want to express, we could use these as a basis for generating a formal specification that can be validated statically.

The most obvious area where research is needed is in fact the generation of such a contract language for components. It is unclear at this point whether such a language is feasible, given the issues of scale that arise even with the limited techniques currently available. However, we believe that it would be a worthwhile exercise to attempt such an extension to one of the BISLs (since they are much more expressive than the design by contract techniques). Issues that could be addressed include quality of service attributes or valid protocols of interaction. Another area of research that could prove quite fruitful would be to look at domain specific contracts. For example, to determine if there are particular types of constraints that are important to document and mechanically check in certain domains. One possible area to look at is the security aspect of components composed in e-Commerce systems.

In terms of tool development, we foresee many opportunities. For example, a tool that can generate a contract by poking and prodding a component through its interface(s) would be very useful. Another area where tools are useful is for contract repositories. Given a set of reusable components with specifications interleaved with their interface definitions, we could use such a tool to aid in component selection and integration based on requirements. A third area where tools may be useful is for the development of an environment supporting runtime composition of components, including contract negotiation at each binding. Technologies that should be investigated in this case would include web services, where we may wish to aggregate many services together, and there may be multiple choices for each of the constituent services.

There is also work to be done to investigate particular issues for some of the existing languages, such as scalability issues in BISLs or performance issues in DbC languages (particularly if we expect to leave contracts turned on after deployment). It would also be interesting to investigate whether any of these techniques can be applied hierarchically, i.e. with an overall contract description for the component, and another set of contracts on the underlying objects.

Of course the basis for all of this is that informal documentation in the form of comments is ambiguous. It would be interesting to study the extent to which this is true. This is perhaps more of a psychology experiment than computer science, but it would certainly be interesting to examine a wide range of existing components and determine the extent to which their interfaces are conducive to reuse.

We believe that syntactic component interface descriptions are insufficient, and that interleaved formal specifications are a practical and feasible solution. Although current techniques do not appear to be sufficiently expressive for the types of constraints that we care about when composing systems from components, we strongly feel that there is potential for valuable and interesting research in this area.

References

1. Barnett, M., and Schulte, W.: Spying on Components: A Runtime Verification Technique. In: Workshop on Specification and Verification of Component-based Systems, OOPSLA 2001, Technical Report #01-09a, Iowa State, October (2001) 7–13

2. Bastide, R., Sy, O., Palanque, P., and Navarre, D.: Formal Specification of CORBA Services: Experience and Lessons Learned. In: ACM Conference on Object-Oriented Programming, Systems, Languages, and Applications (2000)

3. Blom, M.: Semantic Integrity in Programming Industry. Master's Thesis, Computer Science, Karlstad University (1997)

4. Booch, G., Rumbaugh, J., and Jacobson, I.: The Unified Modeling Language User Guide. Addison Wesley (1999)

5. Carillo-Castellon, M., Garcia-Molina, J., Pimentel, E., and Repiso, I.: Design by Contract in Smalltalk. In: Journal of Object Oriented Programming, November/December (1996) 23–28
6. Cicalese, C. D. T., and Rotenstreich, S.: Behavioral Specification of Distributed Software Component Interfaces. In: IEEE Computer, July (1999) 46–53
7. Clarke, E. M., and Wing, J. M.: Formal Methods: State of the Art and Future Directions. ACM Computing Surveys 28(4) (1996) 626–643
8. Cline, M. P., and Lea, D.: Using Annotated C++. In: C++ At Work 1990, September (1990)
9. Cline, M. P., and Lea, D.: The Behavior of C++ Classes. In: Proceedings of the Symposium on Object-Oriented Programming Emphasizing Practical Applications, September (1990)
10. D'Souza, D. F., and Wills, A. C.: OOA/D and Corba/IDL: A Common Base. ICON Computing (1995) Available at: http://www.iconcomp.com.
11. D'Souza, D. F., and Wills, A. C.: Objects, Components, and Frameworks with UML: The Catalysis Approach. Addison-Wesley, USA (1999)
12. Guttag, J. V., Horning, J. J., and Wing, J. M.: The Larch Family of Specification Languages. In: IEEE Software 2(5), September (1985) 24–36
13. Finney, K.: Mathematical Notation in Formal Specification: Too Difficult for the Masses? In: IEEE Transactions on Software Engineering 22(2), February (1996) 158–159
14. Gamma, E., Helm, R., Johnson, R., and Vlissides, J.: Design Patterns: Elements of Reusable Object-Oriented Software. Addison-Wesley (1995)
15. Hoare, C. A. R.: An Axiomatic Basis for Computer Programming. In: Communications of the ACM 12(10), October (1969)
16. Hölzl, M.: Design by Contract for Lisp. Available at: http://www.pst.informatik.unimuenchen.de/personen/hoelzl/ tools/dbc/ dbc-intro.html
17. Jones, C. B.: Systematic Software Development Using VDM. In: International Series in Computer Science. Prentice Hall, Englewood Cliffs, N.J. (1990)
18. Karaorman, M., Hölzle, U., and Bruno, J.: jContractor: Reflective Java Library to Support Design-by-Contract. Technical Report TRCS98-31, University of California, Santa Barbara (1998)
19. Kramer, R.: iContract-the Java Design by Contract Tool. In: Proceedings of TOOLS 98 (1998)
20. Leavens, G. T.: Larch FAQ. Available at: http://www.cs.iastate.edu/~leavens/larch-faq.html
21. Leavens, G. T.: The Java Modeling Language Home Page. Available at: http://www.cs.iastate.edu/~leavens/JML.html
22. Leavens, G. T., Baker, A. L., and Ruby, C.: JML: A Notation for Detailed Design. In: Behavioral Specifications for Businesses and Systems, Kluwer (1999) 175–188
23. Luckham, D. C., von Henke, F. W., Krieg-Brueckner, B., and Owe, O.: Anna, a Language for Annotating Ada Programs: Preliminary Reference Manual. Technical Report CSL-TR-84-261, Stanford University, July (1984)
24. McIlroy, M. D.: Mass-Produced Software Components. In: Proceedings of the 1968 NATO Conference on Software Engineering, Garmisch, Germany (1969) 138–155
25. Meyer, B.: An Eiffel Tutorial. Available at: http://citeseer.nj.nec.com/meyer01eiffel.html
26. Meyer, B.: Object-Oriented Software Construction, 1st Edition, Prentice-Hall (1988)

27. Meyer, B.: Eiffel: the Language. Prentice-Hall (1992)
28. Plösch, R.: Design by Contract for Python. In: Proceedings of the Asia Pacific Software Engineering Conference (1997)
29. Schmidt, D. , and Kuhns, F.: An Overview of the Real-time Corba Specification. IEEE Computer, June (2000)
30. Sivaprasad, G. S.: Larch/CORBA: Specifying the Behavior of CORBA-IDL Interfaces. TR #95-27a, Department of Computer Science, Iowa State University, November (1995)
31. Spivey, J. M.: The Z Notation: a Reference Manual. Prentice Hall International Series in Computer Science, 2nd Edition (1992)
32. Warmer, J., and Kleppe, A.: The Object Constraint Language. Addison-Wesley (1999)
33. Wing, J. M.: Writing Larch Interface Language Specifications. ACM Transactions on Programming Languages and Systems 9(1), January (1987) 1–24

eCots Platform: An Inter-industrial Initiative for COTS-Related Information Sharing

Jean-Christophe Mielnik[1], Bernard Lang[2], Stéphane Laurière[2], Jean-Georges Schlosser[3], and Vincent Bouthors[4]

[1] Thales Research and Technology, Orsay, France
jean-christophe.mielnik@thalesgroup.com
[2] INRIA, Rocquencourt, France
{bernard.lang, stephane.lauriere}@inria.fr
[3] EDF, Chatou, France
jean-georges.schlosser@edf.fr
[4] Jalios, Rocquencourt, France
vincent.bouthors@jalios.com

Abstract. The goal of the eCots[1] project is to setup an open portal for collecting, sharing and improving accurate information on software COTS products and producers. The core information will be freely available on the Internet [1], with secure replication mechanisms available under subscription, allowing enterprises to synchronize their private intranet information with the portal data. The eCots project is based on the in-depth formalization and standardization of the COTS related data, as well as innovative business and legal approaches related to this kind of open information sharing and content collaborative production, inspired by the open source initiative.

1 Information on COTS: A Crucial Strategic Involvement

As a downside to the expected reduction on total cost of ownership, the growing use of commercial off-the-shelf (COTS[2]) software components, instead of in-house developments, is accompanied by a non-negligible loss of control of the systems in which they are used, and increases dependency on COTS component producers, critical particularly in the case of obsolescence.

This loss of control and this dependency can be compensated only by extremely reliable, accurate and continuously updated knowledge of the software component market and its trends. It is a matter of factual data, not subject to interpretation, both on the actors (producers, distributors and consulting companies) and the products in this market. These data must be processed on the

---

[1] A French initiative supported by the RNTL (National Network of Software Technologies).

[2] COTS are software products, components or libraries that can be identified by a name, one or several producers and a version number. COTS can be used locally or through a network: hence COTS include Web services. COTS can have any type of license policy, free or proprietary.

H. Erdogmus and T. Weng (Eds.): ICCBSS 2003, LNCS 2580, pp. 157–167, 2003.
© Springer-Verlag Berlin Heidelberg 2003

technical, commercial, economical, financial and legal dimensions. The choice of integrating a software component into a system requires very detailed characterizations. In the case of open-source components, the code availability would not eliminate the need for reliable specifications. However, factual data are often missing and the general opacity of legal, commercial and technical information about COTS is worsened by the fact that marketing strategies often lead to announcements describing an idealized reality.

1.1   Difficulty to Get, Qualify, and Update COTS Information

Most industrial groups try nowadays to organize the collection of COTS information in order to make it available in-house, but the effort is considerable due to the size and variability of the software component market and the difficulty to collect and update information. This assessment and selection phase is consequently a hard task for enterprises, particularly for SMEs, which cannot invest enough time or money into COTS management to gain qualified information.

Although specialized companies dedicated to technological analysis and market monitoring can bring help, the analysis they provide is often expensive and short-lived. In addition, this information market has not developed a standard for COTS description.

Raw data are actually available: it is held by the COTS producers and the very large community of users. Yet, the information supplied by COTS producers is rather unequal in quality (insufficient most of the time), extremely heterogeneous in location, form and accessibility. The users must compensate, with in-house investments, the difficulty to understand the semantics of the off-standard description elements provided by producers.

The community of commercial software users is neither aware of its accumulated usage information quality and quantity (assessment and experience feedback), nor of the tremendous impact of sharing this information..

1.2   Existing Catalogs Emphasize the Need for a Common Description Model

Different types of software catalogs exist on the Web. However, these catalogs suffer from several drawbacks: on portals like Freshmeat.net or Linux Software Map sites, the user only gets an overview of the technical and legal features of COTS softwares; proprietary catalogs like Cxp.fr or Softdatabase.com cover a succinct part of COTS scope with a low level of accuracy and cannot be enhanced in a collaborative way; UDDI catalogs contain only Web services descriptions; finally, community portals focused on one particular type of COTS, like The-ServerSide.com for J2EE server components, contain abundant and accurate, however unstructured information.

The main flaws of these catalogs rely upon their lack of accuracy and interoperability. A common COTS description model would undoubtedly give synergy and momentum to these various cataloging efforts.

1.3 COTS Description Standards

Several organizations like OASIS (Organization for the Advancement of Structured Information Standards) [2] or UN/CEFACT (United Nations Center for Trace Facilitation and Electronic Business) [3] drive the development and adoption of e-business standards. To our knowledge, none of these organizations have yet installed a work-group specifically dedicated to the emergence of COTS characterization standards. A first attempt towards less ambitious standardization can however be seen in open-source related projects like COOPX [4], aiming at defining "a standard format based on XML to exchange information on projects hosted by facilities such as Source-Forge, Serveur Libre, Tuxfamily or Savannah".

The creation of a consortium leading the standardization process regarding COTS knowledge management might be a necessary stage in the collaborative construction of a well-structured consensual COTS catalog.

2 The Genesis of the eCots Project

The eCots project is the outcome of two complementary sources: the Thales and EDF industrial know-how in COTS management and in-house capitalization, and the Inria research expertise in open-source development and collaborative work.

2.1 The Importance of Intra-company Pooling for COTS Management

The software evaluation and selection approach of Thales is based on COTS detailed descriptions: technical and purchasing experts define new forms on a yearly basis which identify the priorities of the group[3]. Then, to lead to a short list, several lists of selected producers are established, data on their products are collected in accordance to the established descriptions. These data eventually result in a group recommendation associated with commercial negotiations.

This procedure is one of the foundation stones essential for an effective management of COTS and is already used for regrouping a major part of the COTS management costs. Thales could obviously set up this organization and benefit from it because its pooling surface is large enough. However, producers benefiting from a monopoly are reluctant to comply with the framework proposed by a single industrial group. Moreover, assessment campaigns are not frequent enough when organized by a single actor.

2.2 The Commonplace Idea of eCots: Increase of the Pooling Surface, Promotion of Annotation and Open Communication

Thales Group capitalization on COTS information has totally demonstrated how advantageous it is is both to formalize COTS detailed descriptions and associate the producers to the information concerning their products, but a lever

---

[3] For example, in the past, these forms were defined for real time operating systems, relational database management systems and EJB application servers.

was missing for encouraging a larger participation of the producers in this approach, and for enhancing the content and decreasing the maintenance cost of this capitalization and analysis base.

Unexpectedly, the solution came from ideas developed by the free software environment via the Inria proposal to Thales, which suggested to communicate on a large extent and freely all or part of the content outside the group, instead of keeping this capitalization in-house, therefore inviting the growing community of users to participate more directly with a view to contribute to the qualification of this information.

2.3   Openness and the Dynamics of Free/Open-Source Access

The idea of creating an open information portal for COTS takes place in the current movement of so-called free or open-source resources. The elaboration of operational constructs (i.e. subject to experimental reality check, or corresponding to von Hippel's "innovation networks" [5]) like open science and free software is not exactly the proper model for us. We are rather dealing with information about products, and possibly communication among their users, or between users and producers. Fortunately, the open communication model has been recently experienced in many other areas and implemented in a variety of open cooperative structures (von Hippel's "content networks").

Content networks come in a wide variety. They probably started informally with USENET newsgroups, and then evolved into specialized forms according to both the need to handle specific communication issues (emergence of the concept of FAQ, need for moderation, persistence of information) and the desire to take advantage of new communication paradigms and techniques (forums, web logs, on-line collaborative editing with Jalios, Zope, Wikis and other technologies).

Part of the eCots project consists of the analysis of the various types of existing content networks and the relevant literature, to understand and select the organizations and technologies which seem to be the most appropriate for our goals (technical, economic and legal) and forS the type of content we are considering (COTS information).

Despite the differences, some of the benefits, now almost traditionally expected from open source software, have their counterpart in open content networks. Typically, the hopefully large number of active users of the portal with differing, possibly conflicting, interests will leave less room for misrepresentation, descriptive errors, or inaccuracies due to misuse of the COTS in reported experimental situations. More field experience will become available and errors will be caught faster. It is however essential to follow the teaching of similar networks/portals: low transaction costs encourage interaction, and some way of rewarding, at least morally, the contributors (pseudonymously when requested) encourage more wide-spread participation.

Another issue that will have to be dealt with, is the quality assessment of contributions. Here again, a wealth of techniques have been developed in content networks for turning users into evaluators, and assessing their effectiveness as evaluators. The whole idea is to mechanically manage a rating process that mimics the structure of peer evaluation in open science. It includes selecting dynamically the most capable contributors (or increasing their weight) to assess the value of all contributions [6].

3   eCots Platform: Vision, Difficulties, and Means

The main objective of the eCots project is to implement the vision described below. This implementation is supported by a thorough analysis of the industrial, human, economical, legal and technical difficulties and by the use of solutions tailored to each difficulty.

3.1   eCots: The Vision

This section presents the initial vision of the project to which the current work is now converging.

The portal core is composed of the detailed description forms of actors and products. In both cases these data conform to XML schemas, which are a first attempt towards standardization. An underlying UML model has been designed and can be transformed either to XML schemas, Java classes or other formalisms like SQL or RDF so that a wide range of processing possibilities can be applied to the data in order to create value-added services.

Basic services around the portal core include COTS identification, COTS characterization, experience feedback, discussions and rating services. Based on the rating service, collaborative filtering functionalities could be added to the platform so that eCots would become a COTS recommender system, helping users to select COTS that are the most suitable to their project's constraints.

Other services will be available under subscription. The management of the information provided within the scope of a subscription will be made easier when companies acquire the Jalios platform as it will propose synchronization mechanisms facilitating the collection of data from the master portal. The secure replication mechanism will allow the companies to have access both to their own confidential information–in local mode–and to the data managed by the portal– in central mode–the public contents being the only ones to be synchronized.

Initially, the project founders only considered user-oriented services, such as the use of warning mechanisms in the case of obsolescence detection. However, the necessity to commit COTS producers to the role of effective actors of the portal also requires the availability of specific services dedicated to them. Even though user requirements were at the origin of the creation of the portal, the purpose is not to oppose the producers against the users, but on the contrary, to provide conditions for an enhanced collaboration thanks to the creation of a common language and medium.

3.2   The Economic Model of an Open Portal

As one would expect from an industrial project, the primary purpose of eCots is economical: it consists in providing its users with a maximum of quality-controlled information at the lowest possible price. Different categories of potential contributors have to be catered for with different incentives so that they can collaborate efficiently: COTS producers, COTS users and analytical information providers such as journalists, benchmarking and/or labeling organizations.

Hence, eCots has to evolve into a structure that will be economically sustainable, and will adapt to this variety of users. Economically sustainable means:

- reducing costs as much as possible by automating most of the portal and keeping human intervention to a minimum,
- finding funding sources.

Funding is probably the least understood issue regarding open-content networks. This can probably be attributed to the novelty of the concept, both regarding existing formal economic analysis and regarding lack of experience and confidence of decision makers.

Many existing content networks or portals rely on both goodwill donations (notably for computer hosting and network bandwidth) and voluntary work and contributions, sometimes combined with some direct revenue from subscriptions and advertising [6].

In order to maximize voluntary contribution, the portal must provide a service to all potential or desirable contributors. A major difference with most existing content networks is that, rather than individuals, eCots is mainly addressing a corporate community which is much less inclined to risk taking and goodwill and much more sensitive to costs and returns (as opposed, for example, to desire to communicate, moral incentives and ego boosting). This makes it much harder to draw on existing experiences, and forces us into some novel experimentation.

The service to COTS users is obvious, and is the initial motivation. Still, contributing information requires work, and may entail risks (notably legal, security, confidentiality). Hence, there may be a strong temptation to use the portal as a free rider without contributing any experience report. To prevent it, the first approach is to provide a maximum of flexibility to contributors in their participation. This may allow them to test the system at minimal cost, build confidence into it, slowly master its capability, and assess potential costs and risks. In a way, this is related to a general requirement of content networks that transaction costs must be low, as witnessed by the differences in the success of two collaborative web encyclopedia, Nupedia and Wikipedia [6].

The service to COTS producers is mostly in terms of immediate visibility of their products to a large audience, and possibly of an implicit or explicit labeling by existing on the portal. While such a service will undoubtedly be sought by the smaller and less visible publishers, the larger software houses may be at first reluctant to contribute for a return they may see as negative, since it puts them on equal footing with the smaller firms. This is naturally a chicken and egg problem. If the eCots portal is successful, it will impose itself on all players since being absent from it, or poorly represented, would mean a potential loss of customers.

The service to professional information providers is more difficult to assess. There may be some publicity if the portal is known but that may not be a sufficient motivation. Hence, editorial information, analysis and benchmarks may, at least in part, have to be provided as complementary value-added services available on subscription.

However, even with voluntary contributions of content, there will be infrastructure and maintenance costs, plus the necessary intervention of a human in case of problems, especially legal ones. Advertising could prove an effective means of financing for a highly professional portal, but there is an obvious danger of editorial pressure from advertisers, or of suspicion of existence of such pressure. Another better source of income could come from value-added service, rather than content, around the portal. One such service is the facilitation of private replication of the portal, or synchronisation of a private extension with it, for companies needing to preserve confidentiality on some of their activities and interests. Other opportunities for value-added service should emerge as we gain experience with the use of the resource.

Our intent is to draw any necessary additional funding from membership fees to an association in charge of managing and developing the portal, which is currently being constituted. Hopefully there will be enough membership without further incentive, so as to keep the portal open to all. After all, for companies that manageiCOTS information internally, this is only a partial externalization of the service, with an increased effectiveness. For companies that do not, eCots portal represents the opportunity to access to the same facilities as their larger competitors. Thus the association members should consider the return on investment sufficient, so that they will not mind free riders. Note that free riding can be in terms of monetary or informational contributions, or both. Still, all free riders should probably be seen as potential future contributors. But, as we said, the economics of open portals is still in infancy.

3.3 Legal Issues

Free software and free content networks are much perceived as libertarian endeavors, as marginal structures outside the legal system. Nothing could be further from the truth. First, of course, because no one can be outside the legal system. More importantly, because the very organization of open source is generally built and protected by a very ingenious use of the legal system, and especially the copyright laws. Contributions being automatically protected by copyright, the issue is to design licenses so as to strike a balance between freedom of use, modification and redistribution on the one hand, and constraints that preserve the integrity of the work or certain aims of the author regarding its evolution on the other hand. A formal approach to a fine control of licensing strategies with respect to openness of contributions is developed by the Creative Commons project [7].

In the case of the eCots portal, four different types of legal problems have to be considered:

- ownership and licensing of the documents provided by the portal,
- ownership and licensing of the portal as a database,
- legal responsibilities and liabilities due to the documents and activities of the portal,
- finally, the legal organisation of the association managing the portal (which is not an issue worth discussing here).

In content networks, the ownership of contributions is often left with the author(s) of the contributions. There are good reasons for that choice:

- proper transfer of ownership (as opposed to licensing) would probably require some formal exchange, and would thus entail a higher transaction cost, both for the portal and for contributors,
- transfer of ownership may displease some potential contributors, hence reducing the incentive to contribute,
- it implies that the portal accepts legal responsibility for the content that is published, a responsibility that cannot be exercised in an automated way.

On the other hand, open content networks often adopt a uniform licensing policy, requiring that all contributions adopt a unique license. This obviously simplifies many issues, and particularly the interactions of users with the network. Typically, Wikipedia [8] imposes the GNU Free Documentation License [9] to all contributors. The licensing strategy of the eCots portal will restrict the possibilities to a very small set of licenses in order to keep things simple. We expect that some contributors (producers) will want to keep tight control of their texts and data, while other contributors may be willing to participate in open cooperative elaboration of commentaries. The choice of licenses may also possibly depend on the type of documents and the medium: data sheets, COTS detailed description forms, white papers, benchmarks, or posts in a discussion forum.

The issue of ownership and licensing of the portal as a database of documents on COTS is a specifically European problem, since corresponding laws exist only in Europe. This point has not yet been fully explored, but the choice will go toward "no claim for ownership". In a nutshell, if a competitor thinks he can do better with our data, let him do it—we are interested in the availability of a good service, rather than in owning it. A licensing scheme similar to the GNU GPL could prevent anyone from taking total control of the database. It is also to be noted that some document licenses (such as the OR license [10]) preclude application of the database *sui generis* legislation.

The most delicate legal issues concern liability as authors and/or publishers of information, especially regarding libel or commercial practices. It is economically impractical, and counterproductive with respect to portal dynamics, to screen (moderate) all contributions. Hence, we will try to have the portal recognized as a communication provider, responsible only for ensuring that information is deleted when a legal request is made, and for keeping enough connection information to identify, if legally requested, the authors of litigious contributions (since contributors may have to use pseudonyms). For better protection of all, the system automatically notifies the concerned companies when a COTS product is being commented, and provide means to contact directly the contributor (without giving his identity).

This legal scheme is only a first approximation, and many details will have to be worked out or refined as experience is acquired. It is only hoped that a system that can help improve considerably industrial practice, and hence public welfare, will not bog down in the legal quagmires being developed for the Internet.

3.4 Technical Infrastructure

The main qualities of the adopted technical solution are lightness and flexibility. An operational prototype is available. Several adaptation cycles will be necessary to provide a fully efficient service. Thus, the commercial models, the access rights and contribution mechanisms will have to be developed. Likewise, the assessment forms and the data consulting modes will be dedicated to each group of COTS.

The solution is based on *Jalios JCMS*, a content management platform supporting files of various formats and structured data. These structured data can be imported/exported in XML and edited from a browser. This remark holds for the schemas of these data: the definition of the data structure can be edited from a browser and can be imported/exported in XML (XSD standard). The platform complies with the J2EE standards.

The solution meets the requirements of eCots whose spectrum ranges from communication site to cooperation space. This cooperation is structured around the assignment of roles and rights to the various members or groups. A workflow process guarantees that the data validation rules are complied with. Multiple recommendations can be associated with each publication. Finally, forums, FAQ and glossary services favor collaboration.

Data can be consulted either by navigation per category or by explicit interrogation of the database. Various types of requests are supported: full text, per category or per field, along with refinement by intersecting these criteria. The database is journalized in XML and is made natively accessible in Java with no need for access via the API DOM, which improves the flexibility and performance of the solution.

An originality of the solution relies on the replication service among several machines. The service operates on the basis of an optimistic protocol authorizing any typology and managing conflicts in a programmable manner to eventually ensure consistency. Replication requires only one interaction for synchronizing two replicates; it can thus be set up via networks disconnected from external environment.

As can be noticed, we emphasized the collection, validation and distribution of the information to favor the bootstrap of the eCots service data pooling. We expect other services to develop in the future along with new functions, based on the same or another platform, however using the same data exchange standards.

4   Conclusion: Current Status and Future of eCots

The eCots project associating Thales, Inria, EDF and Jalio, has obtained the support of the French ministry of industry within the framework of the RNTL [11] research and development program. The RNTL label was granted late 2001, and the portal will officially open by mid 2003, at the following address: http://www.ecots.org.

The first prototypes were available mid-2002 and used for iterative experimentation, developments and validation. The demonstration of the latest prototype before opening is scheduled during the ICCBSS 2003 conference.

The eCots portal is based on the logics of an enlargement of the pooling surface. This approach was widely communicated all over Europe via the ECUA network [12] (European COTS Users Working Group), supported by the European Commission within the scope of the 5th Framework program [13]. The members of the ECUA network are favorable to this enlargement which will be proposed to the Commission within the scope of the 6th Framework program in the form of a synergy between the ECUA network and the eCots portal. The purpose will be to become the reference platform in Europe for what concerns COTS information and management. Enlargement outside Europe is scheduled for a next phase.

The basic idea ruling the portal is so simple and obvious that upon each presentation, all the comments state how surprising it is that the portal[4] and the associated standards and services are not yet available. This statement emphasizes the difficulty of the task which requires grouping the technical, commercial and legal skills and promoting major changes in the inter-industrial practices. The need is universal and the eCots founders, fully aware of these difficulties, are proposing an innovative and realistic approach which should make this project a success.

References

1. eCots. Available At: http://www.ecots.org
2. Organization for the Advancement of Structured Information Standards. Available at: http://www.oasis-open.com
3. United Nations Centre for Trade Facilitation and Electronic Business. Available at: http://www.unece.org/cefact/
4. COOPX. Available at: http://coopx.eu.org/
5. Von Hippel, E.: Open Source Software Projects as User Innovation Networks. Working Paper No. 4366-02, MIT Sloan School of Management, In: Conference on Open Source Software: Economics, Law and Policy, Toulouse, France, June (2002)
   Available at: http://www.idei.asso.fr/Commun/Conferences/Internet/OSS2002/Papiers/VonHippel.pdf

---

[4] The Cebase portal (http://www.cebase.org) shares some ideas with eCots in its approach, but is intended to share best practices rather than structured description data and apparently ex-cludes the explicit mention of COTS producers, probably due to legal restrictions within the USA.

6. Stalder, F., and Hirsh, J.: Open Source Intelligence. In: First Monday 7(6), June (2002)
   Available at: http://firstmonday.org/issues/issue7_6/stalder/index.html
7. Creative Commons. Available at: http://www.creativecommons.com/
8. Wikipedia. Available at: http://www.wikipedia.com
9. GNU Free Documentation License. Free Software Foundation, March (2000)
   Available at: http://www.gnu.org/copyleft/fdl.html
10. OR Magazine License. June (1999)
    Available at: http://www.openresources.com/magazine/license/
11. RNTL. Available at: http://www.industrie.gouv.fr/rntl
12. ECUA. Available at: http://www.esi.es/ecua
13. European Commission. Available at: http://www.cordis.lu

COTS-Based Development: Taking the Pulse of a Project

Ed Morris, Cecilia Albert, and Lisa Brownsword

Software Engineering Institute, Pittsburgh, PA, USA
{ejm, cca, llb}@sei.cmu.edu

Abstract. Commercial-off-the-shelf (COTS[1])-based systems demand new indicators for determining a project's progress and it's potential for success. Research by the COTS-based system (CBS[2]) Initiative at the Software Engineering Institute (SEI) has shown that organizations building, acquiring, or supporting systems that rely on COTS products experience a consistent set, or pattern, of problems. These patterns provide the foundation for SEI seminars and workshops that present high-level keys to success along with activities or artifacts to look for in successful COTS-based system projects. These same patterns underlie the SEI COTS usage risk evaluation (CURE) technique for conducting a detailed risk analysis of the use of COTS products within an ongoing project. This paper reports on work that expands these efforts to provide an easily used mechanism to help organizations avoid inadequate practices and employ improved ones—in effect, to allow program managers to take the pulse of their COTS-based projects.

1 Introduction

While the use of COTS products to implement business or mission related capabilities is becoming more common, it has presented a number of unforeseen problems. Too many of these problems are recognized late in the process; when a project is already late or over budget.

A particularly disconcerting—yet hopeful—finding is the *consistency* of problems related to the use of COTS software across a wide range of organizations and system types. Experience shows that successful projects employ an identifiable set of shared practices that are harbingers of success. This set of successful and unsuccessful practices underlies much of the work at the SEI. The "Keys to CBS Success" [1] provide project leadership with insight into the business, contractual, and engineering issues they should address when building, acquiring, or supporting software intensive systems that employ COTS products. In keeping with this goal, the Keys are high-level directives that address broad areas

---

[1] We consider a COTS product to be one that is sold or licensed on a for-profit basis to the general public by a vendor that retains intellectual property rights.

[2] We call systems that make important and extensive use of COTS products, COTS-based systems (CBS)

H. Erdogmus and T. Weng (Eds.): ICCBSS 2003, LNCS 2580, pp. 168–177, 2003.

of concern for project personnel. The COTS Usage Risk Evaluation (CURE) [2] represents a detailed rendition of the same basic practices used to develop and prioritize a list of project-unique COTS-related risks and suggested mitigations.

This paper reports on ongoing work to extend the Keys and CURE to provide a mechanism that allows a manager to readily establish current state and progress of a project employing COTS products. The approach relates the practices for successfully developing COTS-based systems to information that is observable as part of one or more development artifacts. This will allow a project manager to:

- take the pulse of a COTS-based development effort in order to determine whether the effort is on track.
- determine whether the project is sufficiently prepared to move on to subsequent steps in the project's process or schedule a major review (e.g., Milestone or Anchor Point review).

The paper provides a brief discussion of critical activity patterns for successfully developing COTS-based systems. It decomposes each pattern into a partial set of criteria that indicate the extent to which the pattern is present in a given project. For each success criteria, examples of directly observable artifacts are provided.

2   Success Patterns, Criteria, and Observables

Known patterns of success for building COTS-based systems can be grouped into two categories: those that address engineering practices, and those that address business practices. These patterns focus on the new or modified practices that are critical for a project employing COTS products. Note that following the advice represented in the patterns alone is not sufficient to assure a successful project, since there are many non-COTS considerations that can lead to a project's success or failure.

2.1   Engineering Practices Must Evolve COTS-Based Systems Continuously

The use of COTS products introduces unique, marketplace dynamics into a system. A chief attribute of these dynamics is volatility. Marketplace changes may cause rethinking of closely held and seemingly stable engineering decisions—during both development and maintenance of a system. The impetus for these changes may range from new versions of products that force other system changes, to withdrawal of a core COTS product from the marketplace. In any case, changes will happen, they will cause rework, and they may be costly.

It is tempting to freeze the system baseline using a specific version of a COTS product (or specific versions of multiple products) to maintain a stable system. This may be successful—for a while. However, for long-lived systems (e.g., 5 years or more), product and version changes are inevitably forced on a system by changes to operational requirements and underlying infrastructure. The practical way to avoid obsolescence or catastrophic rework is by continuously monitoring the marketplaces for indications of change and judiciously evolving the COTS-based system.

Engineering practices for successful COTS-based systems must change in a number of ways to reflect the reality of using components over which the project has limited—or no—control. These changes are widespread and affect the way in which engineers work with users, the knowledge engineers need, and the techniques they employ. Five patterns, discussed in turn, focus on engineering activities:

- Leverage the Marketplace.
- Avoid COTS Modification.
- Reconcile Products and User Operations.
- Engineer an Evolvable Architecture.
- Make Tradeoffs Simultaneously.

Leverage the Marketplace. Successful COTS-based system projects recognize that, as customers, they must be informed and assertive to maximize the benefits of using COTS products. As informed consumers, they build their knowledge of products and product vendors into a model of the forces that drive individual vendors and relevant marketplace segments. They use this information to plan the project and evolve the system.

Successful projects attempt to gain leverage on vendors through market research, participation in user groups, and active roles on standards committees. Leveraging the marketplace, however, also means maintaining a realistic view of the project's limits for influence. It is seldom in the interest of the vendor—or the consumer—for a product to focus too narrowly on the needs of a few.

Avoid COTS Modification. A primary source of failure in COTS-based system efforts is the well-intentioned attempt to modify COTS products to fit operational processes[3] more closely. *Any* tailoring or modification[4] to a product that causes deviation from the "out-of-the-box" capability and configuration potentially increases maintenance effort across the life of the system. Project management should consider the type of modification or tailoring required, the level of skill and engineering needed to maintain the system (initially and for each product upgrade), and the likelihood that supplied tailoring mechanisms will change over time in deciding what form of modification or tailoring to allow.

---

[3] The term "operational process" refers to both business and technical processes or capabilities.

[4] We differentiate modification, which tends to be outside the predefined expectations of the vendor, from tailoring, which is consistent with the vendor's intent for use of the product.

Table 1. Sample Criteria and Observables for *Leverage the Marketplace*

Success Criteria	Observable in Artifacts
Information about relevant market segments is current and useful	* Organizations with similar business needs and uses of COTS products are identified * Major marketplace trends and key drivers of product development are identified * Key vendors in the marketplace and their relative market shares are identified
Information about COTS products is current and useful	* Key product behavior is demonstrated in a relevant environment using hands-on methods * Information about product attributes that affect, or are affected by, the rest of the system solution is captured * The evolution history of key products is captured and used to predict future trends * The definition and rationale for the COTS product evaluation methods is captured
Enterprise objectives are aligned with the marketplace and product trends	* The organization participates in user groups, industry associations, and standards bodies * A library of related publications is maintained

In some cases, the vendor makes the modifications. If some party other than the vendor does the modification, it is almost inevitable that they underestimate the complexity of the modifications and end up degrading the product. Whether the vendor or another party does the modification, it is likely that the modified software will be outside of the vendor's mainstream release process. This can result in the system lagging behind current product releases to accommodate the effort required to rework the modifications with each product release.

Table 2. Sample Criteria and Observables for *Avoid COTS Modification*

Success Criteria	Observable in Artifacts
Long term risks and consequences of modification and tailoring are considered and addressed	* The factors that led to any tailoring/modification decisions are described * The expected complexity of implementing and maintaining tailoring/modification is described * The risks for the life of the system associated with tailoring/modification are described * The approach to maintaining tailoring/modifications across releases is described

Reconcile Products and User Operations. When building a custom system, it is common to first specify the desired, "to-be," operational process and then to construct the system to that specification. When constructing COTS-based systems, however, successful projects engineer operational processes to match the processes implicit in the COTS products. This requires that mismatches between products and preferred processes are identified early, and the implications of those mismatches are considered carefully.

When a mismatch is identified, the preferred strategy is to change the stakeholders' expectation, and not the product. Of course, not all expectations can be changed. The project must differentiate between those stakeholder expectations that are truly required and are therefore inviolate—to change them would render the system unusable—and those that represent preferences that can be changed to improve the match with a COTS product. Stakeholders who are subject to the change must understand the necessity for change, support the nature of the change, and agree to implement any required updates to business processes.

To put this in common terms, avoiding business process reengineering (BPR) is not an option when building COTS-based systems. BPR is made mandatory by the fact that there is an almost guaranteed mismatch between existing processes and COTS products. Further, to be successful, BPR must be conducted simultaneously with design and evolution of the system's architecture during system development and maintenance.

Table 3. Sample Criteria and Observables for *Reconcile Products and User Operations*

Success Criteria	Observable in Artifacts
The critical behaviors of the solution are identified, prioritized, and negotiated to meet business objectives and leverage the marketplace	* Stakeholders absolute requirements and preferences are differentiated * Coverage of available and forecast COTS products against the critical system behaviors is known and acceptable to stakeholders * Stakeholders concur that the current definition of the system will meet their needs * Plans (including cost and schedule) to manage any necessary changes to operational processes are in place
Any process/product mismatches are identified early	* Affected stakeholders participate in early hands-on product evaluation to identify and resolve mismatches between COTS products and operational processes * Mismatches are identified and tracked, resolution of mismatches is captured * Required domain and COTS product expertise is available to the project

Engineer an Evolvable Architecture. For any computing system, the system and software architectures embody design decisions that affect attributes of the system like performance, reliability, and maintainability. For a COTS-based system, where COTS products are outside the direct control of the project, the architecture will also accommodate—or constrain—the ability of the system to evolve efficiently as components change.

Constructing an architecture that allows the system to evolve to accommodate product changes involves more than adhering to a predefined corporate architecture or selecting products on a pre-approved list. It involves assigning skilled personnel to analyze how technology is changing, gather insight into developing standards, and determine how best to isolate the rest of the system from rapidly evolving products. It then involves protecting the investment by using these same skills to maintain the architecture until the system is retired.

Table 4. Sample Criteria and Observables for *Engineer an Evolvable Architecture*

Success Criteria	Observable in Artifacts
Consensus exists among stakeholders on general direction and high-level features of the solution	* Scope and boundary conditions are defined and agreed to by all stakeholders * The target architecture is validated through an executable prototype * Alternate architectures are evaluated and the rationale for the selected architecture is captured * The impact of COTS products on the architecture and ramifications for products imposed by the architecture are captured
The architecture is able to respond to anticipated business, technology, and COTS product evolution	* The expected evolution of the system and the affect of COTS products is described * The affect of technology trends on COTS products and the system is captured * Alternate architectures that focus on functional and technical stress points are analyzed

Make Tradeoffs Simultaneously. Successful COTS-based system projects make continuous tradeoffs among three spheres of influence: the system context[5], the system architecture, and available COTS products. Each sphere is defined and understood concurrently, and allowed to co-evolve and influence, but not overwhelm, decisions on system design and implementation alternatives. No single sphere is defined in isolation or first.

---

[5] System context includes requirements, end-user processes, business drivers, characteristics of the operational environment, policies to be supported, and constraints (e.g., cost, schedule)

A subtler affect of allowing system context, architecture, and product decisions to co-evolve is the need to maintain the specification of each sphere at a similar level of detail. Otherwise, a more fully defined sphere will interfere with the consideration of factors in a sphere that is defined at a more general level. For example, early, detailed specification of requirements will often prevent consideration of the full range of alternate, but viable, architectures and products.

Table 5. Sample Criteria and Observables for *Make Tradeoffs Simultaneously*

Success Criteria	Observable in Artifacts
Realistic accommodation of requirements, architecture, and products to each other	* All affected stakeholders are involved in tradeoffs between requirements, architecture and products, and rationale for the resolution of conflicts is captured and maintained * Risk and cost-centric analysis of alternatives is available to support contingency planning
An executable representation demonstrates the common understanding and feasibility of the solution negotiated among all affected stakeholders	* The critical tradeoffs made (including non-functional expectations) are demonstrated in and operational scenarios * Stakeholders agree that the executable representation will meet their needs

2.2   Business Practices Take the Long View of System Acquisition

Expecting short-term payoffs from COTS-based systems is frequently unrealistic. To achieve the desired benefits, the decision to build a system around COTS products involves a long-term commitment. COTS-based systems depend on the vendor(s) for long-term maintenance of key components and on forces in the marketplace for technology insertion opportunities.

These dependencies require investment early in the project (for example, extra engineering effort to perform hands-on evaluation of COTS products and to create an evolvable architecture) with the payoff in the mid- to longer-term. They require continued investment until the system is retired in order to adjust to potentially disruptive marketplace events (such as deletion of key features or vendor demise). A program that fails to maintain its investment in a COTS-based system may not be able to recover.

Taking a long-term view mandates changes to the business practices associated with management of an organization's software assets. Three patterns have been identified that focus on updated business practices common to successful COTS-based system projects:

- Live by the Business Case.
- Realign Budgets for COTS Realities.
- Negotiate Licenses and Manage Vendor Relationships.

Live by the Business Case. Many organizations build a business case to support the implementation of a new system or to make initial "make vs. buy" decisions. Fewer organizations use that business case to guide their decisions throughout the implementation process. Still fewer use it to guide decisions about a system during long-term maintenance—until, of course, it is time to build a new system.

In reality, successful projects use key components of the business case, such as developing clear objectives, considering alternatives based on return on investment and total cost of ownership, and identification of risks and strategies for mitigation, as a driving force throughout the life of the system. However, to remain a useful touchstone, the business case must evolve as the system and the marketplace change. Part of living by the business case involves updating it periodically to reflect current conditions.

Table 6. Sample Criteria and Observables for *Live by the Business Case*

Success Criteria	Observable in Artifacts
Decisions are based on analysis of value in meeting business objectives	* The rationale for building the system is current, agreed-upon, and compelling * Alternative solutions have been explored and feasibility studies conducted to weigh business, engineering, and contractual issues * Business rationale exists for selection of a particular system approach or COTS product * Measures exist to indicate success in meeting business objectives
The business case covers the life of the system including long-term implications of using COTS products (upgrade and end of life)	* Analysis of the impact of COTS products on life cycle cost is current * Costs and organizational implications of changing operational processes are identified * Long-term funding is adequate to support ongoing engineering until the system is retired

Realign Budgets for COTS Realities. Whether the ultimate cost across the life of a COTS-based system is more or less than a custom system is debatable. However, it is clear that the costs for a COTS-based system are apportioned *differently*. Successful projects have generated strategies for accommodating the budget volatility that comes from uncertain product upgrade schedules and changes to products that make them more or less viable to the system.

Successful projects recognize the unique demands of building and owning a COTS-based system. They identify sufficient funds and staff for monitoring current and emerging COTS products and technology. They make provision for reintegration, retesting, and redeployment of COTS products following a product upgrade. They maintain experimentation facilities where both engineers and end users can examine new COTS products through the life of the system.

Table 7. Sample Criteria and Observables for *Realign Budgets for COTS Realities*

Success Criteria	Observable in Artifacts
Life-cycle cost estimates are realistic	* Expected frequency of minor and major COTS product releases and product update strategies are described * The effort required to evaluate new releases, adapt them to the system, and to adapt other system components is estimated * Costs for reengineering of operational processes, process change management, and data cleansing and conversion are included * A rationale for all cost estimates is provided
Project budget accounts for new costs associated with COTS-based systems	* Resources for technology forecasting, market research, and product evaluation are included * Budget for product upgrade, reintegration, testing, and data migration is accommodated * Budget for subject matter experts and support services is accommodated * Resources (budget, facilities, staff) for a robust experimentation facility are included

Negotiate Licenses and Manage Vendor Relationships. A COTS vendor does not typically respond to direction as a subcontractor might. A vendor is likely to be far less interested in the particular needs of one project. While this lack of control is rightly a concern, it also provides unexpected protection from COTS modification—many vendors are reluctant to change their product to meet the unique needs of a single project. Successful projects negotiate hard, but recognize that the vendor requires a fair profit and other incentives to support the project over the long term.

The project should develop a trusting—but contractual—and mutually beneficial relationship with the vendor. This will often lead to better insight into vendor releases and long term plans, and may provide some influence over the direction of the product. This usually demands commitment of significant project resources.

Table 8: Sample Criteria and Observables for Negotiate Licenses and Manage Vendor Relationships

3   Summary and Future Work

The organizational impact of adopting a "consider COTS first" approach to building or acquiring systems is widespread. End users need to surrender the degree of control provided by a "bulletproof" specification and accept the possibility of negotiating an acceptable, albeit imperfect, solution. They must be prepared to actively participate in defining those solutions. Engineers must develop new skills in negotiating with stakeholders, evaluating the marketplace, selecting products, and "diagnosing" problems and error conditions across mul-

Table 8. Sample Criteria and Observables for *Negotiate Licenses and Manage Vendor Relationships*

Success Criteria	Observable in Artifacts
Roles and responsibilities of all parties are clearly defined	* Roles and responsibilities of vendors and the procuring organization are contractually codified
Defined management approach for vendor relationships forms a "win-win" partnership	* Responsibility for critical vendor relationships is assigned and endorsed by management * Contractual and non-contractual relationships with vendors that provide mutual incentives for project success are in place
Contract vehicles are flexible enough to accommodate projected risks	* Mechanisms for additional or changed resource allocation in response to marketplace or product changes are in place
Vendor support for the long view is incentivized	* Contract incentives exist for staying current with technology, evolving and maintaining system architectures, etc.

tiple products. Managers need to work with engineers and vendors to form and select the best solution available, and then continue to work so that the solution stays viable over the life of the system. Engineers need to identify opportunities to use COTS products and ways to work with the degree of initial uncertainty this may bring to the project. Vendors should be encouraged to find better ways of working with the project—and should be rewarded for doing so.

This work begins to address how project managers can, through the use of information from project artifacts, assess the extent to which an organization has embraced the business and engineering changes required to successfully build and maintain COTS-based systems. In addition, the criteria provided can help take the pulse of the project and determine when the project is ready for completion of a major milestone. A more complete technical report on the topic will be published in late 2002.

Future work will determine the level of maturity and completeness of observable artifacts expected at critical project decision points in the development process (e.g., the Anchor Points: Life Cycle Objectives, Life Cycle Architecture, Initial Operational Capability; or Department of Defense Project Milestones: A, B, C).

References

1. Oberndorf, P., Brownsword, L., and Sledge, C.: COTS-based Systems: Program Manager Keys to Success. In: Course Slides, Software Engineering Institute, Carnegie Mellon University (1999)
2. Carney, D.: COTS and Risk: Some Thoughts on How They Connect. In: SEI Interactive 3(1), March (2000) Available at:
   http://interactive.sei.cmu.edu/Columns/COTS_Spot/COTS_Spot.htm

Estimating the Cost of Security for COTS Software

Donald J. Reifer, Barry W. Boehm, and Murali Gangadharan

University of Southern California
Center for Software Engineering
Los Angeles, CA 90089
d.reifer@ieee.org
{boehm, murali}@usc.edu

Abstract. This paper describes enhancements being made to the University of Southern California's **CO**nstructive **COTS** (COCOTS) integration cost model to address security concerns. The paper starts by summarizing the actions we have taken to enhance COCOMO II to model the impact of security on development effort and duration. It then relates the COCOMO II approach to the COCOTS estimating framework so that the enhancements proposed can be incorporated into the COCOTS model. After summarizing the team's progress in developing counterpart COCOTS security cost drivers and expert-consensus cost driver parameter values, the paper points to the steps that will be taken to validate the findings and calibrate the model.

1   Introduction

As the software engineering community incorporates more and more COTS software into its systems, security becomes a more important concern. The reason behind this worry is that firms are becoming increasingly apprehensive that their critical operations will be disrupted as they integrate and use more and more commercial components into their systems. For example, spyware inserted in commercial operating systems have made it easy for non-authorized parties to collect proprietary information about an individual's or firm's usage habits. Additionally, viruses, worms and Trojan horses inserted in COTS packages have infected entire systems and brought them down for prolonged periods of time. What's worse, according to the National Research Council's recent report of Trust in Cyberspace [1], many of the threats posed by COTS components are simply ignored by firms because they don't know how to deal with them.

Understandably, there are many factors that make COTS security hard to address [2]. Predominate among them is the fact that COTS software is provided by third parties to firms in executable form without full disclosure of what the software functionality and performance is. While it is relatively easy to analyze source code for security flaws, checking binaries is a labor intensive and arduous task. The situation is further confused by the fact that most COTS packages are in a variable state of flux much of the time. This is due to the fact that

H. Erdogmus and T. Weng (Eds.): ICCBSS 2003, LNCS 2580, pp. 178–186, 2003.

new versions of the package are released frequently and inconsistencies between vendor offerings only become apparent when usage patterns change over time during operations.

Many COTS users would like to do more when it comes to security. But, they don't understand what factors drive the costs of additional assurance and are concerned that the effort will be too time-consuming and expensive relative to the benefits derived. They need help in understanding the consequences of their actions in terms of dollars and cents. In response, the Center for Software Engineering at the University of Southern California (USC/CSE) has mounted an effort to address these concerns as part of its active COTS software integration and maintenance cost modeling efforts. This paper reports the initial results of our efforts to date in structuring and analyzing the effects of required security on COTS integration effort.

2   The COCOTS Model

USC/CSE has been researching the topic of COTS costs for several years. We have worked with clients to understand the factors that drive the cost. Using this information, USC has developed a cost-estimating model called COCOTS (**CO**nstructive **COTS** integration cost model [3]). COCOTS builds on the popular USC/CSE COCOMO II model [4] to predict the effort involved in integrating COTS software products into applications using the activity-based approach shown in Fig. 1. In the COCOTS model, the assessment activity refers to the process by which COTS components are selected for use. Tailoring refers to those activities undertaken to prepare the selected COTS packages for use. Glue code development refers to development and testing of the connector software, which integrates the COTS components into the larger application.

In Fig. 1, software systems are assumed to comprise of a mix of new, modified, reused and COTS components. The central block in the diagram indicates that to determine the total effort, the COCOTS estimate must be added to the numbers predicted for the non-COTS software by the COCOMO II model. The relative size of the effort in each of the blocks is a function of the size of the final application. The terms Life Cycle Objective (LCO), Life Cycle Architecture (LCA) and Initial Operational Capability (IOC) refer to project milestones in the USC MBASE life cycle model. The COTS part of the estimate is developed for each of these four activities using formulas that take component size and volume of work into account. Cost drivers like staff experience and desired reliability are used by the models to address variability of costs to operating conditions across organizations.

The total cost of incorporating COTS packages into an application becomes the linear sum of the three sources of effort as follows:

**Total COTS Cost in COCOTS (staff-months of labor) =
Assessment Effort + Tailoring Effort + Glue Code Effort**

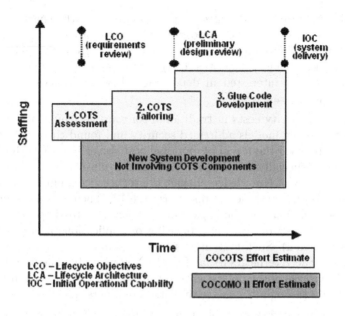

Fig. 1. COCOTS Activity-Based Costing Elements

We have studied each of these activities in depth during the past three years. Using data collected on 20+ projects, we were able to identify the significant factors that influenced project effort and duration and determine their relative impacts on cost [5].

3 Security Enhancements for COCOMO II and COCOTS

Neither the COCOMO II nor the COCOTS estimating model currently includes security as a cost driver. This was not an oversight in either model's design. Until recently, security was considered a significant factor only for military projects. Several cost models addressed security from this vantage point. But, none of these models considers current threats posed by the current state-of-the-art of information munitions. We all are familiar with the threats posed by viruses, worms and denial-of-service attacks like those posed by Code Red. PC World magazine [6] reports that as many as 200 to 300 such viruses circle the globe in any given month. What's worse, the Software Engineering Institute reports that this number is rising with over 26,000 incidences reported just in the first quarter of this year as compared with 21,756 incidences reported in the year 2000 (see www.cert.org/stats/ for details). As the threat increases, our ability to deal with attacks diminishes. For example, a recent article [7] reports that the conventional "layered security" and "defense-in-depth" security strategies used by many firms to combat current threats have major holes. As another example, spyware can be covertly inserted into commercial applications via COTS software to perform industrial espionage. As a final example, tampering with binaries and COTS software represents yet another set of threats as adversaries try to exploit other's work and steal other's technology (key algorithms, protection schemes, make techniques, underlying frameworks, etc.). For these reasons, many commercial firms now are now interested in determining how the costs of implementing different security strategies.

To address security costs in traditional software developments, we have analyzed how existing models addressed security and found them deficient. In response, we proposed the use of an optional cost driver in COCOMO II [8] that we developed especially for security. As Table 1 illustrates, this driver builds on the large Body of Knowledge [9] that the security community has developed over the past decade and the Common Criteria [10]. The motivating force behind use of these techniques is the expansion of business into the world of systems of systems (i.e., network-centric processing of applications in a geographically distributed fashion). Such systems network organizations and applications together across the Internet, Virtual Private Networks, Intranets and Extranets and permit wireless and mobile access to provide subscribers with instant access to information through linkages with distributed, persistent knowledge bases.

Using the framework in Table 1, we conducted a Delphi exercise to obtain some initial expert-based cost driver values for the relative cost of security for the COCOMO II model. This scheme views security from a design, protection and physical security perspective. We circulated a survey to USC-CSE's Affiliates to rate the cost of implementing different strategies within organizations, both aerospace and comercial. The goal was to develop and calibrate a security cost driver that firms and government agencies could use if they needed to. In the COCOMO II software that we freely distribute from our web site at http://sunset.usc.edu, we permit users to employ a user-specified cost driver to address the additional cost of parameters of interest. Because cost drivers are chosen to be relatively independent random variables, variation in one can be considered without considering conditional relationships with other parameters. Using the information presented in Tables 1 and 2, the expert consensus indicates that the delta cost per instruction for implementing software supporting a layered defensive security strategy would be forty-one percent higher than for taking the nominal passive defense strategy.

Unfortunately, the scheme we devised for COCOMO II will only apply to the glue code portion of COCOTS. For completeness, we will have to determine the delta effort associated with the two additional activities in this model as illustrated in Table 3 and sum them to develop an estimate for the total security effort associated with securing a COTS package in staff-months. As the Table indicates, our initial poll of experts believes that security adds a nominal fifty percent to the cost when of COTS. Furthermore, they believe the range of impact on effort is between ten and ninety-five percent and schedule between five and forty-three percent. Of course, there could be no impact. This would be true if security was not a concern and protection did not have to be built into the system to limit the negative impact.

Table 1. Proposed Security Cost Driver Rating Scheme for COCOMO II

Rating	Design for Security	Operational Security	Development Constraints
Extremely High (XH)	Defense-in-depth strategy is planned for. The design is formally verified. The resulting model is supplemented by a formal specification of the requirements and high-level design. Evidence of developer "white box" testing and complete independent confirmation of developer test results is provided along with correspondence proofs. Security controls are supported by a measurable life-cycle model that supports selected protection mechanisms.	The defense-in-depth strategy for protection is implemented. The security policy is represented as a formal model. Protection against insider and outsider attacks is provided using intrusion detection systems, proxy servers and firewalls. Hardware write-protected audit trails are maintained to capture forensic evidence. Independent vulnerability analysis and penetration tests performed by external teams. All communications and storage are encrypted.	Physical security is strengthened even more to include the most biometric devices and other modern access control.
Very High (VH)	Layered defense strategy is planned for. The design is verified using a semi-formal representation. Security is supported by a modular and layered approach to design, and a structured presentation of the implementation. Independent search for vulnerabilities is performed to ensure high resistance to penetration attack. Systematic analysis of covert channels is performed. Security controls are supported throughout development by a standardized life-cycle model that embraces selected protection mechanisms	A layered defense strategy is implemented to protect the system. Audit trails are maintained and access to the system are strictly controlled. All external communications are encrypted. Message digests and integrity verification programs used to monitor activities for penetration attempts. Intrusion detection systems, firewalls and proxy servers are used to protect the network.	Specialized facilities are used to provide even more physical protection (SCIFs). Facilities are secured against emissions of spurious radiation. High levels of vigilance are maintained.
High (H)	A perimeter defense strategy is planned for. The design is tested and reviewed in depth to ensure security requirements are satisfied. The low-level design is analyzed to ensure proper protection. Testing is supported by an independent search for obvious vulnerabilities. Security controls are supported by the life-cycle model selected, tools, and the configuration management system.	A perimeter defense strategy is implemented to protect the system. An unclassified network is used for external communications with no co-mingling of access with the project's secure networks. An incidence response team is put into practice. Audit trails are maintained to track incidences. Data redundancy is used to ensure continuous availability of sensitive information.	Guards, cameras and other perimeter defense measures are put into place to provide additional physical security protection.
Nominal (N)	Security requirements are formulated for the system and its design using high- level guidance documents. Developer tests validating that these requirements are satisfied are independently verified. Black box and vulnerability analysis are performed.	Security policies are well specified. Reasonable password and virus protection practices are put into place along with database integrity and privacy controls. Project has administrator to monitor security controls and improve them as needed. Proper guidance documentation is in place for both the administrators and the users	Development personnel co-located with cipher lock or other protection to guard against unauthorized access.
Low (L)	No security requirements. No security protection other than that provided by the vendors built into either the product or the software engineering environment.	No organization-wide security policies. Ad hoc use of security practices. Some use firewalls and virus protection, some don't.	No unique facility requirements

Table 2. Security Cost Driver Values

	Ad hoc Defense (L)	Active Defense (N)	Perimeter Defense (H)	Layered Defense (VH)	Defense in Depth (XH)
Average Rating	0.94	1.02	1.27	1.43	1.75
Range of Ratings	0.91 to 1.0	1.0 to 1.05	1.1 to 1.4	1.2 to 1.6	1.4 to 2.0

Table 3. Range of Delta Effort and Duration Due to Security

Activity	Nominal Effort	Delta Effort	Nominal + Effort	Range of Impact Effort	Duration
Assessment	Done in two passes: * Initial filtering effort * Detailed assessment effort	Adds a third pass: * Try before you buy	15%	+ 12 to 20%	+ 5 to 10%
Tailoring	Estimated assuming an average effort adjusted for complexity	Adds a second pass: * Assess vulnerabiliti es during setup	10%	+ 8 to 18%	+ 5 to 10%
Glue code development	COCOMO II-like model that uses cost drivers to address parametric variations	Add a new cost driver for security to glue code model	30%	+ 0 to 75%	+ 0 to 33%
+5 to 43%			+ 50%	+10to95 %	+5to43%

The COCOTS assessment effort estimation model includes security as one of 17 attributes being assessed for COTS suitability. For each attribute, the assessment effort is determined as (Number of Products assessed)*(Average assessment effort per product), without further guidance on the latter factor, using Table 1, we can provide a graded sequence of assessment activities needed for increasing security assurance. At the "Low" level, for example, organizations would tap into user communities to see if the COTS has any reported security holes. They would next follow up with the vendors to see if the security problems have been fixed in a timely manner. At the next level, they would embrace a "try the package, before buying it" philosophy. Evalutators would then acquire the COTS package using an evaluation license and test it for viruses, worms, covert channels and a variety of other known security issues. Next, they would try to identify vulnerabilities, isolate problems and determine potential damage inherent to COTS software by running a series of regression tests that they have prepared for such an examination. Further, they would search for dependencies and try to identify configuration-sensitive parameters and platform-sensitive behavior. As expected, this extra analysis and testing takes additional time and effort. Based upon our analyses as illustrated in Table 3, the range of the deltas involved in assessment due to security can add between twelve to twenty percent to the effort and five to ten percent to the duration of this activity.

The tailoring activity configures the COTS package for use within a specific context. Tailoring refers to the normal actions that would be undertaken to adapt a product to the specific host computing environment's configuration like parameter initialization, screen layout and/or report setup. Again, security can add effort and time to the job especially if those involved have to do more than scan each file before incorporating it into the configuration to determine whether or not it is free from viruses, worms, Trojan horses and other types of information munitions. The more secure the application, the more work involved. For example, those involved might perform sophisticated dynamic scans of the COTS software using some a threat simulator to test it for hijackers, hitchhikers or masquerades during setup if you were using it in a critical application. They might also have to examine the behavior of active applets with another threat simulator if you were using Java or other software with known security issues. Such scans are context sensitive and time-consuming to run. Again, as shown in Table 3, based upon our analysis the range of deltas for the extra time and effort involved in tailoring can add between eight to eighteen percent to effort and five to ten percent to the duration of this activity.

The glue code development activity is also impacted when security becomes a concern in the system. Because protection must be built into the system, generic wrappers and bindings build to interface COTS components to the operating system or middleware are hardened. This also takes more effort and time to accomplish. These resources can be easily assessed using an additional cost driver for security. Like in the COCOMO II model, such a security driver can be employed as a user-defined parameter in COCOTS because it uses a like mathematical formulation to predict effort and duration. However, driver ratings for COTS may be rated differently than those developed for COCOMO II to prevent a mismatch between the security level of the product and the application into which it is integrated. In addition, security ratings must be done in a manner that minimizes overlap between contributing parameters. For these reasons, we have developed the separate rating scheme in Table 4 for the proposed additional security cost driver that we are adding to the COCOTS model.

Based upon our analysis, the range of impact as shown in Table 3 is between zero and seventy-five percent for effort and zero and thirty-three percent for duration depending on the extent to which wrappers and bindings have to be hardened and the operational software has to be protected.

Table 4. Proposed Security Cost Driver Rating Scheme for COCOTS

Rating	Protect with	Value
Very High (VH)	Agents used to dynamically search for potential security breaches as connectivity is established and maintained across system in real-time. All of "High" plus top level anti-tamper and data integrity analysis.	1.45
High (H)	Hardened wrappers and bindings used to isolate access to operating system and middleware. All of "Nominal" plus lots of vendor liaison to ensure that adequate security protection is built-in the product.	1.29
Nominal (N)	COTS wrapped and layered for "plug-and-play" to minimize potential threats. COTS scanned both statically and dynamically for information munitions. Vendor error reports checked to ensure that there are no open security holes and all patches have been installed.	1.15
Low (L)	No protection. COTS scanned statically for viruses, worms, Trojan horses and other information munitions	1.00

4   Next Steps: Model Validation and Calibration

We have initiated an effort to validate statistically that the model accurately predicts the impact of added security on effort and duration. We have started with the values developed by experts via our Delphi exercise. Next, we will survey the 20 projects that we have used to initially calibrate the model to collect and analyze the actual impact of security considerations. In parallel, we will use the enhanced data collection forms to gather data from the additional projects that we are working with to determine whether the initial security calibration that we have derived makes sense and holds up when estimates are compared with actual costs. As the database grows, we will glean greater insights into what security strategies work for COTS, under what conditions, and at what cost. Our goal is to refine the initial model developed by experts using actual data provided by projects. As our work progresses, we will provide additional reports summarizing our results.

Acknowledgements. We would like to thank the following groups for supporting the development of COCOTS: the USAF, the FAA, the Office of Naval Research, the Software Engineering Institute, the USC-CSE Affiliates, the members of the COCOMO II research group and most especially the organizations and individuals that have participated in our Delphi exercises and supplied the data upon which our model is calibrated. Particularly valuable contributions have come from Arthur Pyster, Marshall Potter, Roger Cooley, Pat Lewis, Jim Thomas, and Pat Heyl of the FAA; Chris Abts of Texas A&M University, and Betsy Bailey of Software Metrics, Inc.

References

1. Committee on Information Systems Trustworthiness, Trust in Cyberspace. National Academy Press (1999)
2. Lindqvist, U., and Jonsson, E.: A Map of Security Risks Associated with Using COTS. In: IEEE Computer, June (1998) 60–66.
3. Abts, C., Boehm, B., and Clark, E. B.: COCOTS: A Software COTS-Based System (CBS) Cost Model—Evolving Towards Maintenance Phase Modeling. In: Proceedings of ESCOM (2001)
4. Boehm, B. W., Abts, C., Brown, A. W., Chulani, S., Clark, B. K., Horowitz, E., Madachy, R., Reifer, D., and Steece, B.: Software Cost Estimation with COCOMO II. Prentice-Hall (2000)
5. Abts, C., Boehm, B., and Clark, E. B.: COCOTS: A COTS Software Integration and Cost Model—Model Overview and Preliminary Data Findings. In: Proceedings of ESCOM (2000)
6. Luhn, R., and Spanbauer, S.: Protect Your PC. In: PC World, July (2002) page 92
7. Mackey, R: Layered Insecurity. Information Security, June (2002) 61–68.
8. Reifer, D. J.: Security: A Rating Concept for COCOMO II. Center for Software Engineering, University of Southern California, May (2002)
9. Allen, J. H.: The CERT Guide to System and Network Security Practices. Addison-Wesley (2001)
10. Common Criteria for Information Technology Security Evaluation—Part 3: Security Assurance Requirements. Version 2.1, CCIMB-99-033, August (1999)

Bringing COTS Information Technology into Small Manufacturing Enterprises

John Robert[1], Charles Buhman[1], Suzanne Garcia[1], and David Allinder[2]

[1] Software Engineering Institute, 4500 Fifth Ave., Pittsburgh, PA 15213
{jer, chb, smg}@sei.cmu.edu
[2] Duquesne University, 452 Rockwell Hall, Pittsburgh, PA, 15282
allinder@duq.edu

Abstract. Due to increasing competitive pressure, many small manufacturing enterprises (SMEs) are considering COTS software technology improvements to increase productivity. However, SMEs are generally not as prepared to bring COTS software technology into their company as are medium and large organizations. SMEs face unique COTS issues due to organizational constraints, limited interaction with vendors and a passive role (in terms of technology and business process) in the manufacturing supply chain. This report describes these unique SME COTS software challenges as observed in several hands-on technology demonstrations conducted over a two-year period as part of the SEI Technology Insertion Demonstration & Evaluation (TIDE) program.

1   Introduction

Small Manufacturing Enterprises (SMEs), defined as companies having 500 or fewer employees, have an important role in today's global economy. In the United States, the National Association of Manufacturers estimates there are 329,000 small manufacturing firms employing 7 million workers [1]. In the United Kingdom, some reports within the last decade have estimated as many as 94% of manufacturing enterprises employ less than one hundred people [2]. These SMEs impact the global economy not only by directly employing thousands of people, but also by supplying critical parts to larger manufacturers in lean or just-in-time supply chains. Therefore, a healthy SME community is considered a key to success for national governments concerned with economic development and for large manufacturers concerned with building reliable and productive supply chains.

The important economic role of SMEs is driving stakeholder interest in strengthening SMEs. Specifically, governments (both regional and national) and large manufacturers are interested in improving SME productivity to counter the following challenges:

1. Global competition: SMEs face increasing competition in the global economy.
2. Supply chain expectations: Large manufacturers are mandating that SMEs implement information technology and quality standards to improve supply chain productivity.

H. Erdogmus and T. Weng (Eds.): ICCBSS 2003, LNCS 2580, pp. 187–195, 2003.

In response to this increasing pressure to improve productivity, some SMEs are turning toward commercial-off the shelf (COTS) technologies and tools. However, there is concern that SMEs are significantly different from medium and large manufacturers in their levels of resource and control and may not be prepared to identify and manage the risks associated with COTS technology.

This report identifies lessons learned concerning the insertion of COTS technology into SMEs. It provides a short description of each lesson and a summary of the implications of COTS issues for SMEs.

1.1   The Importance of Identifying COTS Issues for SMEs

There are many ways to view SME productivity improvement, including supply chain optimization, organizational change management, technology adoption management or business process reengineering. This report adds a COTS-oriented view to the SME productivity improvement discussion by drawing upon the existing COTS knowledge and applying it to the SME case. This approach highlights COTS issues that are critical to successful COTS adoption for SMEs with particular attention to issues that are distinctive or disproportional as compared to those encountered in medium or large organizations.

Given that an SME is essentially a small business, one might assume that SME COTS issues or lessons learned are the same as for any other business. There are some commonalities, but a number of government and supply chain customers are recognizing that SMEs face additional barriers to growth, including COTS technology adoption, due to their unique characteristics. For example, the PRIME Faraday Partnership in the UK released a technology report [3] providing a detailed listing of SME characteristics in comparison with those of medium and large manufacturers (in Appendix 1). In addition, it summarizes the growing productivity demands on SMEs and the barriers to adoption of the productivity enhancements. Although not explicitly identified in the report, a general COTS implication is that SMEs are not the drivers of the COTS technology effort, but are part of a larger supply-chain-level productivity improvement effort that has an associated COTS technology implication. Therefore, SMEs do face unique COTS challenges due to their environment:

– a lack of control over divergent supply chain level COTS requirements.
– a scarcity of resources and skills to address COTS issues.

A final point on COTS issues for SMEs is that this report does accept as a given that COTS technology adoption is an important strategy of SMEs in order to survive. There is evidence that information technology adoption has a positive impact on the business success of an SME [4]. In addition, the fact that many large manufacturers have set minimum requirements, including information technology requirements, for qualified small suppliers demonstrates that COTS technology is an important part of how small manufactures attract and keep supply chain customers.

1.2   Terminology

The term COTS technology has a very broad meaning and is often not recognized by SMEs. SMEs commonly refer to all COTS software or COTS technology as simply commercial software or information technology (IT). Some SMEs refer to a commercial (COTS) software application as a, "software tool". This reflects the fact that many SMEs view COTS software as simply a tool to develop the final manufactured product.

This report covers COTS software technology (sometimes called a COTS tool) defined as any commercially available software application that can be utilized as part of a product development and manufacturing life cycle. This definition does not include software developed in house, but can include commercial software provided as part of an assembled and delivered system. This definition does not include non-software technologies (such as milling machines), but some of the issues discussed in this report may also apply to adoption of these manufacturing specific technologies.

1.3   Background of This Report

This report was created as part of the Technology Insertion, Demonstration and Evaluation (TIDE) Program at the Software Engineering Institute of Carnegie Mellon University. The goal of the TIDE program is to demonstrate the cost savings and efficiency benefits of applying commercially available software and information technology to small manufacturing firms that supply goods and services important to the national defense. Although the focus of the TIDE program is small defense-manufacturing firms, many of the findings are applicable to any small business relying on software and information technologies.

The TIDE program has three major thrusts, including software technology demonstration projects, technology development projects and workforce development courses [5]. This report is based upon hands-on experience gained from several technology demonstration projects at three SMEs as summarized below:

- SME #1 manufactures high fidelity missile seeker test equipment.
  Demonstration 1: Finite Element Analysis (FEA) tool adoption.
  Demonstration 2: System modeling tool adoption.
- SME #2 manufactures high end vacuum chambers.
  Demonstration 1: 3-D Computer-Aided Design (CAD) tool adoption.
  Demonstration 2: Manufacturing resource planning and scheduling system adoption.
- SME #3 manufactures powdered metal tools.
  Demonstration 1: Manufacturing resource planning system adoption.

In addition to the specific hands-on experience gained in the technology demonstrations, a broad understanding of SME issues was achieved through interviews/discussions with other SMEs, large manufacturers, and COTS tool suppliers. The authors have also reviewed many of the lessons described within this report with TIDE program affiliates that have a nationwide vision for SMEs, including the National Institute of Standards and Technology (NIST) and the Department of Defense Manufacturing Technology program.

2   Lessons Learned

The SME COTS lessons learned are categorized as follows:

- SME Organizational Issues.
- Vendor and Training Provider Issues.
- COTS Research Issues.

An important observation is that the following list of lessons learned is not comprehensive and is intended as a supplement to existing COTS research and knowledge. Unless otherwise noted, typical COTS lessons and issues apply as much to SMEs as they do to any organization. An excellent resource that provides a summary of COTS lessons for a manufacturing system is [6]. Where appropriate, suggestions or techniques to address the issues are also provided.

2.1   Lessons on SME Organizational Barriers

The following are SME organizational issues and lessons learned.

Insufficient definition and understanding of the As-Is business processes is the standard among SMEs. SMEs, like any organization, must begin a COTS technology strategy with a good understanding of the As-Is business process. However, SMEs have only a very high-level understanding of their business processes. This limited understanding has at least three root causes:

1. SMEs do not formally define their processes and tend to use tribal knowledge (meaning that the process and knowledge required to perform tasks exists solely in the minds of employees and is not otherwise captured by the SME).
2. SMEs use flexible processes as a competitive advantage and take pride in that flexibility. Changing this approach is difficult, because many SMEs equate process flexibility with having undocumented processes.
3. The culture within SMEs is one of informal teamwork and therefore is resistant to formalism or change.

The documentation of the As-Is process is an important key to success for any COTS technology adoption effort and should be performed even if the SME management insists that they "know where the problems are." However, documentation of the As-Is process should proceed only until sufficient detail is reached in which the process can be described clearly with consensus among the employees. Further detail may not be possible because individuals may perform the processes steps differently. These differences should be understood and noted, but further formalism may not be required or even beneficial.

SMEs believe they are too busy and do not have time to do any COTS planning activity. SMEs are literally working day-to-day or week-to-week. The flat management structure and small size means that employees and even managers rarely pause to plan the next step or perform analysis to make the next decision. SMEs may oppose spending one day a week for a few months to perform a COTS evaluation or even resist taking an hour away from a key employee to support the COTS evaluation effort.

A clear example of this lack of time attitude can be seen when an SME is offered "free" consulting or planning support. Even if there is no charge and the consultant will come to the SME's facility, the SME will likely decline unless there is clear and immediate benefit.

Part of the solution to this issue is to demonstrate the cost of not performing the COTS planning activities. In addition, every COTS activity must be short and provide clear benefit to the stakeholders.

SMEs employees, particularly managers, wear many hats within the company. SMEs compress several roles into every employee, particularly in terms of management responsibility. The SME flat organizational structure can change typical COTS management and planning activities into strange combinations of questionable value. Using an accounting system as an example, a conventional COTS activity is gathering the key stakeholders for a requirements meeting. Typical attendees include the owner, financial officer, data entry clerk, billing clerk and the purchasing agent. However, in an SME, all of these positions may be filled by only two people, the owner and a close relative (such as a spouse or sibling). This example raises at least two issues: 1) the small size of the team may indicate a lack of required skills within the organization and 2) other relationship dynamics can overpower the original purpose of discussing and determining system requirements.

To address this common issue, SMEs often need a disinterested third party consultant or an unbiased mentor. In the example given, the SME may need part time support from a consultant who is knowledgeable in commercial accounting packages and can work with the SME to perform a COTS evaluation. This consultant may also act as a mentor by working with the SME to identify risks, create the COTS adoption plan, and monitor the COTS implementation.

This example also indicates a fundamental lack of understanding about IT management in addition to COTS management. SMEs typically have few, if any, available IT skills within the organization. To follow up to the above example, adding the SME IT person to the team may mean adding a person who has only basic IT skills. Because manufacturing is the focus of this small enterprise, not IT, there may be little room set aside for developing or staffing broader IT skills.

SMEs lack awareness of available COTS technologies and the potential benefits they can provide. Given that SMEs have little time for and little focus on IT skills, it is not a surprise that they are typically unaware of available COTS technologies. This barrier may be the most difficult to address, because it is not a skill that an SME can readily hire a consultant to provide.When consulting of this nature is available, it is often limited in scope and is expensive.

To address this issue, SMEs should pick people within their organization to monitor and research an area of technology. For example, a designer who uses a 3D CAD system may be a good person to watch the changing market and identify additional tools to improve productivity. Although this approach can work, the SME owner or manager must sponsor an employee to take the necessary time away from other day-to-day tasks.

2.2   Lessons on Vendors and Training Providers

The following are vendor and training provider lessons learned.

Vendors do not target, and may specifically avoid, marketing to SMEs. Vendors are focused on maximizing their sales by getting as many seats/licenses as they can per sales call. Many vendors believe that SMEs require more time to sell to because SMEs may not have the organizational skills and people resources needed to evaluate and purchase the product. In addition, an SME may buy only one or two copies of a COTS tool (like a CAD tool), but a larger manufacturer may buy dozens or even hundreds.

This lack of vendor focus on the SME market appears to be a shortsighted strategy. The medium and large manufacturing markets are saturated with products, so SMEs are the only real growth market. In any case, the lack of vendor attention to the SME market is adversely contributing to the COTS awareness issue discussed in 2.1.4.

There is a training gap between COTS training providers and SMEs. Training is an important part of any COTS adoption plan and most vendors do provide training for use of their product. However, vendors provide general training and do not provide the SME with the explicit training needed to apply the tool to support the specific needs of their business. The result is a training gap that SMEs may not have the resources to fill, meaning that SMEs may believe they do not have time to let an employee investigate the new COTS software tool and figure out how to capitalize on the new technology to provide real business value.

One solution is for SMEs to utilize vendor consulting services as part of the COTS adoption planning and implementation. In addition to getting the COTS tool moving quickly by bridging the training gap, this approach also helps SMEs identify and manage COTS implementation risks.

2.3   Lessons on COTS Research

The following are COTS research issues that are known in the COTS community, but are particularly challenging to SMEs.

The risks and benefits must be evident for an SME to consider investing in COTS software technology. Adopting a COTS software technology is just one of several opportunities to improve SME productivity. Capital is a scarce resource for SMEs, and the COTS software must compete with other worthwhile projects for time and money. As such, the costs and benefits of the COTS software adoption effort must be evident early when investment options are considered. For example, if an SME can spend $50,000 on a COTS CAE tool or a milling machine, which choice is the best to improve productivity?

The correct investment decision requires SMEs to consider the less quantifiable, but very important impact of COTS software technology-on strategy, operations and customers. There are many IT appraisal techniques as listed in [7]. However, successful application of any of these techniques requires training SMEs to identify and consider the all costs and benefits of COTS software technology.

SMEs tend to avoid risks because they can't afford mistakes. As mentioned in 2.1.2, SMEs feel that they do not have the resources to conduct COTS planning activities, including evaluation of several technology options. This issue can result in an SME trying to cut corners and adopt a COTS technology without conducting the proper analysis and risk management activities. Eventually, this results in a costly (and potentially fatal) business mistake that becomes a poster board example within the SME community. Because an SME is small, they can't afford big or expensive mistakes. In fact, some SMEs believe a COTS investment is somewhat irreversible because they don't have the resources to overcome difficulties that may arise.

Continuing with the example from above, other SMEs hear of this COTS failure and simply avoid COTS technologies altogether because COTS technology is not the focus of their manufacturing business. In other words, SMEs avoid the risks associated with COTS technology because they believe they can survive day-to-day operations without COTS technology. To overcome this tendency to avoid COTS, SMEs must be educated on COTS evaluation techniques, COTS technology adoption risk management and the benefits of using COTS technology.

The COTS technology adoption risk management (as opposed to simply COTS risk management) is sometimes overlooked in the COTS research community in that there has been more focus on COTS evaluation or COTS integration techniques. To address the adoption risks for SMEs, the TIDE program has developed a training course called, "Approach to Mitigating Risks: Beyond the Vendor Checklist" [8].

COTS technology must be clearly tied to an SME's business objectives with metrics in place for measurable impact. Of course, every COTS project should have a clear business objective with metrics in place. SMEs in particular do not have the resources or time to invest in long-term, indeterminate benefits. The most difficult part of this challenge is to educate SMEs about identifying and implementing the metrics needed to use quantify the impact. For example, if an SME adopts a Computer Aided Engineering (CAE) tool that enables an SME to reduce product prototypes, how are the savings tracked?

This issue requires SMEs to pay additional attention to the stakeholder buy-in for identifying COTS options and establishing metrics. In addition, SMEs must maintain a list of savings and regularly communicate it to management. This is important to both maintain the existing COTS technology and to transition support of a COTS tool during employee turnover. Because most SMEs use a tribal knowledge system, even a good COTS success will diminish with employee turnover if there it is not given regular attention.

3   Summary

Adopting COTS manufacturing tools such as commercial CAD and CAE products is demanding for organizations of any size, but small manufacturing enterprises (SMEs) are particularly challenged. International competition and supply chain expectations are pressuring SMEs to adopt COTS software technology to improve productivity.

However, SMEs face a number of COTS adoption challenges, including a limited IT capability within the organization and little time or resources to evaluate COTS options. In addition, SMEs are largely unaware of the capabilities of available COTS products due to their lack of attention to this area and a distinct lack of vendor attention aimed at the SME market. Even when SMEs do adopt a software technology, they must overcome a training gap to fully utilize the technology and gain real business benefits.

SMEs face some particular challenges of interest to the COTS research community, including a strong need to align the COTS technology to the business strategy and to consider costs and befits before selecting a COTS technology. SMEs tend to avoid COTS technology due to perceived risks and a belief that they can not afford failure.

As large manufacturing companies move toward design, assemble, test activities, they are offloading more manufacturing responsibilities to SMEs. This shift toward charging SMEs with even more production responsibility indicates that the successful SMEs of tomorrow may be defined by the degree to which they can manage COTS technology and change.

References

1. 2002 Report on Small and Medium Manufacturers: Today's Small and Medium Manufacturers (2001) Available at: http://www.nam.org
2. Denton, P. D., and Hodgson, A.: Implementing Strategy-led BPR in a Small Manufacturing Company. In: Fifth International Conference on FACTORY 2000—The Technology Exploitation Process Conference Publication No. 435 (1997) 1–8

3. Prime Faraday Technology Watch: Fundamental Productivity Improvement Tools and Techniques for SMEs. May (2001)
   Available at: http://www.primetechnologywatch.org.uk/documents/productivity-improvement.pdf
4. Williams, G. A., Pearce, J. W., and Mechling, G. W.: Evolution of the Information Technology/Manufacturing Technology Interface Within Small Manufacturing Firms. Annual Meeting of the Decision Sciences Institute, College of Business, Western Carolina University, November (1994)
5. TIDE Homepage. Technology Insertion Demonstration and Evaluation (TIDE) Program. Available at: http://www.sei.cmu.edu/tide
6. Brownsword, L., and Place, P.: Lessons Learned Applying Commercial Off-the-Shelf Products: Manufacturing Resource Planning II Program. CMU/SEI-99-TN-015, Software Engineering Institute, June (2000)
7. Irani, Z., Ezingeard, J. N., and Grieve, R.J.: Investment Justification of Information Technology in Manufacturing. In: International Journal of Computer Applications in Technology 12(2-5) (1999) 90–101
8. Garcia, S.: Approach to Mitigating Risks: Beyond the Vendor Checklist. In: TIDE Conference 2002, September (2002)

COTS Acquisition Evaluation Process: The Preacher's Practice

Vijay Sai

Software Engineering Institute, Carnegie Mellon University, Pittsburgh, PA 15213
vsai@sei.cmu.edu

Abstract. This paper reflects an effort to apply commercial off-the-shelf (COTS)-based engineering principles to a software acquisition by the Financial and Business Services (FABS) and Information Technology (IT) departments at the Software Engineering Institute. The team responsible for the execution of the project was guided by the principles taught in the "COTS-Based Systems for Program Managers" and "COTS Software Evaluation for Practitioners" training programs conducted by the COTS-Based Systems Initiative at the Software Engineering Institute. Some of the major expectations set and realized included precise comprehension of requirements and preferences, ability to identify weak links in the proposed solutions, support for the "buy versus build" decision and the product recommendation, the promise of a shorter implementation phase, and brimming confidence based on a well-informed project approach.

1 Introduction

In late 1999, Carnegie Mellon University (CMU) had implemented the Oracle Enterprise Resource Planning (ERP) System, a suite of business applications. The ERP system replaced the then existing transaction processing systems, with the promise of extending standardization—across the global organization—of the way financial transactions would be recorded, managed, and maintained. The Software Engineering Institute (SEI) was among several constituents of CMU that were to be served with this system through a central Information Technology (IT) services deployment. The system afforded several extraordinary capabilities for automating bookkeeping and consolidation functions. But it had certain shortcomings: one was an inability to maintain budgets in a manner that would serve the business goals of the SEI. This was a major concern. The situation warranted the continued use of the faltering budget system that had been built internally several years prior (1993). The system was faltering because it needed to be modified substantially to accommodate several new needs created by the advent of the Oracle ERP system.

We found that the dream of an ERP system eliminating all the problems would elude us. We were trying to establish dependencies between two systems that had no capability built in to support such an effort. Thus arose the need to find a suitable solution to a serious problem. We saw two choices:

H. Erdogmus and T. Weng (Eds.): ICCBSS 2003, LNCS 2580, pp. 196–206, 2003.

1. Change the business process to suit the ERP system.
2. Appropriately change the existing in-house system.

We chose the second option and ran into the wall, since reality does not allow the molding of one product to fit another's needs without adverse consequences. Challenges were posed; we would meet a challenge and attempt to move on. The monster would raise its head and exhibit a different behavior and be tamed again until all the troubles surfaced at once, taking us to a point of no return. We found the main ill effect of this phenomenon to be the tremendous effort directed at keeping the business process from failing. Other effects were declining productivity, user frustration, delayed decisions, quick workarounds, and questionable numbers. At this juncture, we reached a decision to scour the marketplace in an effort to find a commercial off-the-shelf (COTS) solution. A team of five members—a combination of technical and business domain experts—were called upon by management to handle the task of steering the rocky boat to calmer seas. This paper attempts to shed light on the process with the hope that it can serve as a reference for readers who expect to embark on projects involving COTS acquisitions.

2   Preparing for the Process

Finding a COTS product proved problematic, partly because the peculiarities of our FFRDC (Federally Funded Research and Development Center)/ Higher Education financial process were not entirely addressed by the marketplace. Therefore, the Chief Financial Officer requested that the COTS Program specialists provide guidance on the project, with intent to procure an off-the-shelf solution. We are thankful to him for that decision. Training in COTS software acquisition techniques soon followed. The techniques learned were applied in the product evaluation process. The COTS Program specialist(s) presided over meetings. Techniques learned were applied to the product evaluation process, hereafter referred to as the PECA (Plan evaluation, Establish criteria, Collect data, Analyze data) process. Each subsection below maps to the process recommended in the COTS training, and was tailored to suit our situation.

2.1   Problem Statement Definition

We needed to understand the problem in depth to determine needs and separate them from preferences. This would ensure a proper evaluation, and prevent the recurrence of previous problems through despite another expensive implementation expensive solution. We verified that all options available within the organization were not usable for resolving our needs. We felt that this knowledge would help us evaluate solutions offered by the vendors.

2.2   Defining Stakeholders

The PECA process taught us to have the right mix of stakeholders so we could draw upon their expertise to guide the project to success. Their participation was necessary since multiple systems would be involved in the final integration.

2.3   Definition of Requirements and Preferences

COTS solutions can only be evaluated for their ability to satisfy the requirements that initiated their quest. Thorough knowledge of requirements is essential and takes considerable time and effort to acquire. While it's not uncommon industry practice to select the vendor and then have the requirements drafted, this approach opens the doors for modifying a vendor's system to fit requirements. The benefits of this approach rarely outweigh the risks. It's important in COTS acquisition that the customer spells out the needs in no uncertain terms. The right stakeholders must be available to support requirement definition. Because we got this clear upfront, we expect our project costs to be stable. Defining the requirements and preferences also helped us to look for what we needed in the proposed solutions. The resulting Functional Specifications document served as an attachment to the Request for Proposal (RFP) and a reference point for evaluations.

2.4   Definition of Expectations from the New System

To ensure requirements are satisfied, COTS software acquisition techniques provide methods to define expectations and identify the capabilities of the proposed solutions. To assist in the PECA process, we drafted the expectations and the means to assess the capabilities. These represented desired characteristics and features of the proposed systems, and were grouped into appropriate categories: System Environment, Operating Environment, Functionality, Vendor Attributes, COTS Characteristics, etc.

2.5   Definition of the Grading Scale

The PECA process recommends using some reasonable method to quantify inferences drawn about a product's ability to satisfy expectations. While automated packages exist, we chose to define a scale (see Sect. 5.1) for the purpose. The scale was to recognize the degree of functionality, ability to modify, ease of modification, system compatibility with the current technical environment, perceivable cost impact, etc.

3   The Search for a Solution

This section discusses the evaluation aspect of the PECA process that is critical to a sound acquisition strategy. It helps one refrain from dealings with novice vendors that are exploring avenues to enter the field, and in turn prevents wasteful use of time and resources over meaningless proposals—or being wedded to one.

3.1   Representation at Key IT Conferences

To understand the latest market developments, it's important to participate in the right conferences. Participation will provide opportunity to network with vendors and members of other organizations and to alert ERP vendors to their products' shortcomings.

3.2   Short Listing Probable Vendors (COTS & Custom Solution Providers)

Researching and creating a list of probable vendors was a difficult task. Conferences hosted by the ERP system vendor, Oracle Corporation, were targeted for our quest. The vendors we met there were affiliated to Oracle's business and technical strategy and dedicated to the financial software arena. Soon we were talking in detail with a large number of vendors. Our defined requirements and related documents proved useful, and reflected sufficient seriousness to attract mostly capable vendors. The degree of reciprocal seriousness helped in shortlisting the vendors.

3.3   Request for Proposal (RFP)

To establish the vendors' familiarity with the business context and their competency to undertake the task, a series of teleconferences, site visits, and product demonstrations soon followed. An RFP was released to the vendors with intent to

- obtain the best possible bid.
- provide an honest exchange in the marketplace and transparency to the vendors.
- ensure Department of Defense (DoD) guideline compliance for IT acquisition.

3.4   On-Site Pre-bid Conference

A day-long on-site meeting, with technical and business domain experts on hand, covered the technical and the functional aspects of the project, and communicated and clarified requirements. A post conference Q & A email exchange was circulated to all.

3.5   Proposal Receipt and Opening

We received proposals from 7 of the 11 vendors that attended the meeting. Three dropped out for reasons unknown; one decided to refrain from participation, as its product was not aligned to the business process discussed—a notable advantage resulting from the approach. All stakeholders were invited to the meeting. We all agreed to evaluate custom proposals only if the four COTS solutions did not satisfy the technical and functional requirements.

4 Knowledge of the Need

The PECA process advises an absolute understanding of the needs refined by appropriate give-and-take efforts between the various system owners and the users groups. This understanding was reflected in the functional specifications document discussed earlier. A questionnaire elicited stakeholders' thoughts on planning, forecasting and budgeting solutions to improve program management. Brainstorming sessions with key players began with a view to establish what might have changed in

- the way business is being done.
- the way information is gathered, processed and analyzed.
- the business drivers.
- the key performance indicators.

Table 1. Sample Requirements

Requirements	Description
Data extracts from General Ledger/Grants Management System and Human Resource Information System (HRIS)	The system should extract data from the Oracle ERP and HRIS systems through suitable interfaces
Burdening	Should be capable of complex conditional transformations and validation of burden structure and negotiated rates for the appropriate funding type, expenditure and task
Flexible Reporting	Should be capable of providing highly flexible reports run for different user selected criteria and presented in multiple formats as reflected in the sample reports provided (*Note: Schedule C of the RFP contained hard copies of current/ mocked up reports to illustrate flexibility*).

The consolidated comments drove the effort to freeze the scope. Table 1 encapsulates part of our understanding. Interestingly, we stumbled upon a quote that read "Producing a system from a specification is like walking on water. It is easier if it is frozen. Reality is that it will always change; therefore you must plan for, and accept, change." In retrospect, this is what was done; the scope (the boundaries of the application functionality) was indeed frozen. Knowing the dangers of scope creep is imperative. Changes with potential to derail the application, if not already factored in, must be prioritized for inclusion into the scope. For example, as this paper is written, a plan develops to upgrade the ERP system for the second time in a year. The selected vendor has been cautioned and will factor the impact into implementation strategy. So the process of educating oneself and the vendor on matters affecting the enterprise-level infrastructure is continuous, expected to bear fruit at the appropriate time. This approach has brought a common understanding of project goals across the lifetime of the project, and helped us assess the need for process changes, and to determine the need to modify the application or our infrastructure. The approach also would later benefit the buy vs. build decision process. Evaluation of COTS solutions preceded custom solution evaluation for obvious reasons— time to market, reduced risk, etc.

5   Proposal Evaluation

The knowledge-gathering phase affects proposal evaluation tremendously, providing necessary guidance to search proposals for evidence of appropriate system attributes. Our structuring of the RFP, functional specifications and vendor survey brought us information in a meaningful format. The difficulty of the proposal evaluation aspect of the PECA process dawned early in the project's lifecycle. Proposals would be evaluated for reflected ability to mitigate problems defined in the problem statement.

In late December 2001 (the project stalled for a period of seven months due to the ERP system upgrade) an RFP was released. The wait was warranted by the absence of key resources and the intent to implement in an upgraded environment.

- Proposal Evaluation criteria.
  These were made known to the vendors through the RFP; but not their order of importance, lest proposals be fabricated to win the contract. This arrangement reflected no disrespect to the vendors. Rather, it serves as insulation against misrepresentation, while retaining the ability to attract good proposals.
- Functional Specifications document.
  The comprehensive Functional Specifications document referred to earlier described the situation, the problem, the environment and the goal.
- Vendor Survey.
  A vendor survey seeking to understand the usefulness of the RFP and related documents helped us to gather feedback to assess the need for improvement.

5.1   Process Definition

The project team sought the guidance of the COTS acquisition program specialists for insights into the method for defining the criteria. This lead to brainstorming sessions that helped crystallize the evaluation criteria. Expectations were set for each of these criteria to assist in the evaluation of the systems. Capability statements were to be identified and/or inferred from the proposals. They were mapped to the criteria. Tables 2 and 3 illustrate a sample of the criteria and the grading scale respectively.

All stakeholders were given clear guidelines for evaluation at the proposal-opening meeting. Some interesting characteristics of this process were

Table 2. Illustration of the Evaluation Template: a Sample

Proposed Budget System Proposal Evaluation Template		Vendor Name:			
Requirement	Expectation	Capability	Grade	Comments	
Client/Server Application					
Performance	Should be quick and scalable as the user base grows. Average response time should optimize on speed, bandwidth, traffic, process, etc.				
Compatibility	Should be compatible with the current technical environment. Windows NT/2000 or UNIX Solaris 2.6 or higher, Oracle 8.1.6 or higher, SQL Server 2000, Oracle AMG APIs.				

Table 3. Illustration of the Grading Scale Used: a Sample

Grading Scale for the New Budget Solution Proposal Evaluation	
10	Fully addressed in current version
8	Partially addressed in current version; low-cost, no-impact/low-impact minor modifications will return fully desired functionality.
7	Not addressed in current version; low-cost, no-impact/low-impact modifications will return fully desired functionality.
6	Partially addressed in current version; high-cost, no-impact/low-impact modifications will return fully desired functionality.

- Stakeholders felt respected by the level of participation afforded.
- Core technical staff members voiced happiness to be involved in the process.
- Common understanding of the capabilities of the solutions existed.
- Most stakeholders turned in their valuable evaluation comments.
- Grades appeared to be based on their understanding of the proposal.
- Experts were used to review the proposals for better understanding.
- New questions were generated for the vendors' clarifications.

5.2   Consolidation of Comments and Grades

All comments and grades received were consolidated for each COTS vendor in the fray. The results were interesting in that less than half a point separated three of the four COTS solution contenders (the last was discarded on grounds of incompetence). The first three fell within the threshold (above 8 as in Table 3) set for accepting a COTS solution as competent to deliver the project objectives.

5.3 Reference Calls and Research Group Analysis

The PECA process was not devoid of advice in the situation. Over a dozen references were called. These were spread across the country and involved organizations large and small—universities, FFRDCs and corporate bodies—that implemented one or another of the products in question. Recourse to product research analyses pointed to significant adversities through maintenance, implementation and modifiability concerns and scarce skilled resources, leaving just one fully capable COTS solution.

5.4 Recommendation

Based on previous experiences, we felt preparing the recommendation would have been a Herculean task if not for the PECA process. The recommendation with the supporting material was ready in good time for management's consideration; this is also attributed to the PECA process. The frequent updates to management and the strength of the PECA process helped clear us quickly for further vendor negotiations.

5.5 System Design: A Perception

To assist in the resource allocation efforts with an aim of reducing the cost of implementation, we embarked on an effort to design the proposed system architecture, as we perceived it, for meaningful reasoning. The approach also fostered an amazing amount of understanding. Figure 1 illustrates the run-time design of the proposed system called "SEI New Budget Solution" along with its interactions with external systems. The components seen above and below it represent the ERP & HRIS systems that the new system will rely upon and offer guarantees to. The design helped identify our contribution to the implementation and the expertise we need to seek externally from CMU and the vendor. The integration points to be satisfied are also clearly represented. The net effect was that there was huge trimming of the consulting costs. We relied on several definitions on software architectural views to develop artifacts similar to the one in Fig. 1. Such views helped us understand and reason out issues related to dependencies, rely-guarantee, security, maintainability, and available skills. They reflected a need for early education to comprehend the implementation activity to be undertaken by the vendors.

6   Value in Approach

The manager of Financial and Administrative Systems anticipates a culture change in future COTS acquisitions, based on the positive experiences derived through use of COTS techniques in the course of this project.

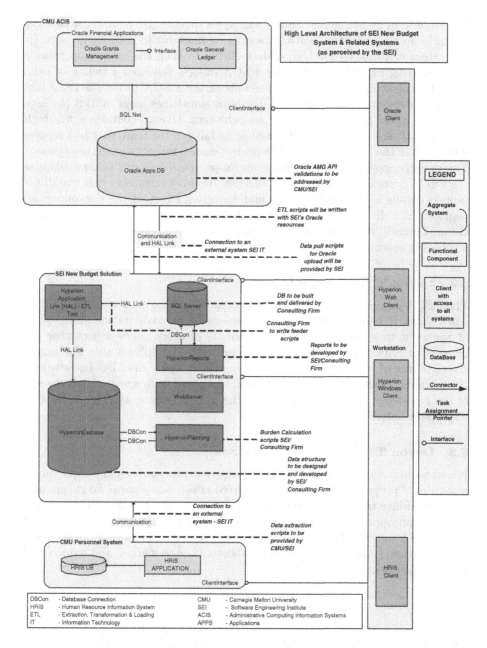

Fig. 1. Functional View of Proposed System

6.1   Lesson 1: Faith Is Fifty Percent of Healing

If religiously practiced, the COTS acquisition techniques—known for their robustness in capturing intricacies and weaknesses ahead of the selection—offer the promise of strong gains. Simple examples include: (i) realization that one strong contender relied on software services vulnerable to security attacks; (ii) realization of the need for high coding efforts to keep the system operational in an evolving IT environment. The PECA process rendered a feeling of being in control most of the time. The demands of the PECA process were so high that a tendency to compromise the discipline sometimes crept in. But the hope of success in the final analyses kept us persistent. Overall confidence was high. Management and stakeholders reposed great faith in the team that had reposed great faith in the PECA process. The project earned respect due to the approach. The vendors cooperated through the entire process. We can't assume adopting the PECA process is a warranty for success. We must remember that the PECA process entails a good deal of time and concerted effort. If these resources are deployed in a disciplined manner, the likelihood of making an ill-informed decision is greatly reduced, particularly when several brains and pairs of eyes are involved in reaching the decision.

6.2   Lesson 2: Knowledge Is Power

The PECA process fostered a deep understanding of the goals and the means to reach them. It helped field the right questions to the vendors and stakeholders at the right time. It promoted the reasoning of every single aspect that was relevant or critical to the success of the project. The difficult side was finding the right mix of stakeholders and managing their aspirations. The knowledge of the team responsible for the project should be equal to or greater than the sum of the knowledge of the stakeholders as the project progresses. This is the only way power balance could be maintained.

6.3   Lesson 3: We Reap What We Sow

It's important to support the PECA evaluation process with the right mix of resources, a proper schedule and a concerted effort. Some gains we experienced were the ability to make well-informed decisions; ability to take calculated risks through appropriate tradeoffs; thorough comprehension of the known; preparedness to seek out and face the unknown; anticipated reduction in negative surprises; wisdom from thorough analysis; shorter time to market; and reduced risk of bad investment.

Expectations

We expect the final leg of the project to be short, due to the PECA process. This expectation stems from all players involved in its implementation being well and informed about project goals, process goals, roles, responsibilities, accountability, etc. Though the final outcome is months away, it seems the project is poised for a smooth journey ahead. Watch for the facts in other papers in the Preacher's Practice series, which is committed to reinforcing the software engineering discipline with facts from the home turf, the Software Engineering Institute, Pittsburgh, PA 15213, USA.

References

1. Bass, L., Clements, P., and Kazman, R.: Software Architecture in Practice. In: Reading, MA:Addison-Wesley Longman (1998)
2. Brownsword, L., Oberndorf, P., and Sledge, C.: COTS-based Systems for Program Managers. In: Course Material, Software Engineering Institute, Carnegie Mellon University, Pittsburgh, PA (1999)
3. Garlan, D., and Perry, D.: Introduction to the Special Issue on Software Architecture. In: IEEE Transactions on Software Engineering 21(4), April (1995)
4. IEEE Recommended Practice for Architectural Description of Software Intensive Systems. IEEE Std 1471-2001, NY: IEEE, Inc., New York (2000) Available at: http:// www.idi.ntnu.no/~letizia/swarchi/IEEE1471.pdf
5. Oberndorf, T., Brownsword, L., and Sledge, C.: An Activity Framework for COTS-based Systems. CMU/SEI-2000-TR-010, Software Engineering Institute, Carnegie Mellon University, Pittsburgh, PA (2000)

BiCom: An Evaluation Framework for COTS Components

Fadrian Sudaman and Christine Mingins

School of Computer Science and Software Engineering
Monash University, Australia
fsudaman@mosca.csse.monash.edu.au
cmingins@csse.monash.edu.au

Abstract. A major problem facing businesses is the proper evaluation of COTS components and its impact on the cost and quality of the target systems. In the evaluation phase, vendors and purchasers often have conflicting interests over component access. Vendors need to retain control for protecting intellectual property while purchasers need complete access for effective evaluation. Currently, evaluation is often limited to documentation or access to function/time-limited versions of the software. In these circumstances, customers are often forced to purchase candidate components for evaluation purposes. This paper introduces an approach that allows vendors to provide access to their components for evaluation, while retaining control over the implementation. Purchasers can perform extensive evaluation as if they have direct access to the implementation. To achieve this, we have developed a toolkit referred to as the BiCom Framework, which presents two views of a component simultaneously, satisfying both the vendor's and purchaser's requirements.

1 Introduction

The myth that all COTS components are thoroughly tested and come with comprehensive documentation is in stark contrast to reality. COTS components are frequently marketed based on the features described in the accompanying documentation, and COTS product selection is similarly often not based on a strong business case or extensive analysis, but instead is often based on web searches, advertising in journals, or fancy demonstration ware [4]. After a component is purchased, developers may realize that the documentation accompanying the selected COTS component is inadequate for understanding the component behaviour deeply enough to integrate it successfully into the target system. Moreover purchasers are typically not provided access to the source code for tracing the component's behaviour during testing, debugging and integration. Consequently, it is likely that the component might not be used appropriately according to the vendor's intentions, thereby compromising the reliability of the target system [5,17]. On the other hand, component designers are unable to predict the range of possible future uses for a component. Thus it is not possible to test and provide satisfactory documentation to cater for the integration of a component

H. Erdogmus and T. Weng (Eds.): ICCBSS 2003, LNCS 2580, pp. 207–218, 2003.

in all possible target projects. In the end, the use and suitability of a COTS component in a project is subject to the consumer's need rather than the vendor's intentions. Other factors such as time and cost constraints also contribute to lack of comprehensive documentation. Even when a vendor provides sufficient documentation, it is insufficient to eliminate the risk of miscommunication and subsequent purchasing of an unsuitable component. Textual descriptions of software components (including text, images, and diagrams) can be ambiguous and fuzzy as it often focuses only on the context that is intended by the designers or vendors. Eliciting information from the documentation for judging the capabilities of the components to be used in different contexts becomes a difficult task [5]. In addition, discrepancies between the interface and the capabilities supported by a binary component as stated in the documentation always exist; it is almost unavoidable for any software element that has evolved over a substantial period of time. Some common discrepancies are that the vendor may not deliver features promised in the documentation, there may be variations in interface signatures, undocumented dependencies and limitations. Due to all these, information provided in the form of specifications and manuals is often an inadequate basis for deciding to purchase and adopt a component. A proper evaluation technique to exercise the component is required in order to discover the true behaviours and capabilities of the component prior to acquisition.

Currently, the most common method of verifying that a piece of software meets requirements is to acquire and test a trial version [10]. However, limitations are usually imposed on trial versions. It has been the norm that software vendors only provide limited information about the software to the public and full documentation is only provided upon purchase [6]. Usually, additional information can be acquired by contacting individual vendors or their nominated distributors. Some vendors also make evaluation copies of their components available for download prior to purchase. However, many evaluation components have limitations imposed such as limited lifetimes, limited functionality, limited licensing, "nag" screens or combinations of these. Often additional development effort is required to impose these limitations [10,16]. All these impositions are intended to protect vendors' intellectual property and to ensure that vendors do not lose control of their components. From the consumer's perspective, these impositions hinder the evaluation process and may interfere with the smooth development of the target system. Purchasing software is always viewed as risk-taking [1]. The amount of perceived risk is dependent on the amount of investment required, and the degree of confidence in the software being purchased. Any deficiency in the evaluation process may result in uncertainty and anxiety about the consequences and thus result in overall lack of confidence in the purchase and high-perceived risks [7,8].

In this paper we propose an evaluation framework, called a Binocular Component (BiCom) Framework. It is achieved by combining a number of enabling technologies. It is called "Binocular" because it aims to satisfy both vendors' and consumers' views of a component, and their needs in providing and acquiring COTS components. In Sect. 2 we describe the overall architecture and examines the role of each software entity in this framework. In Sect. 3 we establish two significant scenarios illustrating the case for using this framework for COTS component evaluation. Section 4 gives a brief overview of the Framework infrastructure. The benefits of adopting such a framework are discussed in Sect. 5. Section 6 summarises the work done, some of the limitations of the current implementation and sketches future work.

2   The BiCom Architecture

The term "evaluation" is defined as an assessment technique using systematic methods and procedures to obtain and process information within the scope of the system for the purpose of future planning and decision-making. In order for evaluation process to be carried out effectively, COTS vendors must provide or supply sufficient information and resources for the consumers to determine the candidate components, and later to examine them and assess their suitability for the target system. On the other hand, COTS vendors always treat their COTS components as intellectual property and hence refuse to give away too much detail about them [10].

The architecture of the Binocular Component (BiCom) framework seeks to satisfy the two divergent views above by employing mediating components. This framework enables consumers to exercise COTS components' capabilities seamlessly through a distributed architecture; it enables vendors to provide distributed access to a component without giving away its implementation. Figure 1 below shows the entities in this framework and their collaborations. It is important to note that the BiCom framework requires network resources, hosting facilities and also that there will be a consequent performance degradation. The labels on the arrows in Fig. 1 indicate the sequence of the operations in the description below.

2.1   Vendors, Resellers, and Consumers

A vendor is defined as a company or individual that produces and supports COTS component(s) based on their own domain knowledge or customer requirements. In a similar manner to any product manufacturer and other software vendors, COTS vendors try to profit from selling their components to consumers through a supply and distribution chain [9,15]. Despite the fact that the software component market is still new, a supply and distribution chain for software components has started to evolve, especially in virtual stores on the Internet. A vendor will normally have his own Internet presence, where information and details about his organization, products, services and marketing material is listed and available publicly. Vendors may often seek one or more business partners (resellers) where their components will be advertised and promoted. COTS resellers normally maintain a catalogue of all available component categories and offer facilities such as search and online shopping [3,13].

A consumer is defined as a company or individual that evaluates or purchases COTS component(s) provided by the vendors or resellers, for integration into their target systems.

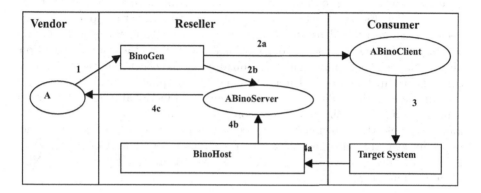

Fig. 1. Binocular Component Framework

In Fig. 1, entity A is the component produced by the vendor. The reseller (this could be the vendor or a third party) is responsible for hosting the BiCom Framework. When a component is presented for reselling, the *BinoGen* element will automatically generate a *BinoServer* element, hosted at the Reseller site by the *BinoHost* and a *BinoClient* element, to be downloaded to the client site. These two elements cooperate to provide the illusion of full component functionality on the client side while the implementation is retained on the vendor site. When the consumer integrates *ABinoClient* into his target system, the execution of any functionality in *ABinoClient* will automatically trigger interactions with *ABinoServer* via the *BinoHost*. A more detailed description of each element of the framework follows.

2.2   BinoGen

BinoGen automates the generation of the BinoServer and BinoClient components from the vendors' component. It encapsulates sets of rules and algorithms that govern the mapping and code generation from the source assembly to the two mediating components, each with their own distinct responsibilities. In practice, it takes as input a Microsoft .NET [18] assembly file (a DLL) and generates a pair of BinoClient and BinoServer DLLs and associated source files. Typically, the BinoServer component will be offered as a service at the reseller end, hosted by the BinoHost element. The BinoClient component will be distributed to consumer locations for evaluation purposes or pilot integration to target systems. BinoGen utilizes many of the rich features provided by the .NET metadata (Reflection) [14] and code generation (CodeDOM) frameworks [11] in order to automatically analyze the target component and generate the server and client proxy components.

2.3   BinoClient

BinoGen constructs each BinoClient component from an individual component. It contains no business logic implementation; instead the implementation is restricted to providing program access and interaction with the BinoServer services. To allow for persistence of object state, the BinoClient component is engineered to connect to a dedicated BinoServer instance. An instance of BinoServer will be created for each instance of BinoClient. This allows the complete functionality of the original component to be mirrored at the client site; the BinoClient component can be used as if it is the vendor's component, local to the target system. Besides the ability to access the complete functionality provided by the vendor's component, the BinoClient component is also designed to be reusable and extensible through inheritance (see Fig. 2 for example), This feature, not generally available in other client-server systems to our knowledge, is possible thanks to the use of wrapper [2] and remoting features in the Microsoft .NET Common Language Infrastructure [12].

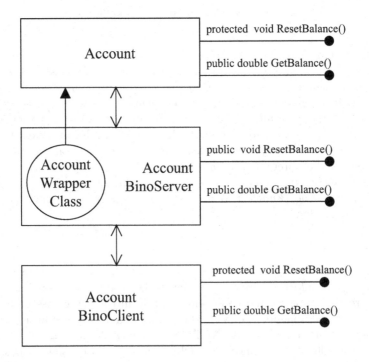

Fig. 2. BinoClient, BinoServer and Vendor's components interaction

2.4   BinoServer

Each BinoServer component is specific to a particular vendor's component. As with the BinoClient component, the BinoServer component contains no business logic implementation. It acts as a gateway for providing public interfaces and services to the BinoClient component to perform operations on the vendor's component (see Fig. 2). In order to replicate the complete functionality of the underlying component, BinoServer component makes extensive use of object composition and interface programming. Each BinoServer component is engineered to permit hosting as server object as well as exposing a specific interface necessary for automatic hosting by BinoHost. However, the BinoServer component must have direct access to the vendor's original component for successful hosting. This generated component also uses some advanced remoting features in the .NET framework [12].

2.5   BinoHost

All BinoServer components need to be hosted and published so that BinoClient components can access them. BinoHost is responsible for this; it registers each BinoServer component on a specific network channel that is known to the BinoClient components. BinoHost is designed to cater for frequent addition and deletion of BinoServer components with minimum configuration and code changes. BinoHost is also capable of dynamically inspecting, loading and hosting any BinoServer components that vendors/resellers intend to publish. It will watch a designated folder and dynamically load and publish all the BinoServer components placed in that folder and remain active until the program is terminated. This automation tool also utilizes many of the rich features provided by the .NET metadata (Reflection) [14] and code generation (CodeDOM) frameworks [11].

3   The Case for a BiCom Evaluation Framework

The scenarios below describe two key situations where potentially conflicting needs of vendors and purchasers are resolved, with no extra effort and expense involved for either party, using the BiCom Framework.

3.1   Scenario 1: Marketing COTS Components

This scenario demonstrates how the BiCom framework can assist vendors/resellers to market COTS components by providing comprehensive an evaluation mechanism to the consumers with minimal effort and risk to either party.

Ace is a software vendor that uses Microsoft .NET technology to build their new billing system. As part of the development, they built a component called "CCard" that provides functionality to validate credit card numbers. Realizing that there is market for this type of components, Ace decides to resell "CCard".

In order to distinguish this component from their competitors', an evaluation copy of "CCard" needs to be provided. On the other hand, **Ace** is not willing to give away their intellectual property freely for evaluation, nor spend extra development effort to inject limitations into the existing component. **Ace** is looking for an alternative and decides to contact a reseller, **Spade**, who is more experienced in this area. The scenario is as follows:

- **Ace** contacts reseller **Spade** to resell "CCard".
- **Spade** uses the automation tool, **BinoGen**, to generate "CCardBinoClient" and "CCardBinoServer".
- **Spade** uses the automatic hosting program, **BinoHost**, to host "CCardBinoServer" and keeps a copy of "CCard" on the host machine.
- **Spade** distributes/emails "CCardBinoClient" to its existing customers and also make it available for download on his website.
- A potential customer, **Greed**, evaluates "CCardBinoClient" by integration testing it into his transaction system. **Greed** realised that he needs one additional functionality and decides to extend "CCardBinoClient" using the .NET cross-language inheritance capabilities, calling his extended component "CCardGreed".
- **Greed** is satisfied with the evaluation and purchases "CCard" from **Spade**, replacing the "CCardBinoClient" with "CCard" (or extending it to "CCardGreed") with minimal effort.

3.2   Scenario 2: Providing a Service

The scenario below demonstrates the use of BiCom framework to provide a software analysis service, operating on software located on a client machine, a service that can normally only be run at the server site.

The School of Computer Science and Software Engineering (**SCSSE**) at Monash University has developed a .NET Common Language Specification (CLS) Conformance testing suite called CLI-C. This software (component) takes a .NET assembly (.EXE or .DLL) performs conformance checking and produces a report file. Initially, users of this service have had to load their components to the CLI-C server through a web client and receive a report back via email. This process is not satisfactory as clients are reluctant to risk giving away their intellectual property and has little control over the entire process. With the availability of BiCom framework, an alternative approach is proposed. The scenario follows:

- To make "CLI-C" easily accessible, but retain the ownership, **SCSSE** uses **BinoGen** to generate "CLI-CBinoClient" and "CLI-CBinoServer".
- **SCSSE** keeps a copy of "CLI-C" component on the host machine.
- **SCSSE** uses the automatic hosting program, **BinoHost**, to host "CLI-CBinoServer" on their server.
- **SCSSE** distributes/emails "CLI-CBinoClient" to the registered users and also make it available for download on the CLI-C project website.

- Users who have a copy of "CLI-CBinoClient" can start using this tool to test the conformance level of their component on their local machines.
- Users have control over the process, such as controlling the number of assemblies to test, preparing the data (assembly) prior to the test, extract the test result, store or present the test results in different formats.
- "CLI-CBinoClient" only needs to be downloaded once by each client, and can be used "as is" as long as the interface of "CLI-C" remains the same.
- Both SCSSE and Clients retain control over their intellectual property.

4   Benefits of Adopting the BiCom Framework

4.1   Complete Functionality

As described earlier, evaluation software is usually distributed with restrictions and it is difficult to exercise the complete functionality. Alternatively, the use of conventional remoting or client-server architectures, will limit client access to publicly accessible services. Neither of the above techniques offers a solution that allows the evaluation software functionality to be exercised while still protecting vendor's intellectual property. The BiCom framework enables this by combining some advance remoting features, the use of mediating components and sets of algorithms that regulate the client-server mapping and component-proxy interactions. All accessible members and operations in the vendor's components such as protected and public attributes, protected operations and static methods are replicated and made available with the same signatures on the generated BinoClient component. Hence, the relation between vendor's component (X) and BinoClient component (XBinoClient) can be formalised as:

X = X Interface + X Business Logic
XBinoClient = X Interface + Remoting Interaction

As a result, the BinoClient component can be tested and evaluated just as if the consumer has a copy of the vendor's component locally.

4.2   Complete Substitutability

Having the complete functionality at the consumer end also means that BinoClient can be easily substituted with the actual vendor's component for final software release. In terms of development effort, complete substitutability means that minimal or possibly no changes are required in the client source code for the substitution to use the vendor's component. The evaluation component (using BiCom framework) could be built directly into the target system and all the evaluation efforts can directly benefit the final integration process. This also includes the testing process. Unit testing of the vendor's component and its integration to the target system can be performed from the day that the BinoClient component is downloaded. Test cases can be built, test operations can be performed and test results can be collated that will also contribute directly to the final system integration process.

4.3   Cross-Language Interoperability and Extensibility

Until very recently, software component development was compartmentalised within individual vendors' component models and programming environments. Binary component reuse could generally only be achieved through composition. Recent developments in component technology have lifted many of these limitations. The implementation of the BiCom framework described in this paper uses Microsoft .NET component technology, hence it directly attain the features such as cross-language interoperability, to the extent of supporting extension of binary components using inheritance. In order to mirror the complete functionality of the underlying component and support extensibility through inheritance, the use of wrappers [2] and advance remoting techniques are engineered into the BiCom framework.

4.4   Satisfying Both Consumers' and Vendors' Views

Besides the purchase price, many other significant costs are involved in integrating and maintaining COTS software in target systems, such as installation, training, integration and maintenance, costs. Before committing to these costs, consumers also often confronted with the following dilemmas:

- There are no effective methods to measure software functionality and quality and hence consumers cannot simply compare and contrast two software items from different vendors.
- Buying software is never a routine process and a consumer seldom buys the same piece of software more than once.
- When searching for software, a consumer is always confronted with unfamiliar products and brands that meet some of the requirements and each of them may offer additional features that differ from one another.
- There is no one established standard and set of criteria for evaluating software as they all differ depending on the nature and type of application of the software.
- Software cannot be utilized directly out of the box and often requires additional processes such as installation, configuration and integration.

The BiCom framework supports the consumer in facing these dilemmas and helps them build their confidence in the product prior to committing to a purchase decision. The full functionality of the COTS component can be exercised through the use of BinoClient components, and a fuller understanding of the product developed, prior to purchase. All of actual costs or additional expenses can be anticipated and planned for. By promising all these benefits, vendors can also market their COTS components better using BiCom framework without giving away their intellectual property.

4.5   Minimum Effort

The interactions of BiCom framework entities are well defined, plus two automation tools are provided for generating mediating components and hosting the client-server environment. The use of this framework guarantees minimum development and configuration efforts required for vendors, resellers and consumers as listed below.

- Vendor: no development effort is required to build the evaluation software. The use of BinoGen also ensures that there is no extra development overhead.
- Reseller: none or minimum configuration effort is required to host the BinoServer components with the aid of BinoHost component.
- Consumer: the evaluation and integration of BinoClient fits smoothly into the target system development life cycle.

4.6   Continuous Evaluation

"DLL Hell" is a widely known problem of versioning and compatibility problems in Microsoft Windows systems. However, this problem does not only exist with DLLs. In fact the problem is experienced with software upgrades generally. The problem is often only discovered after the purchase/upgrade has been made. Since the BinoClient component imposes the same interface as the vendor's component, the existing BinoClient component should be capable of exercising the newer regardless of changes in the implementation. This could be used as a baseline compatibility measure. In the event of interface changes in the new version, the consumer will have a choice of evaluate and test prior of making upgrade commitment. All these facilities encourage continuous evaluation of the software components and reduce potential incompatibility risks.

5   Conclusion

Documentation and component's behaviour mismatch is almost unavoidable and there is no established approach to verify this mismatch prior to component purchase and integration. Currently, consumers are not able to fully evaluate and test alternative components prior to purchase, hence the perceived risk always remain high for making purchase decisions. Vendors are not willing to make their evaluation software available generally due to the risk of losing control and ownership. The BiCom framework accommodates these two divergent views by enabling the exercise and evaluation of a software component's full capabilities through a distributed architecture. As compared to using web services for providing software evaluation, the BiCom framework has additional desirable features such as ability to evaluate object's static and protected members, extend class through inheritance and persist object's states hence allowing access to object's states and properties during the lifetime of the object. The CLI-C program is used as a real-word test case and test outcomes indicate that for now the BiCom framework alone does not solve all the business problems facing the CLI-C program. However, it provides enough control and flexibility for users to incorporate more services or alternatives that can further reduce the risk of exposing their intellectual properties.

The BiCom framework is currently implemented using the .NET framework and works only with .NET assemblies, however the concept can be implemented in other component technologies, on condition that the underlying technology supports the concept of remoting and reflection. An example of such technology is the Java^{TM} 2 Platform, Enterprise Edition (J2EE^{TM}).

5.1   Limitations

In its current form, the BiCom framework has the following limitations:

- It only works with .NET assemblies.
- It does not support the evaluation of graphical user interface (GUI) components.
- It does not support operations related to file system.

5.2   Future Work

We intend to develop the framework further by equipping it with the ability to support assertions using Design by Contract^{TM}. We view assertions as a powerful mechanism for communicating the intended functionality by the vendor to the purchaser. Contract specification and generation will be built into BinoGen program. BinoClient and BinoServer components will both use contracts—to protect the vendor's software from inappropriate use and to notify the consumers about its correct use. Other avenues of this research will be to extend this framework to enable evaluation of GUI components; support operations related to file systems; and provide support for component assemblies from a range of component technologies.

References

1. Berry, D. M.: Appliances and Software: The Importance of the Buyer's Warranty and the Developer's Liability in Promoting the Use of Systematic Quality Assurance and Formal Methods. Computer Science Department, University of Waterloo, Available at:
   http://www.disi.unige.it/person/ReggioG/PROCEEDINGS/berry.pdf
2. Brant, J., Foote, B., Johnson, R. E., and Robert, D.: Wrappers to the Rescue. In: ECOOP'98 Proceedings (1998)
   Available at: http://www.ifs.uni-linz.ac.at/~ecoop/cd/papers/1445/14450396.pdf
3. Component Source. Available at: http://www.componentsource.com
4. Council, W. T, Heineman, G. T.: Component-based Software Engineering Putting the Pieces Together. Addison Wesley (2001)

5. Haddox, J., Kapfhammer, G. M., Michael, C. C., and Schatz, M.: Testing Commercial-off-the-Shelf Components with Software Wrappers. In: 18th International Conference and Exposition on Testing Computer Software. Washington, DC, June (2001)
6. Harrold, M. J., Orso, A., Rosenblum, D., and Rothermel, G.: Using Component Metadata to Support the Regression Testing of Component-Based Software. In: IEEE International Conference on Software Maintenance, November (2001) Available at: http://cs.oregonstate.edu/~grother/papers/icsm01b.pdf
7. Kotler, P.: Marketing Management Analysis, Planning, Implementation and Control. Prentice Hall International Editions (1994)
8. Kotler, P., Shaw, R., Fitzroy, P., and Chandler, P.: Marketing in Australia. Prentice-Hall of Australia Pty Ltd. (1983)
9. Meyers, B. C., and Oberndorf, P.: Managing Software Acquisition: Open Systems and COTS Products. In: SEI Series in Software Engineering, Addison Wesley (2001)
10. Morgan, G.: Catalogue Shopping and Components. Castek (2000) Available at: 'http://www.cbd-hq.com/articles/2000/001003gm_catalogue_shopping.asp
11. MSDN Library. Availab le at: http://msdn.microsoft.com
12. Obermeyer, P., and Hawkins, J.: Microsoft .NET Remoting: A Technical Overview, MSDN Library, Microsoft, July (2001)
13. Object Tools. Available at: http://www.objectools.com
14. Pietrek, M.: Avoiding DLL Hell: Introducing Application Metadata in the Microsoft .NET Framework. MSDN Library, October (2000) Available from: http://msdn.microsoft.com/msdnmag/issues/1000/metadata/print.asp
15. Sparling, M.: Is there a Market for Components. Castek (2000) Available at: http://www.cbd-hq.com/articles/2000/000606ms_cmarket.asp
16. Szyperski, C.: Component Software: Beyond Object-Oriented Programming. Addison Wesley (1998)
17. Vidger, M. R., and Dean, J.: An Architectural Approach to Building Systems from COTS Software Components. Technical Report 40221, National Research Council (1997) Available at: http://wwwsel.iit.nrc.ca/English/papers/vidger06.pdf
18. Watkins, D.: Handling Language Interoperability with the Microsoft .NET Framework. MSDN Library, October (2000) Available at: http://msdn.microsoft.com/library/default.asp?url=/library/en-us/dndotnet/html/interopdotnet.asp

Assessment of Reusable COTS Attributes

Marco Torchiano and Letizia Jaccheri

Department of Computer and Information Science,
Norwegian University of Science and Technology, Trondheim Norway
{marco, letizia}@idi.ntnu.no

Abstract. Among the main activities involved in COTS-based development there are identification, evaluation, and selection of COTS products. Several techniques have been developed for these activities; all of them are based on measurement of attributes. The effort devoted to these activities is more valuable if the attributes can be reused. Since the evaluation of COTS is a very project-specific activity, the definition of reusable attributes is difficult. Several studies show that it is possible and convenient to develop a reusable attribute framework. We propose a set of simple and generic criteria can be used to validate the set of attributes and improve them.

1 Introduction

The software development process using COTS (Commercial-Off-The-Shelf) products has been studied in a few works such as [10] and [3]. Even if no general agreement has been reached, a group of key practices that has been identified in these studies are related to the identification, characterization, evaluation, and selection of the products.

The common feature in these approaches is the use of a set of attributes to identify, characterize, evaluate and select COTS products. In some studies the attributes are designed to be reusable. The advantage of reusing attributes is to capitalize the effort spent to measure them by reusing the collected information across projects and organization units. The main critic to the reuse of attributes is that each project has different requirements that demand for completely different attributes and criteria. An intermediate solution is to have a core of reusable attributes, which are intended to be extended by project dependent specific attributes.

We assume that reusing evaluation attributes is possible. We address such research questions as: how can we understand how good are the attributes? What are the common problems? How can they be improved, both in terms of selection of attributes and their measurements?

The goal of this paper is to propose a set of assessment criteria for reusable attributes. The problems discovered will be tracked to their causes, enabling a process of continuous improvement.

This work was conducted in the context of a research and educational project (see [7] and [14] for more information). Here we present a set of classification and characterization attributes together with their measurement scale.

H. Erdogmus and T. Weng (Eds.): ICCBSS 2003, LNCS 2580, pp. 219–228, 2003.
© Springer-Verlag Berlin Heidelberg 2003

There were 36 students participating in the project, they evaluated a total of 36 products; each student evaluated four different products and each product received four evaluations. The attributes measured by the students have been collected in a database, which served as a means to record and share the knowledge about the products.

This paper is organized a follows. Section 2 describes related works and provides the motivations for this paper. Section 3 describes the attributes we used the software evaluation course. Section 4 describes the attribute assessment criteria, the results of their application to our attribute framework, and discusses how they can be generalized. Finally Sect. 5 draws some conclusions and describes future work.

2   Background and Motivation

In the literature there is a wide range of works about COTS attributes in terms of how the attributes should be defined and how they can be reused.

We try to resume the most representative positions within this spectrum.

At one end there are the Iusware [12], RCPEP [9] and OTSO [8] approaches, which advocate redefining the attribute framework every time based on the requirements. Their motivations are:

- evaluation is different from simple measurement since it is driven by a well-defined goal.
- the factors that influence the choice of attributes depend on the requirements therefore they vary at each project.

At the other end we find CAP [13], the approach proposed by Boloix et al. [2], and the proposal of the eCOTS [6] and CLARiFi [5] projects. They define a set of generic attributes that can be reused across projects and possibly organizations. Their motivations are:

- COTS evaluation is cost effective only if its outcomes can be reused.
- using a fixed framework allows evaluating a wider set of products and continuous improvement.

We have so fare considered attributes that are aimed at selection of products. Several recent works characterize COTS products by means of attributes with a different purpose. Carney and Long [4] and Morisio and Torchiano [11] used attributes to identify relationship between characteristics of products and their impact on COTS based development. The use of a fixed set of attributes is a key requirement in this case.

3   The Attribute Framework

The attributes framework was defined and used in a software evaluation course [1] of the fifth year in the computer science master degree at Norwegian University of Science and Technology (NTNU), Norway.

We wanted the student to reflect on new software technologies in generals. In particular we decided to use the term "software item" to be as inclusive as possible. Thus the attributes were used to investigate a field much larger than only COTS products.

Since the student started from a large set of items they were invited to reflect on questions such as "What is the difference between 'software technology' and 'COTS product'?"

We defined an attribute framework that is made up of classification attributes and characterization attributes. The classification attributes can be used to identify products and organize them into groups of homogenous items; the characterization attributes provide a more detailed description of the COTS products and form the basis for their evaluation and comparison.

The attribute framework makes use of both qualitative and quantitative attributes. Several attributes have both kinds of values. The rationale for this duality is that, in such an indefinite area as COTS products, qualitative evaluations bring a useful richness of information that is easily lost when coded into quantitative attributes.

Classification attributes are all quantitative, while characterization attributes can be both. But all the qualitative attributes have been coded into quantitative values.

As shown in Fig. 1 it is possible to look at a software item both from a qualitative and a quantitative point of view. Estimation provides an imprecise but reach in content qualitative value; it is possible to measure some feature of an item into a quantitative attribute. A qualitative value can be coded into a quantitative value.

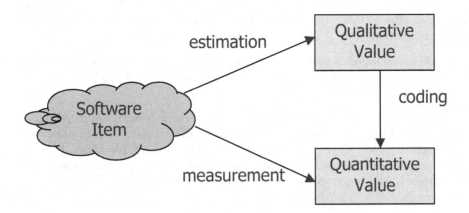

Fig. 1. Quantitative and qualitative attributes

3.1   Classification Attributes

We identified three attributes that are useful in order to classify products: architectural level, artifact kind, and life-cycle phase. Each combination of values of these attributes defines a class.

The possible values of the **architectural level** attribute consist of a pair composed of an architectural pattern and a role defined in that pattern. For the course, we choose to adopt 3-tier architectural style. Thus each software item can play the role of either the client, server, or data.

It is important to find out the **kind** of software. We identified three possible kinds of items: executable, standard, service. Executable items include both source and binary pieces of software. A standard is a prescriptive document publicly available and approved in some forum. A service item consists of a set of functionality provided by a third party, usually through the network; for instance web-based development services (such as project hosting, version control, bug and issue tracking, project management, backups and archives, and communication and collaboration resources).

Another distinction can be found when looking at when, during the life cycle of a system, a given item can be used. We identified two possible values of the **life cycle phase** attribute: development and execution. Development items are tools used to build a software system. Execution items are components used as parts of the system.

3.2   Characterization Attributes

Here we present 16 attributes to characterize COTS products. Only a few attributes have a quantitative scale, most of the attributes were estimated qualitatively, and later on coded into quantitative values. The coding for the qualitative attributes took place when the values were entered into a product database.

Table 1 shows the characterization attributes with their description and how they were originally evaluated. The qualitative column tells whether the attribute has been estimated qualitatively. The quantitative column explains how the quantitative value has been obtained, either by coding the qualitative value or measuring it on the product.

Since the purpose of evaluation attributes is to provide information to select the COTS products and the more trusty the information the better the selection, we collect four independent evaluations for the same product.

4   Assessment

The assessment of the attribute framework aims at finding out whether the attributes are good enough, and how they can be improved for future iterations.

First we describe the assessment criteria and a checklist, then we present the results we obtained on our attribute framework and try to generalize them.

Table 1. Characterization attributes

Attribute	Description	Qualitative	Quantitative
Product maturity	Described by means of a story related to the maturity of the product, e.g. in terms of years on the market and features stability.	yes	coded
Market Share	The ratio/part of the market of similar products that is covered by this COTS product	no	measured (ratio)
Scalability	Measured as the number of users it can scale to without sensible decrease in response time	no	measured (ordinal)
Safety/ Security	The support offered by the product for developing secure or safety critical systems	yes	coded
Reliability	A story describing how fault-tolerant the product is	yes	coded
Hardware requirements	A list of the hardware characteristics required to use the product	yes	coded
Product support	A summary of the facilities offered to support software development using the product	yes	coded
Documentation	What kind (web, on-line, etc.) of documentation is provided together with the product and what is its size (e.g. num of manual pages)	yes	coded
Usability	The degree of satisfaction on a scale from 1 to 5 and a story describing it in more detail	yes	measured (ordinal)
Modifiability	How easy it is to modify this product	yes	coded
Change frequency	How many releases/versions in the last year	no	measured (ordinal)
License Type	The type of license of the product	no	quantitative (nominal)
Cost	The cost for acquiring the product and deploying it	yes	coded
Software requirements	List of required software to run the component	yes	coded
Standard Conformance	List of standard to which the products conforms	yes	coded

4.1 Criteria

We analyzed the products evaluations gathered using the attribute framework, described in Sect. 3 above, to identify the main problems. We focused on generic issues without taking into consideration the specific semantic of each attribute.

The problems we identified are:

- a characterization attribute could not be evaluated because of lack of information.
- it was not possible to assign a quantitative value to an attribute.
- inconsistent values of an attribute were provided by different people for the same product.
- there are no products in some classes.

Based on these problems we defined a checklist to identify them systematically and possibly track them to their causes. Each item of the list consists of the problem to be revealed and of the method to discover it.

C1: Characterization attribute not evaluated: sometimes it is not possible to find enough information to assign a value to an evaluation attribute for a given product. This problem can be spotted looking at the percentage of not evaluated attribute entries for each product and to the percentage of not evaluated entries for each attribute.

C2: Characterization attribute not quantified: it is possible that even though a qualitative evaluation for an attribute is given, it cannot be coded into a quantitative value. A measure of the gravity of this problem can be found looking, for each attribute, at the percentage of entries that have are not codified.

C3: Classification attribute not quantified: a similar problem can occur when an evaluator is not able to decide which value to assign to a classification attribute. A measure of this problem can be found looking at the percentage of the combinations of classification attributes that include at least one "not classified" value over the whole number of entries.

C4: Inconsistent characterization: since several independent evaluations are provided for the same product it is possible to have different people to provide different values for the same characterization attribute. This effect can be revealed looking at the dispersion of the values in the value range. One of the possibilities is to look at the standard deviation of the evaluations.

C5: Inconsistent classification: similarly it is possible that different people classify COTS products in different ways. Since the classification is usually performed by means of nominal attributes, we can measure this issue in a simpler way than the previous one. A simple measure is the number of different classification assigned to a given COTS product.

C6: Empty class: classification of COTS products assigns each product to a specific class. When no product is assigned to a predefined class we have an empty class. Empty classes can be easily found by looking at the number of products assigned to each class.

4.2   Results

We have identified five main possible causes for the problems:

1. the scenario the attributes were designed for does not fit the one that the product is intended for.
2. evaluation or measurement of attributes are affected by the experience or skill of the evaluator.
3. the source of information is scarce.
4. the attribute is not well defined for the following reasons.
   a) the semantic is not well defined.
   b) the coding schema is not well defined.
5. the wrong products have been selected.

We applied the checklist defined in the previous subsection and tried to map the problems to previous list of possible causes.

C1: Characterization attribute not evaluated. This problem is mostly related to a specific product. The main cause can be bad or missing documentation or lack of information on the product web site (3). An alternative cause may be an evaluator not skilled enough to find the information (2).

It is also possible that the kind of information required by an attribute is not easily accessible, not only for a specific product but for a full range of products. In this case either the attribute is not well defined (4.a) or the products being evaluated are off the scope of the attribute framework (1). If a single product has a high percentage of attributes not evaluated probably the product should not be evaluated (5).

In some cases the problem can be solved improving the definition of the attribute.

C1 revealed problems both in getting information about specific products and generic problems regarding attributes. For instance in 39% of the cases the market share of the products could not been determined. This can be explained because product web sites rarely report this kind of information, which on the other end can be found from market research firms.

As a general rule, it is important to use several information sources whenever they are available. Otherwise we should be aware that certain attributes cannot be measured and avoid basing our judgment on them.

C2: Characterization attribute not quantified. This is a major problem can be caused by a misinterpretation of the definition of the attribute, due to either a bad definition of the attributed (4.a) or to an unskilled evaluator (2). It is also possible that the coding scheme for the attribute is not well designed (4.b).

The solution for this problem lies in a better coding schema and a more precise description of the attribute.

C2 revealed that certain attributes could be applied to products of a limited set of classes. For instance 19% of the values of attribute maintainability were not quantified. This can be explained by the dependency that it has on other characteristics of the product, for instance maintainability cannot easily be measured for a product from a third party.

As a general rule it is important to understand and anticipate the dependencies between attributes to avoid this kind of problems.

C3: Classification attribute non quantified. This problem can be due to a limited set of possible values for an attribute (4.b) or an attribute not well defined (4.a). Another possible cause is the presence of a product category that was not considered when defining the attribute (1) or the wrong products are being evaluated (5).

The solution is either to modify the attribute and its coding schema or to filter the set of candidate products.

C3 emphasized the dependency between different classification attributes. For instance 8% of the classifications were Not Classified, Executable, Development, i.e. tools used to develop code for an undetermined architectural level. The explanation is that development tools do not address a specific level, the exception being represented by user interface editors, which are clearly client-level tools. In the case study at first we focused on web-based three-tier systems and then included a wider range of products.

As a general rule it is important to carefully choose the classification attributes, stating the type of products they can be applied to.

C4: Inconsistent characterization. One possible cause is an imprecise definition of the attribute (4.a) or a bad designed codification schema (4.b) leading to different interpretations.

It is also possible that the information provided by the COTS vendor be scarce or misleading (3).

The solution is to minimize the ambiguity in the definition of the characterization attribute and its coding schema.

C4 revealed several problems with the definition of attributes. On the average each product has two different evaluations per attribute. Several cases of inconsistent evaluations were due to imprecise definitions; for instance attribute reliability, which has 2.8 different evaluations per product suffered of both an imprecise definition and inapplicability to certain categories of products.

As a general rule it is important to provide a precise and operational definition for the attributes.

C5: Inconsistent classification. The most likely cause for this problem is the imprecise definition of the attribute (4.a) or a bad designed codification schema (4.b). It is also possible that the product being evaluated is wrong (5). The scarcity of information (3) can also cause this problem.

The solution is to minimize the ambiguity in the definition of the classification attribute and its coding schema.

C5 discovered a problem with products that also embody a standard. This ambiguity was partly due to the choice of very generic classification attributes and served the purpose of make the student reason about the multiple meanings of products names.

In general it is important to identify precisely the products and avoid buzzwords.

C6: Empty class. A give combination of values of classification attributes may be impossible, for instance because the attributes are dependent on each other due to a bad design (4.a).

More likely the presence of empty, or even scarcely populated class, may indicate a bias in the selection of the initial set of COTS products (5).

The solutions to this problem are a better selection of the candidate products and improved attributes.

C6 revealed that several classes are empty. Even if this may be due to the limited number of products, it can also highlight the scarce number of products belonging to a given class on the marketplace.

The relationships between the problem and the possible causes are summarized in Table 2.

Table 2. Problems and causes

Problem	Attribute	Causes
Attribute not evaluated	characterization C1	1) scenario 2) evaluator 3) information 4.a) attribute semantics
Attribute not quantified	characterization C2	1) scenario 2) evaluator 4.a) attribute semantics 4.b) attribute coding
	classification C3	1) scenario 4.a) attribute semantics 4.b) attribute coding 5) wrong products
Inconsistent values	characterization C4	3) information 4.a) attribute semantics 4.b) attribute coding
	classification C5	2) evaluator 3) information 4.a) attribute semantics 4.b) attribute coding 5) wrong products
Empty class	classification C6	4.a) attribute semantics 5) wrong products

5   Conclusions

Our opinion is that in a COTS product evaluation initiative in a large enterprise should be based on reusable attributes in order to be cost effective and gain commitment from all levels in the organization.

If we accept the possibility of reusing COTS-related attributes, it becomes then important to assess the "quality" of the attributes, their measurements criteria, and the collected information. This is the first step in a continuous improvement approach.

Based on our experience we proposed a checklist to perform the assessment of an attribute framework. Each problem can be mapped to a set of possible causes, thus enabling both the evaluation of the quality and the improvement of the attribute framework.

The application of the proposed approach to the case study provided useful insight into the attributes and the collected data.

We found several problems caused by the coding schemas of the quantitative attributes. The main motivation is represented by the educational context in which the attribute framework was defined; its main purpose was pedagogical: make the student reflect about COTS products.

In the next version of the attribute framework we emphasize the pedagogical role of the qualitative evaluations and its imprecise feature. Instead we will improve the quantitative attributes to make them more precise and focused, this will enable collecting more precise data.

As COTS product evaluation becomes a common practice, its assessment gains importance. A lot of work can be done in this area; we foresee two main focus areas:

- development of new and more sophisticate assessment criteria.
- empirical validation of both existing and new criteria.

References

1. SIFT80AT—A Course in New Software Technology (2001)
   Available at: http://www.idi.ntnu.no/emner/sif80at/
2. Boloix, G., and Robillard, P.: A Software System Evaluation Framework. In: IEEE Computer 12(8) (1995) 17–26
3. Bronswortd, L., Oberndorf, T., and Sledge, C. A.: Developing New Processes for COTS-Based Systems. In: IEEE Software (2000) 48–55
4. Carney, D., and Long, F.: What Do You Mean by COTS? Finally a Useful Answer. In: IEEE Software 17(2) (2000) 83–86
5. CLARiFi project home page (2002) Available at: http://clarifi.eng.it/
6. eCOTS project (2002)
   Available at: http://www.industrie.gouv.fr/rntl/FichesA/E-Cots.html
7. Jaccheri, L., and Torchiano, M.: Classifying COTS Products. In: 7th European Conference on Software Quality, LNCS Vol. 2349 (2002) 246–255
8. Kontio, J.: A Case Study in Applying a Systematic Method for COTS Selection. In: IEEE-ACM 18th International Conference on Software Engineering (1996) 201–209
9. Lawlis, P., Mark, K., Thomas, D., and Courtheyn, T.: A Formal Process for Evaluating COTS Software Products. In: IEEE Computer 34(5) (2001) 58–63
10. Morisio, M., Seaman, C., Parra, A., Basili, V., Condon, S., and Kraft, S.: Investigating and Improving a COTS-Based Software Development Process. In: 22nd International Conference on Software Engineering (2000) 32–41
11. Morisio, M., and Torchiano, M.: Definition and Classification of COTS: a Proposal. In: 1st International Conference on COTS Based Software Systems, LNCS Vol. 2255 (2002) 165–175
12. Morisio, M., and Tsoukiàs, A.: IusWare: A Methodology for the Evaluation and Selection of Software Products. In: IEE Proceedings-Software 144(3) (1997) 162–174
13. Ochs, M. A., Pfahl, D., and Chrobok-Diening, G.: A Method for Efficient Measurement-based COTS Assessment ad Selection—Method Description and Evaluation Results. In: IEEE 7th International Software Metrics Symposium (2001) 285–296
14. Torchiano, M., Jaccheri, L., Sørensens, C. F., and Wang, A. I.: COTS Products Characterization. In: Conference on Software Engineering and Knowledge Engineering (2002) 335–338

Implications of Using the Capability Maturity Model Integration (CMMI©) for COTS-Based Systems

Barbara Tyson, Cecilia Albert, and Lisa Brownsword

Software Engineering Institute
4301 Wilson Blvd, Suite 902, Arlington, VA 22203, USA
{btyson, cca, llb}@sei.cmu.edu

Abstract. Using commercial off-the-shelf (COTS) products to meet the needs of business or operational applications is an increasing trend. Practical experience is showing that building systems using COTS products requires new skills and different processes. Practitioners are finding that building and supporting COTS-based systems demands more, not less, management and engineering discipline. Many organizations have derived substantial benefits through process improvement using Capability Maturity Models (CMM©s) and want to leverage previous investments in process improvement to build COTS-based systems. In addition, organizations building COTS-based systems want to begin applying the CMMI©. This leads to the question, "How should the CMMI be interpreted for organizations building, fielding, and supporting a COTS-based system?" This paper provides high-level guidance on interpreting and using CMMI practices in a way that facilitates the definition and development of appropriate processes for COTS-based systems.

1 Introduction

Using commercial off-the-shelf (COTS) products to meet the needs of business or operational applications is an increasing trend. Practical experience, however, shows that building systems using COTS products requires new skills, knowledge, and abilities; changed roles and responsibilities; and different processes [1]. Moreover, practitioners are finding that management and engineering processes for COTS-based systems[1] must be more (not less, as some had thought) disciplined.

Based on knowledge from teaching and applying the Capability Maturity Model© Integration (CMMI©[2]) [2] as well as lessons learned from over 50 COTS-based systems, this paper characterizes the unique aspects of defining, building,

---

[1] A COTS-based system can be one substantial COTS product tailored to provide needed functionality or multiple components from a variety of sources, including custom development, integrated to collectively provide functionality.

[2] Capability Maturity Model, CMM and CMMI are registered in the U.S. Patent & Trademark office by Carnegie Mellon University.

H. Erdogmus and T. Weng (Eds.): ICCBSS 2003, LNCS 2580, pp. 229–239, 2003.
© Springer-Verlag Berlin Heidelberg 2003

fielding, and supporting a COTS-based system and provides high-level guidance to facilitate the definition of appropriate work processes for developers and maintainers of COTS-based systems using the CMMI.

2   Demands of COTS-Based Systems

In contrast with custom development, where a system can be *created* to meet the demands of a particular operating environment, COTS-based systems are, for the most part, *composed* of products that exist "off-the-shelf". COTS products introduce unique dynamics and constraints in that they are developed and enhanced in response to the vendor's perception of the needs of a broad set of customers—the commercial marketplace—not the needs of a particular customer. This introduces new factors that must be accommodated by any set of work processes that build, field, and support COTS-based systems:

- COTS products make implicit **assumptions about the way the product will be used**. These assumptions seldom match the predefined operational processes of the project's end users.
- COTS products make implicit **assumptions about the way the product will interact with other products** and enterprise infrastructure. These assumptions often include dependencies on specific versions of other COTS products.
- The **frequency and content of COTS product releases** are at the discretion of the vendor. In a market segment with significant competition, COTS products may add and/or delete functionality frequently.
- The vendor maintains the COTS product, retains data rights to the source code, and intends for the products to be **used without modification**[3] of the product.

In spite of these differences, many organizations have tried to use the more traditional approach shown on the left in Fig. 1. This approach defines the requirements, then forms an architecture to meet them, and then searches the commercial marketplace for COTS products that fit into that architecture. These organizations rarely find this approach successful—they find COTS products don't "fit." They then either resort to custom development; or, they try to make the COTS products fit by modifying them. In either case, they incur significant cost and schedule impacts that are repeated with each product upgrade.

SEI experience in examining projects attempting to build COTS-based systems shows a fundamental change is required in how COTS-based systems are engineered with attendant management and business process implications. As shown on the right of Fig. 1, this required approach simultaneously defines and performs tradeoffs among four *spheres of influence* (areas of information) over the life of the system:

---

[3] We use the term *modification* to mean changes to the internals of a hardware device or the software code. This does not include vendor provided mechanisms for tailoring the product to specific operational environments.

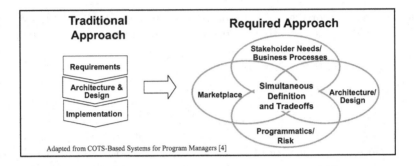

Fig. 1. Fundamental Engineering, Management, and Business Change

- **Stakeholder needs and business processes.** What the stakeholders want and how end users will operate using the system.
- **Marketplace.** What current and emerging products, technologies, and standards are available in the marketplace and how the products are likely to change.
- **Architecture and design.** What engineers can do to structure the system architecturally such that the components work and evolve together.
- **Programmatics and risk.** What the project and end-user community can tolerate in terms of cost, schedule and risk, including the impact of implementing any needed changes to the end user's operational processes.

While three of the spheres in Fig. 1 have analogues in custom development processes, the marketplace is a potent addition. To accommodate the marketplace, forming a solution requires an approach that gathers information from each sphere concurrently as information in one sphere often depends on and drives the information from another sphere. As the information among the spheres is analyzed, needed tradeoffs are identified and resolved through negotiation among the stakeholders. To allow greater use of available products from the marketplace, requirements, end-user operational processes, the target architecture, and/or cost and schedule are modified where possible. In practice, this drives the approach to gather a little, synthesize and negotiate a little, and then gather some more and synthesize and negotiate further. Due to the volatility of COTS products, this approach is not done once at the start of a project. Rather, it will need to continue until the system is retired.

3   CMMI as a Foundation for Improving Work Processes

Capability Maturity Models (CMMs) integrate total quality management, targeted domain best practices and organizational development practices to provide guidance for improving an organizations processes, and therefore its ability, to manage the development, acquisition, and maintenance of products or services.

The CMMs contain "the essential elements of effective processes" and provide "guidance to use when developing processes." Many organizations have derived substantial benefits [3] from process improvement using CMMs and want to leverage previous investments in process improvement to build processes for COTS-based systems. Other organizations building COTS-based systems want to begin applying the CMMI.

The CMMI currently contains four disciplines--*Systems Engineering, Software Engineering, Integrated Product and Process Development (IPPD),* and *Supplier Sourcing.* Each of these disciplines is critical to building, fielding, and supporting a COTS-based system. The *Systems Engineering* and *Software Engineering* provide a basis for the necessary development and maintenance activities. *IPPD* provides for the timely involvement of stakeholders in support of the negotiations among the spheres of influence. *Supplier Sourcing* provides practices for selecting and managing subcontractors that may be extended for relating to COTS vendors.

Process areas[4] are the primary building blocks for the CMMI. Process areas are **not** a process nor are they process descriptions. They are made up of specific practices, that when performed, satisfy CMMI process area goals. The CMMI process areas are grouped in the continuous representation[5] into four categories as shown in Table 1. Although all of the categories and associated process areas are important in a COTS-based system, this paper focuses primarily on the Project Management and Engineering categories with their associated process areas.

4   Developing COTS-Based Systems Work Processes Using CMMI

The practices in the CMMI must be interpreted using an in-depth knowledge of the organization, the business environment, and any other relevant circumstances to define and implement work processes that meet the organization's needs. Experience has shown that work processes for the required COTS-based systems approach (shown in Fig. 1) demand the following behaviors:

-   Simultaneous definition and tradeoffs among the four spheres that begins at project initiation and continues until the system is retired:
    -   Business process engineering integral to system engineering.
    -   Requirements formed through discovery of what is available.
    -   Early definition and maintenance of a flexible system architecture.
    -   Continuous awareness of changes in the marketplace.
    -   Cost, schedule, and risk implications for implementing the system **and** any required business process changes integral to all trades.

---

[4] To distinguish them from generic process names, CMMI **process area names** are underlined throughout this paper.
[5] The CMMI is also available in a staged representation.

Table 1. CMMI Process Areas

Category	Process Areas
Project Management	Project Planning Project Monitoring and Control Supplier Agreement Management Integrated Project Management (for IPPD) Risk Management Integrated Teaming Integrated Supplier Management Quantitative Project Management
Engineering	Requirements Development Requirements Management Technical Solution Product Integration Verification Validation
Support	Configuration Management Process and Product Quality Assurance Measurement and Analysis Organizational Environment for Integration Decision Analysis and Resolution Causal Analysis and Resolution
Process Management	Organizational Process Focus Organizational Process Definition Organizational Training Organizational Process Performance Organizational Innovation and Deployment

- Continuous negotiation among stakeholders.
- Disciplined spiral or iterative practices with frequent executable representations of the evolving system.

In the following sections, selected CMMI process areas are identified for each of these behaviors with guidance for interpreting the process area for COTS-based systems. Due to the brevity of this paper, not all affected process areas are discussed nor is a full treatment of the needed interpretations provided. While our focus in this paper is primarily the Project Management and Engineering process areas, readers will see references to other process areas that we found particularly noteworthy.

4.1   Simultaneous Definition and Trades

As discussed above, an approach for COTS-based systems is an act of reconciling four diverse spheres of influence. Successful development of a COTS-based system requires work processes that fully integrate the discovery of requirements, the design of the solution, and formation of project parameters as stakeholders mature their understanding of the capabilities in the marketplace. COTS products, however, will potentially cause aperiodic disruptions to this discovery. New product releases can affect the requirements and the solution—and these changes can occur at any point in development or maintenance of the solution.

Implications for work processes:

- **Project Planning:** project activities, such as requirements elicitation, market research and solution design start concurrently at project initiation and continue with extensive interaction among them until the system is retired.
- **Decision Analysis and Resolution:** well-established, robust decision processes are required to manage the negotiation among stakeholders.
- **Risk Management:** defining one sphere without adequate understanding of the implications on the other spheres represents a key project risk.
- **Technical Solution:** continuously develop and analyze alternative solutions (including selecting products) to reflect a balance across all four spheres.
- **Verification** and **Validation:** it is important to continuously determine that the information in each sphere is sufficient, complete, and meets real business or operational needs of the organization.

Business Process Engineering Integral to System Engineering. COTS products implement the vendor's assumptions about how end-user business processes operate. This is very different from a custom development situation where the system is created to meet the demands of predefined operational processes. For COTS-based systems it means that the end-user business processes are determined and negotiated simultaneously as more is learned about the COTS products. Through the life of the system, end-user business processes may need to be re-determined and renegotiated as new releases of the COTS product are evaluated for use.

Implications for work processes:

- The CMMI does not address changes to the processes in the functional units of the enterprise. However, the concepts in **Organizational Process Focus** can be expanded in application to explicitly plan and implement enterprise business or operational process improvement.
- **Project Planning:** planning for implementing the agreed upon business processes needs to be integrated with system planning.
- **Organizational Environment for Integration:** a shared vision of success among stakeholders, with suitable incentives, and leadership are critical to aligning business processes with alternative solutions.

Requirements Formed through Discovery of What is Available. For COTS-based systems, defining a detailed set of requirements at the start of a project and forcing the architecture and resulting system implementations to meet that set is unrealistic. Two conditions cause this to be true. First, as end users interact with candidate COTS products and better understand the capabilities in the marketplace their expectations for the solution tend to change.

Second, the marketplace is continually changing product capabilities and introducing new technology providing unforeseen opportunities. Thus, requirements need to be fluid enough to respond appropriately to the marketplace.

Implications for project management:

- **Project Planning:** manage the project to encourage and reinforce the continual discovery (and re-discovery) of requirements while and concurrently establish sufficient stability to deliver a solution.
- **Requirements Development:** to aid in the making trades, prioritizing the requirements is an essential practice for a COTS-based system. In particular, stakeholders must agree on a minimum set of "must-have" requirements (including quality attributes such as evolvability, reliability, or performance thresholds).
- **Requirements Management:** managing requirements in a disciplined and controlled manner must begin at project start. It is critical that changes are tracked and managed as they are identified, the impact on the other spheres is determined, and resolution of mismatch is negotiated.

Early Definition and Maintenance of a Flexible System Architecture.
Since the COTS products are "owned" by the vendors, the framework by which the COTS products and other components of the system are combined to provide desired functionality—the architecture—becomes an important strategic corporate asset. The architecture must be based on current and predictive knowledge of the both the enterprise and the underlying technologies of relevant COTS products and must be carefully crafted and maintained until the system is retired.

In addition, the *evolvability* of a COTS-based system becomes a critical quality attribute of the system. That is, the architecture must retain its structure and cohesiveness yet allow the system to respond efficiently to continuous COTS product upgrades, technology advances, and new operational or business needs. Flexible, evolvable systems do not happen without understanding the nature of potential changes in the marketplace and crafting an architecture than can insulate parts of the system from changes in other parts.

Implications for work processes:

- **Project Planning:** appropriate skills and dedicated resources are necessary to form, evaluate, and maintain the flexibility and evolvability characteristics of the system and its architecture. In addition, project plans need to include the effort to create and maintain the "wrappers" or "glue" and re-integrate the solution as the COTS products change.
- **Product Integration:** composing and evaluating executable representations from the start of the project is a critical mechanism to verify and validate the suitability and evolvablity of the architecture.

- **Technical Solution:** "make-or-buy" analysis continues until the system is retired. Previous decisions may need to be revisited when an existing product changes or a new product becomes available. In addition, the architecture for each alternate solution needs to include an explicit COTS product integration strategy that describes the project standards or protocols that will be used to link COTS products and other system components.

Continuous Awareness of Changes in the Marketplace. Given the continuing volatility of the commercial marketplace, work processes for a COTS-based system must proactively anticipate and track changes to relevant market segments, including market share distribution, other customers, and current and emerging products and technologies. This knowledge is needed not just at the start of a project, but must be updated continuously until the system is retired. Key sources for marketplace information include vendor user groups, conferences, industry associations, standards bodies, and other customers.

Also required are work processes for evaluating and proactively identifying the impact of key COTS products on the solution and the impact of potential changes to determine if, how, and when to accommodate them. Knowledge of the product must be sufficiently detailed to evaluate the potential impact and benefits to the system of sets of COTS products as well as any emerging changes in vendor product direction.

In addition, effective processes to develop and maintain relationships with the vendors who supply key COTS products are needed to *influence* a vendor's product direction (vendor's don't often respond to *direction* from a customer). The vendor is an important stakeholder for the project; they provide unique insights into ways their products work. The specific nature of the relationship will depend on the importance of the COTS product to the solution and the vendor involved. Not all vendors will encourage (or entertain) a close working relationship.

Implications for work processes:

- **Project Planning:** monitoring the marketplace and continuous COTS product evaluation may require significant resources (cost, schedule, experimentation facilities, skilled personnel).
- **Supplier Agreement Management:** license agreements with COTS vendors should be negotiated to meet the needs of the project. Understanding the terms and conditions used by other customers in the marketplace is a valuable asset.
- **Integrated Supplier Management:** establishing and maintaining appropriate relationships with key vendors is critical. Generally, vendors will not allow monitoring of their processes or work products. Hands-on evaluation of each vendor's product releases (including any patches) is more realistic.
- Relationships with key vendors' other customers, while not explicitly covered in CMMI, are a necessary element for COTS-based systems processes.

- **Technical Solution:** informative material states "COTS alternatives may be used with or without modification." Modification of COTS products introduces long term maintenance considerations and sizeable risk to the project and should be avoided whenever possible.

Cost, Schedule, and Risk Implications Integral to All Trades. Each alternative solution developed and analyzed needs to include an understanding of the team skills and expertise required to implement, field and support it as well as the associated cost, schedule and risks. Unique to a COTS-based system is the requirement to include the cost, schedule and risks of implementing business process changes for the functional units who are affected by the solution.

Implications for work processes:

- **Project Planning:** estimates of work product and task attributes need to be generated for each alternative.
- **Technical Solution:** engineering trades must include risk, cost, schedule and other programmatic factors associated with each alternative solution.

4.2   Continuous Negotiation among Stakeholders

Communication and effective decision-making processes are critical to a COTS-based system. Stakeholders must be available to quickly resolve mismatches as they are discovered, and concurrently agree that the evolving definition of the system will meet their needs. In addition, the activities that identify, evaluate, and select COTS products shape the end-user operational processes and define the functionality, cost, and schedule for the system that will be delivered. This has a profound affect on stakeholder involvement through the life of the system; the required level of commitment throughout the life of the system is significant, even unprecedented, particularly for the end-user community.

Implications for work processes:

- The *IPPD discipline:* integrated teaming among disparate stakeholders throughout the development and maintenance is essential.
- **Project Planning:** resources to support stakeholder involvement must be accommodated. Also, the necessary changes to end-user operational processes must be explicitly and continuously managed and coordinated with solution development.
- **Validation:** the informative material says that "often" end users are involved in validating the suitability of the solution. For COTS-based systems, the end users must always be involved to confirm the results of any and all negotiations.

4.3   Disciplined Spiral or Iterative Practices with Frequent Executables

COTS-based systems are particularly suited to spiral development work processes. Spiral development allows the discovery of the critical attributes of the solution through an evolutionary exploration of the highest risk elements of the system. Spiral development also encourages frequent and direct feedback from the stakeholders while reducing the risk of misunderstandings by producing and validating executable representations (prototypes or production releases) of the evolving solution.

Implications for work processes:

- **Project Planning:** if not already implemented, projects may need to revamp their planning processes to align with a spiral development approach.
- **Risk Management:** in spiral development, the highest priority remaining risks are used to directly plan and manage the project.
- **Technical Solution** and **Product Integration:** an executable representation is produced to reflect how the system will operate and the alternative designs explored and negotiated in each iteration.

5   Summary

All disciplines of the CMMI are critical to defining, building, fielding, and supporting COTS-based systems. Developing and maintaining a COTS-based system is more than selecting products—and therefore, more than just applying the *Supplier Sourcing discipline* of the CMMI. Successful projects use insight into what is available in COTS products to form solutions. This demands fully integrated work processes that accommodate the volatility of the marketplace throughout the life of the system

If not already implemented, the biggest change in work processes for COTS-based systems will be the implementation of risk-based spiral development processes to facilitate the simultaneous definition and trades among the competing spheres of influence. In addition, the integration of business process engineering and robust product evaluation as a part of defining alternative solutions will be new to most system development organizations.

The CMMI provides a sound basis for improving the processes used for COTS-based systems. As with any application of the CMMI, the unique aspects of COTS-based systems as well as the specific needs of the organization must drive the development of effective work processes.

References

1. United States Air Force Science Advisory Board Report on Ensuring Successful Implementation of Commercial Items in Air Force Systems. SAB-TR-99-03 (2000)

2. CMMI Product Team: Capability Maturity Model© Integration. Version 1.1: CMMI for Systems Engineering, Software Engineering, Integrated Product and Process Development and Supplier Sourcing, (CMMI-SE/SW/IPPD/SS, V1.1). CMU/SEI-2002-TR-11, Software Engineering Institute, Carnegie Mellon University, Pittsburgh, PA (2002)
3. Goldenson, D., and Herbsleb J.: After the Appraisal: A Systematic Survey of Process Improvement, Its Benefits, and Factors That Influence Success. CMU/SEI-95-TR-009, Software Engineering Institute, Carnegie Mellon University, Pittsburgh, PA (1995)
4. Brownsword, L., Oberndorf, P., and Sledge, C.: COTS-Based Systems for Program Managers. Software Engineering Institute, Carnegie Mellon University, Pittsburgh, PA (1999)

Evaluating COTS Based Architectures

Mark Vigder[1], Toby McClean[2], and Francis Bordeleau[2]

[1] National Research Council of Canada
mark.vigder@nrc.ca
[2] Carleton University
{tmcclean, francis}@scs.carleton.ca

Abstract. The criteria for evaluating the architecture of COTS based software systems is different from the criteria used for custom-built software systems. These differences arise due to the different development and maintenance scenarios that are the business drivers for COTS based software systems. Current architecture evaluation methods must be adapted to take these differences into account. One approach is to use the Architecture Tradeoff Analysis Method^{SM} (ATAM^{SM}) as a basis for the evaluation. This can be done by identifying the Scenarios and Utility Trees that are applicable to COTS based software systems.

1 Introduction

The architecture and design of a software system is driven by the need to meet the stakeholder requirements. These requirements, both functional and non-functional, impose different and sometimes contradictory constraints on the software architecture. Determining the "best" architecture involves developing a set of criteria that can be used to analyze the candidate architectures relative to the requirements and determining where and how the architectural tradeoffs should be performed to best realize the requirements.

The development, maintenance and management processes for custom-built software systems and Commercial Off-the-Shelf (COTS) based software systems are different [17,18]. These differences arise for a number of reasons: insufficient knowledge of the COTS products used to build the system; frequent upgrades and patches to the COTS products; lack of flexibility within the COTS products; and unnecessary and emergent behaviour within the COTS products. Although the process for architectural evaluation can be similar for the two types of systems, the criteria for evaluating the architecture of a COTS-based system and a custom-built system are different. The different architectural evaluation criteria result mainly because the non-functional requirements of COTS-based systems differ from those of custom-built systems (see Sect. 3 for examples.)

This research outlines an approach to architectural evaluation for COTS-based systems that is based on the Architecture Tradeoff Analysis Method^{SM} (ATAM^{SM}) developed by the Software Engineering Institute (SEI) [10,11]. We focus on the evaluation of the architecture rather than the development or generation of the architecture, since for COTS-based systems the architecture is

H. Erdogmus and T. Weng (Eds.): ICCBSS 2003, LNCS 2580, pp. 240–250, 2003.

often constrained by the COTS product selection. This results in requiring an architectural evaluation method that can be applied to an existing architecture.

The ATAM^{SM} defines a method for evaluating software architectures with respect to the non-functional requirements. The ATAM^{SM} approach develops **scenarios** that help in identifying the **drivers** behind the realization of non-functional requirements. These drivers are then used to evaluate the software architecture with respect to the non-functional requirements. In this paper we propose a set of scenarios and drivers that are tailored for the unique requirements of COTS-based systems.

Section 2 gives a brief overview of ATAM^{SM} as applied to a general architectural evaluation. A brief discussion of other architectural evaluation methods that could have been used as well is also included together with reasons for choosing ATAM^{SM} as our model. Section 3 shows how the ATAM^{SM} can be tailored to deal more specifically with the issues associated with COTS-based systems. Section 4 provides some discussion on the application of the approach. Finally, Sect. 5 gives our conclusions.

2   The ATAM Method for Architecture Evaluation

The SEI's ATAM^{SM} provides a context and domain independent method for evaluating software architectures as well as identifying the interaction of non-functional requirements. The ATAM involves all of the software architecture's stakeholders to ensure the highest degree of requirement realization. It draws upon several concepts developed at the SEI including quality attributes [1,3] and attribute based architectural styles (ABAS) [12].

The goal of the ATAM^{SM} is to determine how well the proposed software architecture and the decisions taken satisfy the quality attributes (non-functional requirements) described by its stakeholders. The goal is accomplished by identifying in the software architecture the *risks*, *sensitivity points*, and *tradeoff points* that exist. The *risks* are those decisions that are not well understood, or have not been made. A *sensitivity point* is an architectural element that directly affects the satisfaction of a quality attribute (non-functional requirement). A *tradeoff point* is an architectural element that affects the realization of multiple quality attributes in opposing ways.

The ATAM^{SM} consists of four phases: *presentation, investigation and analysis, testing* and *reporting*. The *presentation* phase consists of an overview of the ATAM^{SM}, the business drivers of the software system and the software architecture. The *investigation and analysis* phase consists in identifying the architectural approaches used, generating the quality attribute utility tree and analyzing the architectural approaches taking the utility tree and ABAS's into account. A brainstorming of scenarios and prioritization of scenarios by stakeholders that are then used for a further evaluation of the architectural approaches, comprise the *testing* phase. Finally the *reporting* phase consists of a presentation of the results to the software's stakeholders. The risk, sensitivity points and tradeoff points are initially identified in the investigation and analysis phase, concretized in the testing phase and presented to the concerned stakeholder's in the reporting phase. The overall process can span several days.

Scenarios are used to elicit the non-functional requirements. The authors of the ATAM^{SM} provide quality attribute characterizations [11] that help in the elicitation of such scenarios. The scenarios are represented in a quality attribute Utility Tree. The root of a Utility Tree is Utility, which represents the overall quality of the software. Below the root are the quality attributes, while the internal nodes between the quality attributes and the leaf nodes are refinements of the quality attributes. The leaf nodes are short scenarios specific enough that they can be prioritized (high, medium and low) along two dimensions; influence on the success of the software and level of risk encountered by the scenario. An example Utility tree for COTS-based systems is discussed in Sect. 3.2.

2.1   Other Architectural Evaluation Methods

Several other methods have been developed for evaluating software architectures. The method of de Bruin and van Vliet [5,6] and the method of Liu and Yu [14] take a more generative approach to the evaluation of a software architecture. They not only perform an architectural evaluation but also assist the designer in making the appropriate design decisions. These methods make explicit the impact of architectural decisions on the satisfaction of stakeholder requirements. Since in COTS-based systems architectural decisions are frequently imposed by the COTS software packages, it was felt these two approaches are more applicable to custom-built systems than to COTS-based systems.

The architectural analysis method of Bose [4] focuses on evaluating the connectors used to coordinate component interaction and the one of Lassing et al. [13] looks specifically at analyzing the flexibility of a software architecture. Although connectors and flexibility are considered to be an important aspect of architectures, in isolation they are not considered sufficiently comprehensive to provide a basis for a complete evaluation of a COTS-based software architecture.

The method of Gannod and Lutz [8] is primarily for product line architectures.

In [16] and further developed in [15] Ncube and N. Maiden outline a method for selecting COTS software packages while attempting to satisfy both stakeholder and architectural requirements. The method presented in this paper differs in that it attempts to predict the satisfaction of stakeholder requirements based on the software architecture that includes COTS software packages. We do not look specifically at the selection of the COTS software packages that are combined to create the overall system.

3   Evaluating COTS-Based Architectures

The drivers behind many architectural decisions are the non-functional requirements defined by the system stakeholders. This has a number of implications for COTS-based systems versus custom-built systems.

First, since implementers are integrating software products of unknown quality, the integration mechanism must provide any non-functional attributes that are required by the system. Integrators cannot depend on the COTS products. Integrators do not control the architecture of the commercial software products; that is under the control of the COTS developer. They do however control the architecture used to integrate the COTS products and it is through this integration architecture that they must realize the non-functional attributes of the overall system. The architecture must provide the attributes even though the attributes of the individual software products are unknown.

Second, because integrators are building systems from large-scale commercial products whose evolution and maintenance remains under the control of the COTS vendor, there are some fundamental differences between COTS-based systems and custom-built systems regarding how they are evolved, managed, and maintained. Since the evolution strategy and release cycle are under the control of the COTS product developer, and do not necessarily conform to the requirements of the system integrator, integrators must adapt their strategy and release cycles to that provided by the various COTS vendors. This means designing systems that plan for a highly volatile configuration of underlying COTS products. As this configuration changes, the characteristics of a system, such as functionality, performance and reliability, will change.

3.1   COTS-Based System Scenarios

The method for understanding and developing the non-functional requirements in the ATAM^{SM} is to develop a set of scenarios that illustrate usage of the system from one of the stakeholder's perspectives. The stakeholders are not only customers who will use the system, but also all others involved with the system such as the developers, maintainers, or managers of the system. ATAM^{SM} identifies three types of scenarios that can be used to concretize the development-time quality attributes: use-case scenarios to describe typical uses of the existing system; growth scenarios to cover anticipated changes to the system; and exploratory scenarios to cover extreme changes that are expected to stress the system.

A number of scenarios can be identified that are unique to COTS-based systems. Examples of these scenarios are listed below:

- A new version of each COTS product in the system becomes available on average every 6-9 months [2]. The average effort for integrating a new version of a COTS product is two person-months.
- Some of the features of COTS product X are not needed or conflict with features of other COTS products. These features are masked out so that users or programmers cannot access them.
- The features of product X that were masked out in the previous versions of the system must now be exposed to the user.
- The vendor of COTS product Y has announced that the product will no longer be supported in six months. The system integrators substitute competing product Z within that time frame.

- The load on the server increases 700%. To improve performance clustering is added to the COTS server that is being used. Clustering involves a reconfiguration of the COTS products.
- The system has failed due to a fault in one of the COTS products. The faulty COTS product can be quickly identified. The vendor can be notified and a workaround quickly developed.
- System performance is becoming a problem. The performance profile of each of the COTS products is generated to determine the bottlenecks within the system.
- A fault in a COTS product is generating erroneous events/values in a critical system; the system minimizes the damage caused by the fault.
- Malicious hackers discover a previously unknown security hole in a COTS product; the system policies prevent the hackers from exploiting the security hole. The insecure product is quickly identified and, together with the vendor, a patch is developed.

Although many of the above scenarios have counterparts in custom-built systems the architectural decisions can be quite different for COTS-based systems. Because the COTS products are black-box and under vendor control, effectively satisfying the criteria derived from the above scenarios can be achieved only through the integration architecture, and not through modification to the individual components. Moreover, the architecture must be sufficiently robust to continue satisfying the criteria while the underlying COTS products change.

3.2   Utility Trees

Within ATAM^{SM}, a utility tree provides a top-down mechanism for translating the business drivers of a system into concrete quality attribute scenarios. From the scenario types that have been identified, the utility tree can be used to derive specific quality attributes for evaluating an architecture.

A **utility** tree always has utility as the root, and this is a measure of the overall quality of the system. Under the utility node are the quality attributes the stakeholders consider important for the system. In the standard ATAM^{SM} model, the typical quality attributes under the root are **performance, modifiability, availability** and **security**. These can be modified as required to adapt to any specific organizational requirements and business drivers. Most of the COTS scenarios that we have identified can be categorized within these four nodes, as shown in Fig. 1.

We have also added a fifth node under **utility**, namely **manageability**. Manageability is the ease with which system administrators and managers can perform the functions necessary to keep all installations of the system up and running in an efficient manner after they have been deployed. The reason for adding this node, is that for COTS-based systems, where initial development cost is often less than for custom built systems, much of the lifecycle cost of the system comes not just from the modification or maintenance activity, but from providing the support necessary to keep a diverse set of products correctly functioning in different environments. This includes, for example: monitoring and logging behaviour including the execution profile and performance of individual COTS products; maintaining configuration management information for all deployed configurations; providing support for each deployment; deploying new installations; and monitoring and upgrading each deployed installation.

Under the quality attribute nodes, are more specific sub-factors for each quality. The sub-factors provide the categories under which a set of measures will be derived for quantifying the quality of the system. The sub-factors are system dependant. However, we have illustrated a set of sub factors that are typical factors in COTS-based systems. Although some of these factors are significant for custom built as well as COTS-based systems, the way the measurement is defined, or how it is used, is different between the two types of systems.

Based on the example scenarios developed in Sect. 3.1, a set of possible sub-factors are developed as shown in Fig. 1. These sub-factors are then further refined into specific architectural goals.

For example, the **modifiability** attribute has three sub-factors: **new product integration, product replacement,** and **product upgrade**. These three items are defined as follows:

- What is the level of difficulty in integrating a new COTS product into the system in order to provide new functionality to the system?
- What is the level of difficulty in replacing a COTS product in the system with a similar product from a competing vendor?
- What is the level of difficulty in replacing a current COTS product in the system with an upgraded version of the same product?

Answering these questions requires developing a set of specific scenarios that provide a measure for these factors. For example, under the product upgrade one scenario might be to upgrade any one of the COTS products in the system. Assuming that the average release time between COTS product upgrades is eight months, the requirement may be to average no more than two person-months to upgrade any COTS product in the system. Determining whether the requirement generated from this scenario has been met can be analyzed by answering questions such as the following:

- What is the number of other system components with which the upgraded component interacts directly? Indirectly?
- Does the software conform to the accepted and open industry standards?
- Do the developers reliably maintain backward compatibility with all their product versions?
- For the procedural interface, what is the level of complexity (measured in terms of number of calls and number of parameters passed) between the COTS component and the rest of the system?

By determining the answers to these questions during the evaluation of the software architecture and design, the stakeholders can assess the level of effort

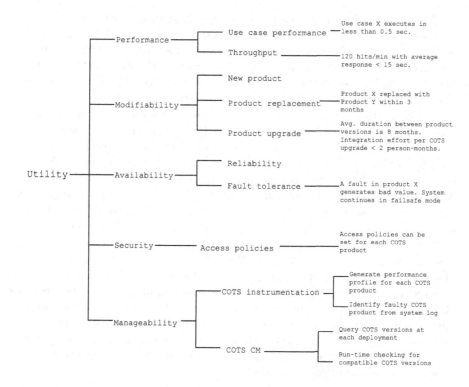

Fig. 1. Example Utility Tree for COTS Based Software System

for a product upgrade and determine whether the requirements as defined by the scenarios are being met.

3.3   Architecture Evaluation

From the specific scenarios developed in the utility tree, a rudimentary evaluation of the architecture can be undertaken. This evaluation can proceed along two dimensions.

- Evaluation of the COTS products relative to the specific scenarios.
- Evaluation of the architecture relative to the specific scenarios.

We shall focus on the latter dimension, as this is the focus of the ATAM^{SM}. The concrete scenarios elicited by the quality attribute utility tree drive the initial analysis of the architecture. These scenarios are prioritized along two dimensions: the importance to system success and the apparent peril in achieving them. Only the highest priority scenarios are used in the analysis of the architecture. The analysis proceeds by extracting the architectural approaches (styles) that have been used in the system architecture.

A significant effort has been but into associating quality attribute character-istics to architectural approaches. The ATAM^{SM} evaluation phase relies heavily on this knowledge. The evaluators map the scenarios onto the architectural com-ponents and connectors that are involved in realizing the scenario. Through this mapping attribute-specific questions are asked that result in the identification of the risks, sensitivity points and tradeoff points.

The evaluation continues with all stakeholders taking part in a brainstorming session in which the highest priority scenarios are identified and compared to those derived from the quality attribute utility tree. These scenarios are then used to further test the architecture to ensure that it meets the stakeholder requirements. The evaluation process is similar to that used in the utility tree driven evaluation. The involvement of all stakeholders can bring to light issues that were overlooked by the architecture and evaluation teams. Following this analysis the risk, sensitivity points and tradeoff points should be concrete.

Continuing with product upgrade example developed in previous sections we will provide an example evaluation. We will assume that product X has been placed in a wrapper, we shall refer to this as "Decision 1". The rationale for the architectural decision is that it will ease the effort in upgrading to new releases of product X. We will assume for simplicity that it has been shown that such an approach increases the modifiability in terms of product replacement and feature exposure while decreases the performance of functionality involving the product.

The architectural and evaluation teams have determined that the following scenarios are of the highest priority:

- Use case X executes in less than 0.5 sec. (S1)
- Product X replaced with product Y within 3 months. (S2)
- A fault in product X generates a bad value. System continues in failsafe mode. (S3)

Through the analysis of the scenarios it is determined that product X is involved in all of the scenarios. Since product X is also involved in "Decision 1" we must consider how that approach affects the realization of the scenarios.

If we first consider scenario S1, knowledge extracted on the use of wrappers shows that the performance is reduced. We therefore have a sensitivity point in the use of a wrapper on scenario S1; using the wrapper approach poses a risk in realizing S1. However, it is widely accepted that the use of wrappers increases the ease of product replacement. Thus a tradeoff point exists with respect to the approach undertaken in "Decision 1".

A similar process would be followed for all other approaches and high prior-ity scenarios present in the system. Upon completion a list of risks, sensitivity points and tradeoff points will exist that are traceable to the scenarios and ar-chitectural decisions. A similar process is undertaken for the scenarios derived by the stakeholder brainstorming session.

4   Discussion

We conclude the paper by discussing the issues of applicability and feasibility of the $ATAM^{SM}$ to COTS-based systems. As with the use of any method there are many pros and cons. The SEI discusses the use of the $ATAM^{SM}$ method in [9]. The focus will remain on issues surrounding COTS-based systems.

While we have focused on drivers specific to COTS-based systems there are many drivers and scenarios that are non-COTS specific that remain important to consider. In particular many of the drivers and scenarios pertaining to security and usability remain relevant whether the system is COTS-based or custom-built. The ideas and sample scenarios have been developed in other $ATAM^{SM}$ literature or are under investigation at the SEI.

To be effective, architectural evaluation should be an ongoing process as the system evolves. This requires that the models associated with the architectural evaluation be kept current and up to date. The models under consideration are the utility tree, scenarios, stakeholder requirements and the software architecture. It is a common occurrence that models used in development are forgotten during the maintenance phase of the system lifecycle. Ideally the evaluation of the architecture should use as little effort as possible and provide a fast turnaround time. However, due to the involvement of all stakeholders in the $ATAM^{SM}$, significant overhead and effort is actually required and it can take up to a week to complete.

One significant advantage of the $ATAM^{SM}$ process is that the decisions taken for the integration architecture are explicitly captured and documented. This is particularly important for COTS-based systems since much of the integration architecture contains elements introduced to overcome deficiencies in the COTS software packages. For example, if a particular style of wrapper is used to overcome security concerns in some packages (such as in [7]), this information is captured and available to future maintainers of the system.

As the researchers in [16] have identified one of the major issues in COTS-based system development is the selection and procurement of COTS software packages. A disadvantage to the process discussed in this paper is that it does not directly aid in the selection and procurement process. It can, however, identify at very early stages through the $ATAM^{SM}$ evaluation process those packages that may cause the system to fail to satisfy the non-functional requirements. In [15,16] a method is under development that helps in the selection of the packages and is our belief that the process outlined in this paper complements that work.

5   Summary and Conclusions

The architecture of a COTS-based systems provides the framework through which the different COTS products are integrated. This framework must guarantee that the requirements are satisfied, or at least identify which requirements are at risk and how to address the risks. The challenge is satisfying the system requirements when the attributes of the COTS products are unknown or are inconsistent with the system requirements.

Our experience with evaluating COTS-based systems has led us to conclude that the requirements and attributes needed in these systems is significantly different from custom-built systems. Architectural evaluation methods must be tailored and adapted to account for these differences and to verify that the software architecture is meeting the requirements. We have found that the ATAM^{SM} is an appropriate approach to the architectural evaluation of COTS-based systems. Its use of scenarios and utility trees to capture the non-functional requirements of the COTS-based system allows the method to identify the risks in the architecture and make decisions regarding the different tradeoff points.

Although the ATAM^{SM} involves significant effort to include all the stakeholders in a formal architectural evaluation, the high evolution and maintenance costs of COTS-based systems means that getting the architecture right is critical for a systems success. Formal evaluations are a necessary step to getting the architecture right.

References

1. Barbacci, M., Klein, M., Longstaff, T., and Weinstock, C.: Quality Attributes. Technical Report CMU/SEI-95-TR-021, Software Engineering Institute, Carnegie Mellon University, Pittsburgh, Pennsylvania (1995)
2. Basili, V., and Boehm, B.: COTS-Based Systems. In: IEEE Computer 34, (2001) 91–93
3. Bass, L., Klein, M., and Bachmann, F.: Quality Attribute Design Primitives. Technical Note CMU/SEI-2000-TN-017, Software Engineering Institute, Carnegie Mellon University, Pittsburgh, PA (2000)
4. Bose, P.: Scenario-Driven Analysis of Component-Based Software Architecture Models. In: First Working IFIP Conference on Software Architecture, San Antonio, TX (1999)
5. de Bruin, H., and van Vliet, H.: Scenario-Based Generation and Evaluation of Software Architectures. In: Generative and Component-Based Software Engineering (2001)
6. de Bruin, H., and van Vliet, H.: Top-Down Composition of Software Architectures. In: Engineering of Computer-Based Systems 2002, Lund, Sweden (2002)
7. Dean, J., and Li, L.: Issues in Developing Security Wrapper Technology for COTS Software Products at COTS-Based Software Systems. In: First International Conference, Orlando, FL (2002)
8. Gannod, G., and Lutz, R.: An Approach to Architectural Analysis of Product Lines. In: 22nd International Conference on Software Engineering, Limerick, Ireland (2000)
9. Kazman R., Barbacci, M., Klein, M., and Carrière, J.: Experience with Performing Architecture Tradeoff Analysis. In: 21st International Conference on Software Engineering, Los Angeles, CA (1999)
10. Kazman, R., Klein, M., Barbacci, M., Longstaff, T. *et al*: The Architecture Tradeoff Analysis Method. In: 4th International Conference on Engineering of Complex Computer Systems (1998)
11. Kazman, R., Klein, M., and Clements, P.: ATAM: Method for Architecture Evaluation. Technical Report CMU/SEI-2000-TR-004, Software Engineering Institute, Carnegie Mellon University, Pittsburgh, PA (2000)

12. Klein, M., and Kazman, R.: Attribute-Based Architectural Styles. Technical Report CMU/SEI-99-TR-022, Software Engineering Institute, Carnegie Mellon University, Pittsburgh, PA (1999)
13. Lassing, N., Rijsenbrij, D., and van Vliet, H.: Towards a Broader View on Software Architecture Analysis of Flexibility. In: 6th Asia-Pacific Software Engineering Conference (1999)
14. Liu, L., and Yu, E.: From Requirements to Architectural Design—Using Goals and Scenarios. In: Workshop 9: Software Requirements to Architectures, International Conference on Software Engineering, Toronto, Ontario, Canada (2001) 22–30
15. Maiden, N., Kim, H., and Ncube, C.: Rethinking Process Guidance for Selecting Software Components at COTS-Based Software Systems. In: First International Conference, Orlando, FL (2002)
16. Ncube, C., and Maiden, N.: COTS Software Selection: The Need to make Tradeoffs between System Requirement, Architectures and COTS/Components. In: International Conference on Software Engineering: COTS Workshop, Limerick, Ireland (2000)
17. Vigder, M., and Dean, J.: Building Maintainable COTS-Based Systems. In: International Conference on Software Maintenance, Washington DC (1998)
18. Vigder, M.: The Evolution, Maintenance and Management of Component-Based Systems, in Component-Based Software Engineering. ISBN 0201704854, Addison-Wesley (2001)

UML-Based Integration Testing for Component-Based Software

Ye Wu[1], Mei-Hwa Chen[2], and Jeff Offutt[1]

[1] Information and Software Engineering Department
George Mason University
Fairfax, VA 22030, USA
{wuye, ofut}@ise.gmu.edu
[2] Computer Science Department
State University of New York at Albany
Albany, NY 12222, USA
mhc@cs.albany.edu

Abstract. Component-based software engineering is increasingly being adopted for software development. Currently, components delivered by component providers only include specifications of the interfaces. This imposes significant difficulties on adequate testing of an integrated component-based system. Without source code, many testing techniques will not be applicable. The Unified Modeling Language (UML) has been widely adopted in component-based software development processes. Many of its useful tools, such as interaction diagrams, statechart diagrams, and component diagrams, characterize the behavior of components in various aspects, and thus can be used to help test component-based systems. In this paper, we first analyze different test elements that are critical to test component-based software, then we propose a group of UML-based test adequacy criteria that can be used to test component-based software.

1 Introduction

In his survey, Allen predicted that by the year 2003, up to 70% of all new software-intensive systems will heavily rely on component-based software [2]. A component-based software system often consists of a set of self-contained and loosely coupled components that allow plug-and-play integration. The components may have been written in different programming languages, execute on various operational platforms, and distributed across vast geographic distances; some components may be developed in-house, while others may be third party or commercial off-the-shelf components (COTS), whose source code may not be available to developers. These component-based software characteristics may facilitate fast-paced delivery of scalable and evolvable software, as well as improve the quality of the final products. However, these characteristics also introduce new problems for testing component-based software systems [17].

This research assumes that individual components have been thoroughly tested by component providers. But when integrating them in a new context,

H. Erdogmus and T. Weng (Eds.): ICCBSS 2003, LNCS 2580, pp. 251–260, 2003.

unexpected results may occur [17]. Therefore, adequate integration of reusable components is the key to the success of a component-based software system. Test methodologies are often categorized into two types: black box and white box. Black box approaches, such as functional testing and random testing, do not require knowledge of the implementation details. But when applied to component-based software, the use of black box approaches may encounter problems similar to those found in the testing of traditional programs, for example the complexity of the actual combination of functions presented in the real system. Thus, white box approaches are often used to complement functional testing to ensure the quality of the programs. However, component-based software has two properties, heterogeneity and implementation transparency (the implementation is not available), which together make it difficult to directly apply traditional white-box techniques to test component-based software.

To overcome these difficulties, we need to precisely represent the behavior of components without source code. The Unified Modeling Languages (UML) [5] is a language for specifying, constructing, visualizing, and documenting artifacts of software-intensive systems. There are several advantages to adopting the UML. First, the UML provides high level information that characterize the internal behavior of components, which can be processed efficiently and used effectively when testing. Second, the UML has emerged as the industry standard for software modeling notations and diagrams are available from many component providers. Third, the UML includes a set of models that can provide different levels of capacity and accuracy for component modeling, and thus can be used to satisfy various needs in the real world. In the UML, collaboration diagrams and sequence diagrams are used to represent interactions among different objects in a component. This research used interaction diagrams to develop interaction graphs that are used to evaluate the control flows of components. Statechart diagrams, on the other hand, are used to characterize internal behaviors of objects in a component. Based on the statechart diagram, we further refine the dependence relationships among interfaces and operations that are derived from collaboration diagrams.

Section 2 of this paper briefly describes background of component-based engineering and software testing. Section 3 introduces a test model for component-based software, and various UML-based test elements are described in Sect. 4. Related research in the area of testing component-based software systems is discussed in Sect. 5, with conclusions in Sect. 6.

2   Background

The component-based software literature has introduced a number of new terms, some of which are still used inconsistently. This section of the paper defines these terms as used in this paper.

There are several definitions of *software components*. Szyperski and Pfister [7] provide the distinctive nature of components from a structural perspective: A component is "a unit of composition with contractually specified interfaces and explicit context dependencies only. A software component can be deployed independently and is subject to composition by third parties." Brown [4] defines a component in a broader aspect: A component is "an independently deliverable piece of functionality providing access to the services through interfaces."

Interfaces are the access points of components, through which a client component can request services declared in the interface and provided by another component. Each interface is identified by an interface name and a unique interface ID. Each interface can include multiple *operations*, where each operation performs one specific service. For clarity, we assume that each interface only includes one operation, and the references to the interface and to the operation are identical.

We define an *event* as an incident in which an interface is invoked in response to the incident. We consider only external events in which the responding entity is external to the invoking entity. The incident may be triggered by a different interface, through an exception or through an explicit user input (such as pushing a button). Some exceptions and user actions that require other components to respond may not occur in any interface of a component. To simplify our discussion, we define a *virtual* interface to account for all these possible incidents. Therefore, in general, we define an *event* as an invocation of an interface through another interface.

3   Component-Based Test Methodology

This section introduces a model for testing component-based software, and then several specific criteria for generating test cases.

3.1   A Test Model for Component-Based Software

When testing component-based software systems, we assume that each individual component has been adequately tested. Therefore, the key to the success of a reliable software system is to ensure the accuracy of interactions among the components.

Components may interact with other components either directly or indirectly. Direct interaction includes invocation of the interfaces exposed by the components, an exception, or a user action triggering an event. Indirect interaction is through a sequence of events. We define four key elements that can model the characteristics of the interactions. These elements must be considered during component-based testing.

Interfaces: Interfaces are the usual way to activate components. Therefore, it is necessary during integration and system testing to test each interface in the integrated environment at least once.

Events: Testing interfaces provides confidence that every interface that can be invoked during run time has been exercised at least once. This scenario is similar to the traditional test criterion that requires every function or procedure to be tested at least once. However, an interface invoked by different components within different contexts may have different outcomes. Thus, to observe possible behaviors of each interface during runtime, every invocation of the interface needs to be tested at least once. Moreover, some events that are not triggered via interfaces may have an impact on the components, which need to be tested as well. Therefore, every event in the system regardless of its type needs to be covered by some test.

Context-dependence Relationships: Interfaces and events testing ensure that every interaction between components is exercised. However, when execution of a component-based software system involves interactions among a group of components, the sequence of event triggering may produce unexpected outcomes. To capture the inter-relationships among events, we define a context dependence relationship that is similar to the control flow dependence relationship in traditional programs. An event $\bullet_2$ has a *context-sensitive dependence relationship* with event $\bullet_1$ if there exists an execution path where triggering $\bullet_1$ will directly or indirectly trigger $\bullet_2$. For a given event $\bullet$, it is necessary to test $\bullet$ with every event that has a context-sensitive dependence relationship with $\bullet$. This allows the tester to observe the possible impact of execution history on the outcome of the execution of $\bullet$.

Context-sensitive dependence relationships not only include direct interactions, but also the indirect collaboration relationships among interfaces and event that occur through other interfaces and events as well. Therefore, testing context-sensitive dependence relationships may serve to identify interoperability faults caused by improper interactions among different components.

Content-dependence Relationships: An invocation of an interface of a component results in an invocation of a function that the component implements. Therefore, when a function declared in an interface $\bullet_1$ has a data dependence relationship with another function declared in another interface $\bullet_2$, the order of invocation of $\bullet_1$ and $\bullet_2$ could impact the results. A *content-dependence relationship* exists between two interfaces $\bullet_1$ and $\bullet_2$ if the two interfaces have a data-dependence relationship. An interface encapsulates one or more signatures, where each signature is a declaration of a function. When an interface is invoked, one or more functions will be executed to perform the requested service. Thus, the interface dependence relationship can be derived from the function dependence relationship, which we have shown elsewhere to be useful information in object-oriented class testing [6]. More precisely, a function $\bullet_2$ depends on a function $\bullet_1$ if and only if the value of a variable defined in $\bullet_1$ is used in $\bullet_2$. Therefore, a content-dependence relationship is formally defined as follows: An interface $\bullet_2$ has a *content-dependence relationship* on interface $\bullet_1$ if and only if $\bullet_1$ contains the signature of $\bullet_1$, $\bullet_2$ contains the signature of $\bullet_2$ and $\bullet_2$ depends on $\bullet_1$.

Both the direct interaction among interfaces and events, as well as the context-dependence relationships, should be included in the control flow interactions of a component-based system. Content-sensitive dependence, on the other hand, can provide valuable additional information in generating test cases and detecting faults.

3.2   UML-Based Integration Testing for Component-Based Software

The test model presented in the previous section has presented a way to test component-based software. However, the implementation of the model faces a technical challenge; how to efficiently obtain the test elements to perform testing, particularly when the source code of the components is not available for COT components. Without source code, we can obtain the specifications of interfaces and events, however, the information needed for context-dependence and content-dependence relationships is not available. These two elements are likely to be effective in detecting component integration faults. Therefore, it is important to develop a methodology to obtain these two elements from the available resources other than the source code. We use the Unified Modeling Languages (UML) [5,11] to capture component relationships.

In this section we describe how to use the UML diagrams to precisely derive context-dependence and content-dependence test elements. In the next section we explore some practical issues of implementing this test model.

Context-dependence Relationships. When integrating components, programmers typically focus on how to specify component interfaces and events. But how these interfaces and events will interact, and their potential risks to the integrated system, are usually not considered. Context-dependence relationships, which model how interfaces and events interact, can be derived through one of the following approaches:

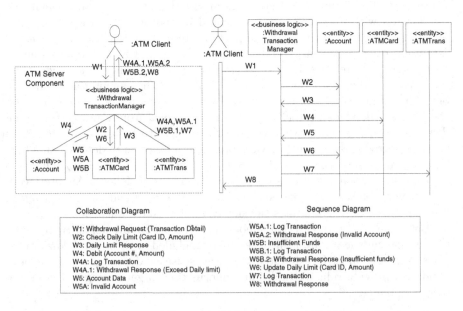

Fig. 1. Collaboration and Sequence Diagrams of an ATM Server Component

Collaboration/Sequence Diagram Based Approach. UML collaboration diagrams and sequence diagrams focus on interactions among various objects within a use case (we refer to a use case as a component.) In UML sequence diagrams, interactions are ordered by time while in collaboration diagrams, the same information is presented with the interactions ordered in numeric message sequence order.

Figure 1 describes a partial collaboration diagram and one sequence diagram of an ATM server component. The sequence diagram only shows one of the possible scenarios ordered by time while the collaboration combines all scenarios in numbered order. In Fig. 1, W5, W5A, and W5B demonstrate three alternatives that can occur after the message W4 is passed by the Withdrawal Transaction Manager object to the ATM Account object.

With the collaboration diagrams, we can refine our context-dependence relationships to be all possible sequences, as shown in Fig. 1 in a collaboration diagram that could be possibly invoked to precisely model how interfaces and events interact with each other.

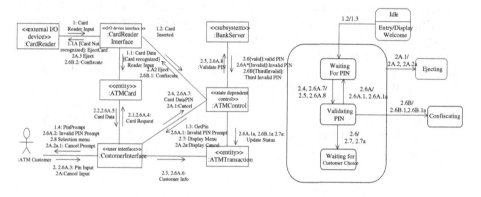

Fig. 2. Collaboration Diagram and Statechart for Validate PIN

Statechart Based Approach. The collaboration diagram itself is not always sufficient to model behaviors of the interactions of components. The behavior of a component can be more precisely modeled by combining the collaboration diagram with statechart diagrams, which are used to describe state-dependent control objects in components.

For example, Fig. 2 shows a collaboration diagram and statechart. As we can see, the sequence "2A-2A.1-2A.2, 2A.2a-2A.3, 2A.2a.1" (2A.2 and 2A.2a are two concurrent messages) is the only sequence that allows the user to cancel. Nevertheless, this sequence can happen in different contexts, such as the user canceling the current transaction after correctly inputting the PIN, or the user canceling the current transaction after incorrectly inputting the PIN. With the help of the statechart diagram, which is shown in Fig. 2(b), we can clearly see that the cancelation sequence needs to be validated in three different scenarios: (1) Waiting for PIN, (2) Validating PIN and (3) Waiting for Customer Choice.

The interactions among interfaces and events can be further refined by using the statechart diagram. Given a statechart diagram, our context-dependence relationships will have to include not only all possible sequences in a collaboration diagram, but all possible combinations of the sequences that are shown in the statechart diagram as well.

Content-dependence Relationships. Context-dependence relationships reflect control sequences of objects in a component with respect to single interactions between actors and the component. Nevertheless, content-dependence relationships among different interactions cannot be obtained solely from control flow information. For example, consider Fig. 3, which shows an extended ATM server component. The component includes two interfaces: withdraw and deposit. Context dependence relationships may depict the interactions within each interface, but the content-dependence relationships across the interfaces cannot be obtained. For instance, the withdrawal interface depends on deposit interface because the deposit transaction will modify the account entity, while the withdrawal transaction will use that entity to verify whether there is enough money in that account. Unfortunately, content-dependence relationships are not directly specified either in the program or in any UML diagrams. To specify the content-dependence relationships, further processing of UML diagrams is necessary. We suggest two approaches below.

Collaboration Diagram Approach. UML collaboration diagrams and sequence diagrams demonstrate interactions of objects within a component. When interactions involve entity classes, collaboration diagrams can demonstrate the

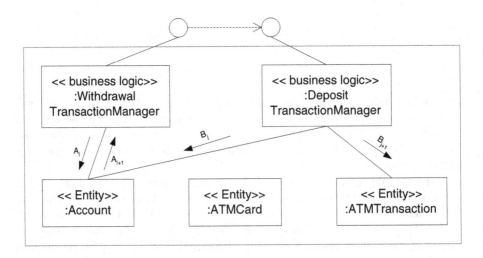

Fig. 3. An Extended ATM Server Component

dependence relationships between two interactions. For example, Fig. 3 shows message $\bullet_j$ flowing into entity class $\bullet \bullet\bullet\bullet\bullet\bullet$, and no information flows out of $\bullet \bullet\bullet\bullet\bullet\bullet$. Generally speaking, message $\bullet_j$ will update information in $\bullet \bullet\bullet\bullet\bullet\bullet\bullet$ objects. We define this to be an $\bullet\bullet\bullet\bullet\bullet\bullet$ message. On the other hand, messages $\bullet_i$ and $\bullet_{i+1}$ flow into and out of $\bullet \bullet \bullet\bullet\bullet\bullet$, which indicates that information of $\bullet \bullet\bullet\bullet\bullet\bullet\bullet$ is retrieved. These are called $\bullet\bullet\bullet\bullet\bullet\bullet\bullet$ messages. Therefore, interactions that include messages $\bullet_i$ and $\bullet_{i+1}$ will depend on sequences that includes message $\bullet_j$. In general, an interface $\bullet$ *depends* on interface $\bullet'$ if and only if a message sequence invoked by $\bullet$ includes an $\bullet\bullet\bullet\bullet\bullet\bullet$ message, and another sequence invoked by $\bullet'$ includes a corresponding $\bullet\bullet\bullet\bullet\bullet\bullet\bullet$ message.

Statechart Diagram Approach. Statechart diagrams can demonstrate content dependence relationships from a state transition point of view. The rationale lies in the fact that if interface $\bullet_1$ depends on $\bullet_2$, the state of the component is $\bullet_1$ after the execution of $\bullet_1$. When executing interface $\bullet_2$, the state transitions from $\bullet_1$ to $\bullet_2$ depend on state $\bullet_1$ and the invocation $\bullet_1$. To model this type of content dependence relationships, we eliminate dependence relations that are not effective:

- If the component remains in the original state $\bullet_1$ after the invocation of $\bullet_1$, the dependence relationship does not affect the behavior of the software; therefore the dependence relationship is not effective.
- From a state $\bullet$, if the invocation of $\bullet_2$ will always bring the state to $\bullet'$, it does not matter if interface $\bullet_1$ is invoked before $\bullet_2$ or not. This indicates that the state transformation is not caused by the dependence relationships.

UML-based Test Adequacy Criteria. Given the UML-based context dependence relationships and content dependence relationships, the test criteria that were provided in our test model has to be modified follows:

1. Each transition in each collaboration diagram has to be tested at least once.
2. Each valid sequence in each collaboration diagram has to be tested at least once.
3. Each transition in each statechart diagram has to be tested at least once.
4. Each content-dependence relationship derived from each collaboration diagram has to be tested at least once.
5. Each effective content-dependence relationship derived from each statechart diagram has to be tested at least once.

4   Related Work

The research results in this paper follow a small but growing body of work in component-based software testing. Weyuker [16] developed a set of axioms to help determine test adequacy and used them to evaluate several program-based testing techniques. Perry and Kaiser [14] further applied these adequacy axioms to object-oriented software and suggested that in the presence of object-oriented features, in particular inheritance and multiple inheritance, subclasses and superclasses require special attention during testing. Stemming from these studies, we developed a class testing technique [6] for testing object-oriented classes and programs.

In component-based testing, Rosenblum [15] proposed a formal model for adequate testing of component-based software, in which a "*C-adequate*" criterion is defined to determine the adequacy of a test set for a given component-based software system as well as for a single component. A number of concepts [8,9, 18] have been proposed to analyze the characteristics of component-based software and suggest ways to test component-based systems. Harrold et al. [9] proposed a testing technique that is based on analysis of component-based systems from component-provider and component-user perspectives. The technique was adapted from an existing technique [10], which makes use of complete information from components for which source code is available and partial information from those for which source code is not available. They further extended their work by proposing a framework that lets component providers prepare various types of metadata such as program slicing [13]. The metadata was then used to help test component-based systems. Ghosh and Mathur [8] discussed issues in testing distributed component-based systems and suggested an interface and exception coverage-based testing strategy.

The UML is increasingly being used to support the design of component-based systems [5,11]. Some of the UML diagrams have also been used to automatically generate test cases. Offutt and Abdurazik first proposed a mechanism that adapted state specification-based test data generation criteria to generate test cases from UML statecharts [12]. They subsequently extended their work to generate tests from UML collaboration diagrams [1]. Similarly, Briand and Labiche suggested using class diagrams, collaboration diagrams, or OCL to derive test requirements [3].

5   Conclusions and Future Work

This paper has presented a new model for describing component-based software and a related approach for testing. The model uses different UML diagrams to model the internal behavior of third party software components. When the source is not available (as is usually the case), these behavioral descriptions can be used as a basis for deriving tests that can help ensure the quality of the component-based system. Our ongoing research directions on this topic are empirical studies of comparisons of the effectiveness of our approach with other approaches, the development of a tool to support automation of the technique, and enhancement of the technique for resolving problems caused by distributed characteristics such as synchronization.

References

1. Abdurazik, A., and Offutt, J.: Using UML Collaboration Diagrams for Static Checking and Test Generation. In: Third International Conference on the Unified Modeling Language, York, UK, October (2000) 383–395
2. Allen, P.: Component-based Development for Enterprise Systems: Applying the SELECT Perspective. Cambridge University Press, Cambridge, UK, New York (1998)
3. Briand, L., and Labiche, Y.: A UML-based Approach to System Testing. In: Fourth International Conference on the Unified Modeling Language, Toronto, Canada, October (2001) 194–208
4. Brwan, A. W.: Background Information on CBD. SIGPC 18(1), August (1997)
5. Cheesman, J., and Daniels, J.: UML Components : A Simple Process for Specifying Component-based Software. Addison-Wesley (2001)
6. Chen, M., and Kao, M.: Effect of Class Testing on the Reliability of Object-oriented Programs. In: Proceedings of the Eighth International Symposium on Software Reliability Engineering, May (1997)
7. Clemens, S.: Component Software: Beyond Object-oriented Programming. Addison-Wesley (1998)
8. Ghosh, S., and Mathur, A. P.: Issues in Testing Distributed Component-based Systems. In: First International ICSE Workshop on Testing Distributed Component-based Systems, Los Angeles (1999)
9. Harrold, M. J., Liang, D., and Sinha, S.: An Approach to Analyzing and Testing Component-based Systems. In: First International ICSE Workshop on Testing Distributed Component-based Systems, Los Angeles (1999)
10. Harrold, M. J., and Rothermel, G.: Performing Dataflow Testing on Classes. In: Proceedings of the Second ACM SIGSOFT Symposium on Foundations of Software Engineering, December (1994) 154–163
11. Heineman, G., and Councill, W.: Component-based Software Engineering : Putting the Pieces Together. Addison-Wesley (2001)
12. Offutt, J., and Abdurazik, A.: Generating Tests from UML Specifications. In: Second International Conference on the Unified Modeling Language, IEEE Computer Society Press, Fort Collins, CO, October (1999) 416–429
13. Orso, A., Harrold, M. J., and Rosenblum, D.: Component Metadata for Software Engineering Tasks. In: Proceedings of the 2nd International Workshop on Engineering Distributed Objects, November (2000) 126–140
14. Perry, D. E., and Kaiser, G. E.: Adequate Testing and Object-oriented Programming. In: Journal of Object-Oriented Programming, January (1990)
15. Rosenblum, D. S.: Adequate Testing of Component-based Software. Technical Report TR97-34, University of California, Irvine (1997)
16. Weyuker, E. J.: Axiomatizing Software Test Data Adequacy. In: IEEE Transactions on Software Engineering SE-1215 (12), December (1986) 1128-1138
17. Weyuker, E. J.: Testing Component-based Software: A Cautionary Tale. In: IEEE Software 15(5), September/October (1998) 54–59
18. Wu, Y., Pan, D., and Chen, M. H.: Techniques for Testing Component-based Software. In: 7th IEEE International Conference on Engineering of Complex Computer Systems, Skövde, Sweden, June (2001) 222–232

Author Index